Advances in Fuzzy-Based Internet of Medical Things (IoMT)

Scrivener Publishing
100 Cummings Center, Suite 541J
Beverly, MA 01915-6106

Publishers at Scrivener
Martin Scrivener (martin@scrivenerpublishing.com)
Phillip Carmical (pcarmical@scrivenerpublishing.com)

Advances in Fuzzy-Based Internet of Medical Things (IoMT)

Edited by

Satya Prakash Yadav
Department of Computer Science and Engineering, GL Bajaj Institute of Technology of Management, Greater Noida, U.P., India

Sudesh Yadav
Dept. of Higher Education, Govt. PG College, Ateli, Mahendergarh, Haryana, India

Pethuru Raj Chelliah
Edge AI Division, Reliance Jio Platforms Ltd., Bangalore, India

and

Victor Hugo C. de Albuquerque
Department of Teleinformatics Engineering (DETI), Federal University of Ceará, Brazil

Scrivener
Publishing

This edition first published 2024 by John Wiley & Sons, Inc., 111 River Street, Hoboken, NJ 07030, USA and Scrivener Publishing LLC, 100 Cummings Center, Suite 541J, Beverly, MA 01915, USA
© 2024 Scrivener Publishing LLC
For more information about Scrivener publications please visit www.scrivenerpublishing.com.

Wiley Global Headquarters
111 River Street, Hoboken, NJ 07030, USA

For details of our global editorial offices, customer services, and more information about Wiley products visit us at www.wiley.com.

Limit of Liability/Disclaimer of Warranty
While the publisher and authors have used their best efforts in preparing this work, they make no representations or warranties with respect to the accuracy or completeness of the contents of this work and specifically disclaim all warranties, including without limitation any implied warranties of merchantability or fitness for a particular purpose. No warranty may be created or extended by sales representatives, written sales materials, or promotional statements for this work. The fact that an organization, website, or product is referred to in this work as a citation and/or potential source of further information does not mean that the publisher and authors endorse the information or services the organization, website, or product may provide or recommendations it may make. This work is sold with the understanding that the publisher is not engaged in rendering professional services. The advice and strategies contained herein may not be suitable for your situation. You should consult with a specialist where appropriate. Neither the publisher nor authors shall be liable for any loss of profit or any other commercial damages, including but not limited to special, incidental, consequential, or other damages. Further, readers should be aware that websites listed in this work may have changed or disappeared between when this work was written and when it is read.

Library of Congress Cataloging-in-Publication Data

ISBN 978-1-394-24222-1

Cover image: Pixabay.Com
Cover design by Russell Richardson

Set in size of 11pt and Minion Pro by Manila Typesetting Company, Makati, Philippines

Printed in the USA

10 9 8 7 6 5 4 3 2 1

Contents

Preface

This book explores the latest trends and transitions concerning the Internet of Medical Things (IoMT). The emerging notion is that IoMT will play an important role in shaping the future of healthcare. Many medical instruments, equipment, scanners, robots, appliances, cameras, handhelds, wearables, and other devices are becoming integrated with cloud-hosted software applications, analytics platforms, digital twins, databases, AI models, etc. This integration adds the required intelligence necessary to exhibit intelligent behavior.

Decision-making in the medical profession is imprecise and fuzzy logic handles the partial truth concept well. Fuzzy logic is advantageous in situations in which the truth-value ranges between completely false and completely true. The combination of the established fuzzy logic concepts with the IoMT systems is a game-changer.

The fuzzy logic theory is an important tool that deals with imprecise linguistic concepts, addresses the loss of precision in the decision-making power of a physician, and ultimately will improve medical science in the ensuing digital era.

Here the main goal is to strengthen medical professionals, caregivers, and surgeons by providing methods for achieving fuzzy logic-based health diagnosis and medication. The health condition and various physical parameters of humans, such as heartbeat rate, sugar level, blood pressure, temperature, and oxygen quality, are captured through a host of multi-faceted sensors. Additionally, remote health monitoring, medication, and management are being facilitated through a host of ingestible sensors, 5G communication, networked embedded systems, AI models running on cloud servers and edge devices, etc. Furthermore, chronic disease management is another vital domain getting increased attention. The distinct advancements in the fuzzy logic field are useful in various advanced medical care functionalities and facilities.

The first chapter focuses on the IoMT paradigm, its healthcare applications, the challenges, how to surmount them, and the distinct benefits.

Chapter 2 illustrates various technical challenges in fuzzy-based IoMT system design and development. Chapter 3 conveys the design and implementation of a novel fuzzy logic-based IoMT framework.

Chapter 4 focuses exclusively on the different aspects of fuzzy logic-based medical image processing. It also deals with how fuzzy logic aids in efficient image processing. Chapter 5 explores the development of a fuzzy logic system for monitoring patients' health conditions and the articulation of solution approaches. Chapter 6 underscores the importance of establishing complete trust between patients and IoT systems using fuzzy logic theory.

Chapter 7 concentrates on articulating and accentuating the proven and potential methods for significantly improving the efficiency of IoMT using fuzzy logic techniques. Chapter 8 is predominantly about fuzzy interference system (FIS) for IoMT. Chapter 9 is a use-case chapter that primarily focuses on leveraging a fuzzy deep learning method to analyze Pap smear images to identify cervical cancer.

Chapter 10 deals with the classification and diagnosis of heart diseases using fuzzy logic-powered IoMT. Chapter 11 describes an implementation of a neuro-fuzzy-based classifier to find Type-1 and Type-2 diabetes. Chapter 12 discusses an efficient implementation of Type-2 fuzzy logic mechanisms in IoMT. Chapter 13 explains the ways and means of doing feature extraction and diagnosis of heart diseases using fuzzy logic-inspired IoMT.

Chapter 14 is dedicated to demystifying the unique capabilities of an intelligent heartbeat management system using fuzzy logic methods. Chapter 15 expounds on a fuzzy logic algorithm for effective monitoring of medical data management systems. Chapter 16 concerns the implementation of IoT's function in healthcare monitoring systems. The importance and value of IoT healthcare systems are discussed, along with the advantages of using such a system. Chapter 17 addresses the integration of edge computing and fuzzy logic to monitor novel coronavirus. Chapter 18 illustrates the aspect of IoT implementation in healthcare barriers and its future challenges.

We wish to express our gratitude to everyone involved in this project for their efforts, as well as Wiley and Scrivener Publishing for their cooperation and assistance in the timely publication of this book.

Editors: Satya Prakash Yadav, Sudesh Yadav, Pethuru Raj Chelliah
and Victor Hugo C. de Albuquerque
January 2024

1

IoMT—Applications, Benefits, and Future Challenges in the Healthcare Domain

E. M. N. Sharmila[1]*, K. Rama Krishna[2], G. N. R. Prasad[3],
Byram Anand[4], Chetna Vaid Kwatra[5] and Dhiraj Kapila[6]

[1]*CIRD Research Centre & RPA First Grade College, (Approved by University of Mysore), Banglore, India*
[2]*Department of Information Technology, Vasavi College of Engineering, Hyderabad, India*
[3]*Department of MCA, Chaitanya Bharathi Institute of Technology, Gandipet, Hyderabad, Telangana, India*
[4]*Department of Management, Pondicherry University Karaikal Campus, Karaikal, Pondicherry, India*
[5]*Lovely Professional University, Phagwara, Punjab, India*
[6]*Department of Computer Science & Engineering, Lovely Professional University, Phagwara, Punjab, India*

Abstract

In the healthcare sector, the Internet of Medical Things (IoMT) is significantly enhancing the accuracy, reliability, and efficiency of electronic devices. Interactions between machines and people or a combination of the two are made possible via the Internet of Things (IoT). The most recent advancements in the Internet of Things technology have helped human daily activities, including rapid service delivery and real-time information access. Our area of interest is the research benefits of the IoT in the healthcare sector though. By enabling the quick and efficient capture of diagnostic information and patient care, this technology has improved healthcare management and delivery, particularly inside medical facilities. The existing literature consists primarily of different investigations. The study focuses mostly on the evolution of the Internet of Things architecture, its accompanying challenges, and its benefits for the general public, with little to no attention paid to the IoT's potential applications in the healthcare industry. This study investigates the effects of utilizing the IoT to close the healthcare management gap.

**Corresponding author*: emnsharmila@gmail.com

Satya Prakash Yadav, Sudesh Yadav, Pethuru Raj Chelliah and Victor Hugo C. de Albuquerque (eds.)
Advances in Fuzzy-Based Internet of Medical Things (IoMT), (1–24) © 2024 Scrivener Publishing LLC

The study offers a thorough examination of how the IoT might be used to improve hospital management systems' operating capabilities. This study investigates prospective new innovations that might aid in development. Systems for managing hospitals are controlled by the IoT technology. Medical practitioners are able to treat patients anywhere and at any time. Patients, especially the elderly, are frequently offered medical care and monitoring. The goal of wearable sensor technology is to improve people's welfare in their homes. Multiple obstacles, such as the production of unnecessary and useless data, worries about the security and privacy of patient information, and the high cost of IoT adoption make it difficult to integrate IoT applications into the field of healthcare. Future research initiatives on the application of the IoT technology in the healthcare industry also include the prediction of stroke and epileptic convulsions as well as the use of prosthetic sensors to gather important information to speed up patient treatment.

Keywords: IoMT, IoT, healthcare, management

1.1   Introduction

Scholars from all over the world have been investigating new methods to use technology to augment conventional healthcare services by utilizing the Internet of Medical Things (IoMT) [1]. This study demonstrates how the use of multi-homing dense networks enhances a hitherto unexplored component of the IoMT deployment, highlighting the significance of each contribution. The convergence process in the healthcare industry presents both new challenges and opportunities [2, 3]. The research aims to highlight cutting-edge research projects that advance the field. A major global challenge for civilization is preserving people's health. The healthcare industry has drawn a lot of scholarly attention in the last 10 years [4]. The current study examines the current applications of the Internet of Things (IoT) in healthcare and the possible benefits it might bring to the industry.

Figure 1.1 describes the IoMT's journey to improve the effectiveness and efficiency of healthcare applications. Researchers are also interested in spotting patterns in developing technologies [5]. An in-depth analysis of the multiple barriers preventing the widespread adoption of effective, reliable, and scalable IoT healthcare applications is provided in this study. New opportunities to raise the level of healthcare and, consequently, human life expectancy are urgently needed. It is envisaged that a reinforcement algorithm be developed and joined to the IoT-enabled healthcare infrastructure to address the issues brought on by duplicated sensory data acquired by wearable sensor devices [6–8]. This is anticipated to take place soon.

Figure 1.1 Journey of the IoMT system.

The Internet of Things refers to a collection of physical elements connected to one another via the Internet to facilitate the storage of shared and aggregated information [9]. These elements include sensor information, data processing, intelligence services, software, and intelligent applications. Potentially, medical institutions and potential patients may communicate via the Internet, opening up access to high-quality healthcare services at any time and from any location [10–13]. As a result, organizations or groups of healthcare experts can create a system that is open and effective. Additionally, the adoption of IoT technologies can make it easier to develop a real-time healthcare delivery paradigm. Additionally, IoT-based healthcare methods have improved the provision of healthcare services from a traditional healthcare standpoint, providing a cutting-edge real-time healthcare system [14]. Thus, the incorporation of bIoTechnology has aided in the modernization of traditional medicine and acted as a key catalyst for the creation of intelligent healthcare systems for hospital administration [15]. Because of its integration, Internet of Things technologies are establishing an innovative healthcare-based hospital management method for providing healthcare services.

Technology makes it possible to create an intelligent hospital management system with access to healthcare data that is frequently referred to as the IoMT [16, 17]. It entails employing wearable medical sensors and Internet-connected smart devices to monitor patient health, confirm medication compliance, predict cardiac events, and obtain the most recent diagnostic information. The healthcare sector is currently being affected by a surge of new trends and technological developments that are quickly gaining traction on a worldwide level. The latest innovations in the development of medical devices improve patient care. The immediate transmission of important data is made possible by emerging technical developments, which range from physical gadgets to intelligent systems. This makes it possible for specialists, medical professionals, and regular people to communicate and spot crucial situations that can jeopardize lives [18]. In order to meet patient needs, the paradigm of medical services being available always, everywhere, and spanning all facets of healthcare is changing. This change is causing the field to generate innovative innovations. At this time, smartphone framework developments have achieved a level of practicality and utility that enables medical practitioners to offer consultations for medical support. A substantial problem is presented by the interconnectedness of IoT regions, which calls for the integration of frameworks related to enormous amounts of data, security, and privacy [19].

Additionally, it gives users the ability to upload, access, archive, and aggregate data, which results in the creation of enormous databases. Transfer, retrieval, storage, and accumulation of data by persons are made easier by information technology (IT). The current study also investigates continuous considerable data streams to derive insightful conclusions in big data implementations across certain domains [20, 21]. Internet of Things technology's structures and automated systems, as well as healthcare systems that handle copious volumes of data to improve decision-making, are just a few examples of the potential digital solutions this study explores in the numerous facts of daily life. Technical developments have a substantial impact on the IoMT, and remote medical services are the main topic of this study.

The Internet of Medical Things makes it feasible for medical device performance to be improved, response times to be accelerated, and healthcare to be more widely accessible. The IoMT can collect health information from patients who are over a long distance to wearable sensors and gadgets connected to Internet health monitoring platforms. The processing of the IoMT is made easier by Wi-Fi-enabled medical devices by connecting to one another and transferring M to M. A cloud server receives data from connected medical devices and stores and analyzes them [22]. The method of continuously monitoring someone's health by tracking his or her activity levels and comparing them to expected future activity levels is known as "remote health monitoring" (RHM). Although RHM may ultimately lead to the provision of clinical services, there are other priorities. Physiological characteristics like heart rate may need to be monitored.

The idea of remote healthcare entails the methodical gathering and evaluation of health-related data to determine the efficacy of a certain program [23–25]. This strategy makes it easier to do fundamental analysis, which helps to get the desired results. Patients can conduct routine tests on their smartphones or wearable technology and submit the results to healthcare professionals in real time by integrating remote health monitoring with healthcare assistance. The use of remote health monitoring and healthcare services has enhanced doctors' ability to supervise and control patients in unusual healthcare settings [26]. RHM uses sophisticated methods to collect health information from people in a specific locality, like a patient's

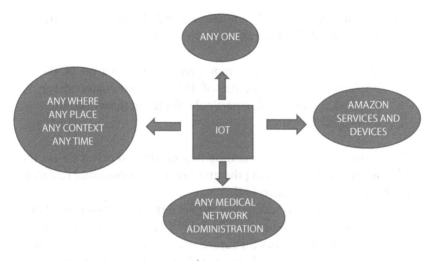

Figure 1.2 Various environments in the IoT.

home, and transfer the information to medical professionals in another location to access the patient and give directions to the nurses.

The concept of the IoMT refers to the Internet-based integration of computer networks and medical devices, allowing the collection of real-time data and enhancing patient participation. The IoMT refers to the concept of connecting animate and inanimate objects through the Internet. The term "things oriented" refers to everyday items that are connected to intelligent systems using cutting-edge interfaces like Zigbee, LAN Bluetooth, Wi-Fi, radio frequency identification (RFID), or other working devices to enable communication in social and client contexts. This concept is encompassed by the IoMT [27]. The object-oriented methodology used in the IoMT module relates to a physiological gadget with cutting-edge technology that permits virtual communication via Internet-based technologies [28]. A patient's physical measures concerning any element of his or her health can be collected and transmitted by the IoMT at any time and place [29, 30]. This is accomplished by utilizing the best services offered by different pathways and networks, as shown in Figure 1.2. People with chronic illnesses can connect remotely to the Internet of Medical Things. This is accomplished by using the physical locations of patients and hospitals, as well as by tracking medicine requests and wearable medical technology [31, 32]. The present study's noteworthy contributions are delineated as follows:

- The significance and rationale behind the creation of the IoT-enabled smart healthcare were emphasized and deliberated upon [33].
- This study presents a comprehensive examination of the implementation of Internet of Things technologies in the healthcare sector, with a particular focus on their utilization in medical hospitals.

The identified challenges pertaining to security and privacy were thoroughly discussed, thereby laying the groundwork for potential research in future avenues in this domain [34].

A major goal is to give academic scholars a thorough assessment of the present state of IoT technologies in the field of healthcare-enabled hospital administration and key issues for future attention. The goal of the essay is to give a critical critique that helps to guide academic discussion on the topic.

1.2   Literature Review

For monitoring epileptic seizures, a dependable and low-power alert system has been created. Conceptual learning and fuzzy categorization form the basis of this system, guaranteeing its efficacy and precision. In addition, a selective data transfer technique has been designed to pick the optimal data transmission mode according to the recognized patient's individual needs.

A mobile app has been developed to facilitate the transfer of health information between individuals, their healthcare providers, and their insurance companies. To ensure a thorough data gathering, this software gathers information from various sources, including wearables, manual input, and medical equipment. Every medical file is kept safely on the cloud, where its authenticity and accuracy can be independently verified. In addition, the blockchain links these documents for even greater security and transparency.

An IoMT healthcare system architecture framework has been suggested for use in the medical profession. The patient's health is tracked in real time through a network of sensors infused into the patient's body. The system's ability to recognize trends and insights on patients' health and offer possible preventative measures directly results from its use of ensemble tree-based learning algorithms. When a patient's health state changes, medical staff receives real-time instructions and alerts to respond quickly to keep the patient alive. Integrating an IoMT-based wearable body sensor network has shown potential for improving patient health outcomes.

Various machine learning (ML) algorithms are applied to enhance the reliability of diagnostic tools in healthcare. The effectiveness of different courses of action is compared, ensuring informed decision-making in medical settings. Moreover, the report addresses open issues and explores possibilities arising from the convergence of the IoMT in the healthcare sector, paving the way for future advancements.

The emerging healthcare applications and specific technological requirements for delivering end-to-end solutions are thoroughly discussed. The focus is on both short- and long-range communication, and a comprehensive analysis of present and future technologies and standards is presented. These discussions provide valuable insights into the potential of technological advancements in healthcare.

In the coming years, artificial intelligence (AI) and machine learning will play vital roles in medical professionals' ability to diagnose diseases accurately, suggest treatment options, and offer recommendations. Additionally, AI is expected to assist in providing cues for image interpretation in medical imaging, further enhancing diagnostic capabilities.

The comprehensive analysis of the IoMT examines various methodologies employed in smart healthcare systems (SHSs). This includes the utilization of radio frequency identification, artificial intelligence, and blockchain technologies. Multiple architectural frameworks proposed by scholars in the field are compared, aiding in the development of robust IoMT solutions.

Ensuring data security in the Internet of Things is of utmost importance. The method that employs an improved version of the Crowd search algorithm has been introduced to detect data manipulation and infiltration in IoT environments. Deep convolutional neural networks are utilized to conduct a comparative analysis, enhancing coordinated data security.

The research efforts dedicated to enhancing the IoMT are comprehensively analyzed, exploring data collected from various sensors that monitor a wide range of aspects, from heart rate to emotional well-being. These efforts contribute to the continuous improvement of healthcare systems and pave the way for personalized patient care.

The increasing frequency of cyberattacks on the healthcare sector is a pressing concern. This analysis seeks to identify the most critical challenges in cybersecurity, examine the solutions implemented by the health sector, and explore areas that require further development to ensure robust security measures.

The Internet of Things has the potential to improve healthcare in a number of ways, one of which is the ability to monitor breathing via noncontact wireless technologies. In this research, the accuracy of ultrasound (US) and Internet of Things-based methods of measuring respiration rate is assessed. The effectiveness and viability of the suggested method are investigated via simulation utilizing a programmable moving surface platform to model chest movement during breathing.

Significant difficulties exist in optimizing IoMT cybersecurity and establishing resilience against cyberattacks. Physical layer risks and the necessity for collaborative efforts to combat crime-as-a-service (CaaS) in the healthcare ecosystem are two examples of the difficulties that must be overcome.

The effective deployment of the IoT technology in healthcare depends on the ability to understand customers' concerns about privacy and security. Understanding the hazards involved with using the IoT technology is important; thus, it is important to have open and safe processes in place.

Consideration of the public's part in the creation and deployment of IoT applications in healthcare is crucial. Acceptance and adoption of IoT solutions in healthcare might be facilitated through public outreach and the resolution of public concerns.

In conclusion, innovations like conceptual learning, wearable sensors, ML algorithms, and IoT integration have the possibility to change the healthcare system. Accurate diagnoses, individualized treatment plans, strengthened data security, and better health outcomes are all made possible by these innovations. Research and analysis of this scale show a persistent dedication to improving healthcare via technology.

1.3   Healthcare System and IoT Overview

The Internet of Things has revolutionized the way intelligent devices interact with the environment. With the IoT, devices like mobile phones, sensors, and Raspberry Pi can connect to the Internet, allowing enhanced connectivity and communication. Thanks to this network, machines can talk to one another, and people can talk to devices. This network is used to conduct operations, keep tabs on patients at home, and keep an eye on the physical facilities of hospitals in real time, among other applications in the healthcare sector.

Interactions between humans and machines let people perform their healthcare duties more efficiently. These duties might include everything from operating on patients to checking on their well-being at home.

In addition, computers may exchange data with one another for convenient access. Sensors may send information to a cloudlet system for short-term storage to make data administration easier.

The scenario above is representative of a typical IoT-enabled healthcare platform. This infrastructure exemplifies how the Internet of Things might transform the medical industry by facilitating seamless information sharing across smart devices.

Figure 1.3 shows the four main parts of a typical IoT-enabled healthcare system. The hospital is the hub where medical staff coordinates and provides inpatient and outpatient treatment. Hospitals may keep tabs on patients' well-being and recovery after being discharged from the facility by using the Internet of Things (IoT) apps. Wearable or implanted medical body sensors may be used to get this information.

Machine learning algorithms and application software are used to process and interpret the obtained sensor data. The sensor data give the hospital staff a visual representation of the outpatient's health at home. If a patient's health suddenly worsens or becomes life-threatening, steps are made to get him or her to the emergency department, such as calling an ambulance.

For patients who are no longer hospitalized or have fully recovered, ambient assisted living devices powered by the Internet of Things come into play. These devices enable individuals to monitor their health in real time from the comfort of their own homes. They can track various parameters like calorie expenditure, blood sugar levels, and heart rate. With the data obtained from these ambient assistive IoT devices, patients can proactively manage any unforeseen health issues that may arise.

By equipping healthcare professionals with timely and accurate data, a competent IoT-enabled healthcare system enhances patient outcomes. It empowers medical professionals to deliver high-quality treatment and care

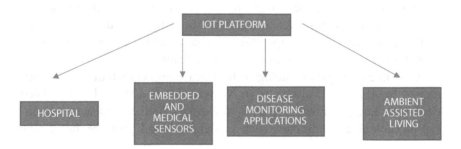

Figure 1.3 Healthcare and the IoT system.

when needed, ultimately improving the overall healthcare experience for patients.

1.4   IoT-Based Healthcare System

The concept of a "Smart Planet" forms the basis of "Smart Healthcare," which is an intelligent infrastructure driven by sensor-based information retrieval. The data collected from various sources are transmitted to a cloud data center, where it is processed into actionable information. This information is then made accessible to healthcare practitioners and authorized patients through the Internet of Things. The demand for excellent and fast healthcare services anytime, anywhere has been a key motivator in the development of efficient healthcare systems.

Innovative healthcare has been defined in various ways, but it generally refers to patient-centric facilities connected within an ecosystem that extends beyond traditional hospital settings. These facilities can include patients' homes, hospital wards, and other healthcare settings. Innovative healthcare aims to improve patient–provider interaction by facilitating the exchange of emotional information, enabling informed decision-making, optimizing resource allocation, and ensuring high-quality treatment. The term "smart healthcare" encompasses advanced interpretation and utilization of medical data.

A healthcare management service enabled by the IoT can be classified as a form of heterogeneous computing. The wireless communication system employed by IoT applications and devices serves as a means of connectivity between patients and healthcare professionals. This enables a wide range of services, including identification, monitoring, observation, and storage of crucial medical and statistical data. Numerous potential applications of innovative healthcare involve devices such as brainwave-measuring headsets, sensor-embedded clothing, blood pressure monitors, glucose monitors, electrocardiogram (ECG) monitors, and pulse oximeters. Additionally, medical sensors integrated into equipment, drug-dispensing systems, surgical robots, implantable devices, and various wearable technologies fall within the scope of innovative healthcare.

A notable example of intelligent healthcare implementation is demonstrated by Ably Medical Centre in Norway, where a smart bed has been deployed. Equipped with sensors, the smart bed can measure essential physiological parameters such as weight, blood pressure, heart rate, and vital signs. This technology enables healthcare professionals to stay updated on the patient's current health status, indicating whether his or her condition is improving or deteriorating in response to medical interventions. Additionally, the smart bed helps prevent falls and allows patients to reposition themselves autonomously, reducing the occurrence of pressure ulcers.

1.5   Smart Healthcare System—Benefits

Figure 1.4 illustrates the benefits of integrating the IoT technology into healthcare systems. These benefits include improved treatment outcomes, enhanced disease management, and increased safety and maintenance of medical facilities.

The use of IoT devices in capturing and processing diagnostic information has led to more accurate and error-free diagnoses, ultimately improving treatment outcomes. Patients receiving improved or high-quality treatment are likely to have increased confidence and trust in the healthcare providers and institutions associated with the hospital.

The Internet enables the general public to access medical advice in real time from anywhere and at a reasonable cost. This accessibility to medical guidance contributes to better healthcare outcomes and empowers individuals to make informed decisions about their health.

Intelligent healthcare systems, enabled by the IoT, play a crucial role in the maintenance and security of healthcare facilities. Continuous surveillance through embedded camera sensors ensures the upkeep and safety of medical establishments.

Furthermore, the IoT technology assists the elderly in effectively managing significant health concerns without the need for frequent hospital visits. Remote monitoring and healthcare applications allow healthcare professionals to evaluate and monitor patients' conditions remotely, reducing the burden on elderly individuals and promoting better health management.

Figure 1.4 Benefits of healthcare and the IoT system.

Overall, incorporating the IoT technology in healthcare systems brings forth a range of advantages, including improved treatment outcomes, enhanced disease management, increased accessibility to medical advice, and the ability to maintain and secure medical facilities.

1.6   Smart Healthcare System—Applications

The organizational structure of companies has undergone significant changes, driven by the development and widespread use of modern technology. However, the e-healthcare industry has been relatively slow in adapting to these transformations, which recently started to experience the reorganization that other sectors have skilled. Similar to other commercial fields, the healthcare industry is witnessing a trend toward technology division and standardization, leading to improved quality and cost-effectiveness in healthcare delivery.

Within the IoMT framework, various types of e-health data are generated and shared among relevant parties. The increasing prevalence of the IoT devices has attracted attention from different industries, including healthcare. The healthcare industry is actively investigating the potential of technologies like ingestible sensors, wearables, moodables, and intelligent video pills to improve medication administration, monitor patients, and support paramedical personnel. The Internet of Things is revolutionizing the delivery of healthcare.

By implementing self-correcting capabilities based on feedback, IoMT devices may further increase the accuracy of their decisions. Doctors may use virtual assistants to research recent developments in the healthcare industry and academic literature and publications. Using virtual assistants in this way has the potential to improve healthcare.

Multiple hashes should be stored on sensor data to guarantee data integrity and patient ownership. By taking this precaution, vital medical records are protected from prying eyes and kept private.

In conclusion, the online healthcare industry is reorganizing to keep up with the rest of the business world. The proliferation of IoT devices offers diverse applications, including improved drug management, patient tracking, and assistance for healthcare professionals. Implementing the IoT technology in healthcare can lead to enhanced decision accuracy and improved patient care. Safeguarding data integrity and patient ownership is crucial to maintain the privacy and security of e-health data.

1.7   IoT Applications

A. IoT Application in Body Centric

Tools or systems that thoroughly interact with the body to gather psychological information are referred to as body-centric applications. The data are then evaluated and sent to healthcare providers for medical evaluation. Wearable and non-wearable medical technology is used in applications that concentrate on the human body. Intelligent sensors that can be implanted or worn as supplemental devices in the human body are referred to as medical wearables. This study shows a number of environmental applications that run on body-centric platforms.

B. IoT Application in Scanner

In areas with poor or nonexistent healthcare infrastructure, the Internet of Medical Things has opened up new possibilities. Since sonography has produced affordable portable ultrasound IoMT equipment that can be used at the point of care (POC), it is commonly employed. It is an independent device that only makes use of one field-programmable gate array (FPGA). By transmitting images to another system's external memory, the system may avoid the need for video processing hardware. Additionally, in distant areas where there is a lack of radiologists, the IoMT-enabled ultrasound technology has advantages.

C. Identification of Skin Disease by the IoT

To identify and track facial skin conditions, a portable application monitoring system is developed. The timely detection of medical issues could be made easier with the installation of sensors at healthcare facilities and public entrance points, reducing the frequency of unnecessary hospital visits. The use of the face detection approach shows promise in the field of monitoring and surveillance applications. In order to recognize face abnormalities, a real-time face disorders detection (RFDD) tool was developed in 2016. The investigators came up with a strategy to identify and separate the damaged area of the visage. The method that was presented was effective in identifying cold, flu, and fever cases. The RFDD has the potential to be employed in high-traffic settings such as medical facilities, transportation hubs, and aviation terminals to identify and mitigate the transmission of contagious illnesses within the populace.

D. IoT for Skin Disorder Detection

In an urgent scenario, it is crucial to quickly and accurately identify important resources. One of the most reliable and effective methods for attaining indoor localization is RFID technology. Devices can recognize things and gather data using radio waves. The two basic components of radio frequency identification technology are tags and readers. Transponders, which are made up of antennas and microchips, act as identifiers connected to numerous devices. Through the use of radio waves, the title is transmitted to and received by interrogators, which are the transmitters and receivers of the readers. Healthcare has adopted RFID technology to help with equipment-tracking systems. To help medical workers quickly identify and keep track of medical equipment, an RFID-based tracking system was created.

1.8   Different Layers in the IoMT

In this section, many writers have described various layers of the IoMT device management system. The construction of a structured framework that distinguishes the physical components of a network and their functional organization and configuration is a requirement of the discipline of architecture. The technology used, the application areas, and commercial concerns are only a few of the variables that have an impact on the Internet of Things' development. As mentioned, the management layer is in charge of controlling monitoring operations utilizing the cloud management tools that are widely used in 10T technology. In Figure 1.5, layer management in the IoMT is depicted.

A. *Sensor Layer in the IoMT*
The framework's sensor management layer is the most crucial part. The research highlights the Raspberry Pi, a remote two-lead EKG, devices, RTX4100, the Arduino platform, pulse oximetry, oxygen in the blood sensor, and smartphone sensors. Sensors capture biological signals. Biosensors could speed up data analysis and treatment by letting individuals monitor others' health. Sensors in healthcare should collect vital data for examination at a remote storage facility.

B. *Network Layer in the IoMT*
The network management layer is involved in a number of network operations, such as subnetting and Internet Protocol (IP) address. Access points, gateways, and routers are examples of tangible components included in this category. Due to the transmission of private information via network devices, the issue of network security has become a major concern in the healthcare industry. The IoMT security of the network layer requires the

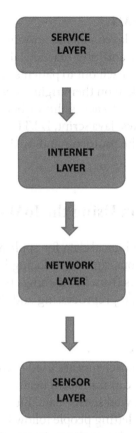

Figure 1.5 Different types of layers in the IoMT.

resolution of a number of issues, including trust management, integrity, confidentiality, authentication, and defense against denial-of-service attacks. Wi-Fi and Zigbee are the IoMT protocols that are most extensively used at the network layer tier. Due to its short range, Bluetooth technology is also used, albeit less frequently, and cannot be used in large spaces like hospitals.

C. *Internet Layer in the IoMT*
The Internet administration layer stores data. Cloud storage simplifies data administration. Cloud storage supports logical pools. Hosting companies own and operate physical storage infrastructure, which may include servers: on-demand algorithms and cloud-based services. Examples are big Query, cloud data stores, cloud SQL, Android, JavaScript, and machine learning algorithms.

D. Service Layer in the IoMT

The service management layer enables instant data access for medical specialists, ERs, hospitals, and pharmaceutical delivery networks. In an emergency, the doctor can reach out to patients remotely, check their medication histories, and check in on them right away. Additionally, the patient can use the offered interface to access his or her medical records anytime and wherever he or she likes. JavaScript, HTTPS/HTTP, and RESTful Web services are just a few of the protocols and methods that the layer is compatible with.

1.9   Data Collection Using the IoMT

In the IoMT, gathering biological data for application use is referred to as data acquisition. Continuous signal-producing biosensors are often used for data acquisition. Signals from living things frequently have low amplitudes and noise. As a result, preprocessing and digitization are applied to the signals above.

A. Facilitating Biosensors

Electronic devices called biosensors are used to monitor and measure biological signals. Biosensors can transform healthcare by linking people and the system. Caregivers get vital sensor data. Biosensors' simple data analysis speeds up diagnosis by letting people follow their health. Wearable and non-wearable biosensor technologies make up the IoMT paradigm. The IoMT uses several wearable and non-wearable technologies.

B. The Detection of Cancer Cells

For the purpose of diagnosing cancer, a patient's bodily samples are frequently taken. The prior case is examined once more to see if any malignant neoplastic cells are present. Obtaining a blood sample is a frequent method used to identify circulating tumor cells (CTCs) in the bloodstream. Contrarily, those receiving cancer therapy may experience considerable negative health effects from blood draws. Because of the use of IoMT devices, researchers have successfully created noninvasive methods for detecting circulating tumor cells.

C. Beds with Advanced Technology

The use of smart beds in hospitals is widespread. The use of technology makes it easier for carers or medical experts to monitor patients from a distance. Biosensors built into smart beds can pick up heartbeat, temperature, and breathing. Users of intelligent bed technology have access to detailed information on their heart rate variations, breathing patterns, and sleeping habits. In the event of an emergency that calls for immediate attention, smart beds have the capacity to sound an alarm or warn carers.

D. Detection of Human Activity

The most important health issues nowadays include cardiovascular disease, obesity, stroke, disorders, and musculoskeletal diseases. Implementing a human monitoring and healthy activity detection system in such situations offers the best chance for fast health recovery guidance and early detection of medical emergencies. By deploying effective wireless sensors, 10T technologies give healthcare personnel the ability to remotely administer healthcare systems and collect precise data. One such instance is the use of wireless sensor networks (WSNs) to identify human activity in a residential environment. The numerous interconnected sensors, however, involve significant deployment and maintenance expenses as well as significant power consumption. However, several coupled sensors need High costs for implementation, maintenance, and power usage. low-power network sensor detects human activities using radar.

E. A Wearable Device for Skin Care

Advanced sensors built into a wearable skin care gadget gather information from the skin and send it through Bluetooth or Wi-Fi to a smartphone app. The mobile application assesses the information based on the skin type and suggests the best LED color and patch. Then, LED-illuminated patches are attached to the skin.

F. An Intelligent Pillbox

The intelligent pillbox is a technological solution designed to assist individuals in effectively managing their medication regimen. With busy schedules and the need for clarity on medication prescriptions, there is a risk of improper administration, which can have negative effects on a person's overall well-being. Over the long term, adherence to medicine is frequently necessary for patients with chronic diseases, making it essential to take the correct dose at the right time.

In particular, older people have trouble taking their prescriptions as directed. Their health is in danger because they could miss doses or take too much of their medicine. These problems need a swift and effective response.

A prototype pillbox was developed as a solution to this problem. This small adaptable gadget can automatically sort medications into nine classes.

Accurate and consistent drug administration may be achieved by selecting the proper dose and time by individuals or their carers.

Better medication management and fewer adverse effects are two of the many benefits of using an intelligent pillbox. This gadget offers a workable answer to help patients preserve their health and well-being by ensuring their medications are taken as prescribed.

1.10   IoT Future Benefits

The healthcare industry has witnessed a significant increase in the adoption of the Internet of Things technology, particularly for monitoring patients' health status. However, there is still immense potential to transform primary healthcare establishments into advanced secondary care facilities, and identifying feasible technologies to achieve this objective is crucial.

One area of research with great importance is the prediction of stroke and epileptic seizures. Stroke is a leading cause of premature mortality globally, and approximately 50 million people worldwide suffer from epilepsy. Real-time prediction of these events holds significant value in advancing healthcare. Machine learning algorithms can be developed to detect and anticipate stroke and epileptic seizures before their occurrence, enabling prompt reactions and preventive strategies. Integrating ML algorithms with IoT-enabled healthcare systems can enhance the accuracy of real-time predictions for these conditions.

Another important healthcare application is the development of sensors for prosthetics using Tactile Internet communication. Deploying intelligent sensors that can perceive and extract relevant information from the environment is critical for prosthetics. Research and exploration of algorithms capable of extracting valuable insights from sensor data are essential in this domain.

The concept of the Internet of Nano Things (IoNT) involves integrating nanoscale devices and sensors into the IoT ecosystem. This emerging technology has the potential to revolutionize various industries, including healthcare, by enabling the collection and analysis of data at an unprecedented scale. However, there are limitations to be addressed in the healthcare sector, such as the finite energy reservoir of the IoNT. Harvesting potential energy can provide solutions for power-limited IoNT networks. Additionally, design concerns related to antennas, interoperable protocols for data sharing, and addressing signal interference within the human body require attention.

Looking ahead, the IoNT can be utilized to develop precision medicine applications. Improved treatment results and fewer side effects are possible using nano-robots that deliver drugs directly to targeted tissues. The growth of the IoNT network needs to provide future communication standards that improve coordination and control within the network.

Overall, there may be considerable improvements in patient care, medical event prediction, and the creation of novel applications for better treatment results if the healthcare industry embraces the IoT technology and explores its possibilities.

1.11   IoT Healthcare for the Future

Rising healthcare expenses and an aging population are two significant obstacles confronting the healthcare sector today. The IoMT shows promise to enhance patient care while decreasing costs. Healthcare practitioners may monitor patients from a distance and respond quickly to emergencies using remote diagnostics and video surveillance to identify signs of injury or illness. This boosts effectiveness while cutting expenses.

Data security and privacy concerns have been raised in response to the expanding connection of healthcare equipment. Protecting patient data and maintaining its privacy and security in storage are critical. Patient information compromised due to a security flaw might be used for identity theft, fraud, or illegal drug distribution. These issues need to be dealt with right now.

Trust is paramount in the healthcare industry when embracing new technologies, such as explainable artificial intelligence (XAI) models. Building confidence requires checking that the model is correct, fair, reliable, reproducible, stable, and comprehensive. For the model to be trusted, keeping its accuracy and precision high while making it easy to understand are crucial.

Cloud computing, which uses remote servers for storage and processing, is often used in designing IoMT systems. This centralized architecture has advantages in dependability, but it also introduces new privacy and security concerns. Due to resource constraints, IoMT devices cannot implement industry-standard cryptographic methods, and relying on remote servers creates privacy and reliability problems. Furthermore, because everything is stored in the cloud, there is just one weak link that might be compromised by anything from a hacker to a software glitch to a power outage.

Sensor data in medical devices must be accurate and precise to prevent patients from receiving false information or being put in harm's way. The functioning of a device must be consistent and reliable across usage, and alerts or warnings should make it easier to execute any necessary maintenance or replacement.

By incorporating various forms of medical data into clinical decision support systems, the IoMT has the potential to enhance the quality of healthcare delivery. Caretakers get invaluable insights into their patients' health conditions via this all-encompassing method, allowing for more efficient and precise therapy. The accuracy of medical treatment may be improved when services like sepsis diagnosis are readily available.

In conclusion, the IoMT has many applications in healthcare, but it also presents particular difficulties in data security, privacy, trust, system design, and sensor data accuracy. If the IoMT is to reach its full potential and be widely used in healthcare settings, these obstacles must be overcome.

1.12   Conclusion

The research conducted worldwide focuses on exploring technological advancements in healthcare by leveraging the potential of the IoMT as a supplementary solution to existing services. The study aims to contribute to novel dimensions of the IoMT usage through the utilization of multi-homing dense networks, addressing both challenges and opportunities within the healthcare system.

The preservation of global health is a significant concern, and scholarly attention has been increasingly directed toward the healthcare industry in recent years. The research examines current trends in utilizing the Internet of Things technology in healthcare and its potential benefits. It also explores emerging trends that hold promise in improving the effectiveness and efficiency of healthcare applications enabled by the IoT, leading to enhanced treatment outcomes.

The article delves into the challenges that hinder the development of reliable, efficient, and scalable healthcare applications enabled by the IoT technology and their adoption. It highlights the need for innovative opportunities and solutions to enhance the quality of healthcare treatment and improve human longevity.

One potential future development mentioned is the use of reinforcement algorithms incorporated into the IoT-enabled healthcare infrastructure. This development aims to address issues arising from the duplication of sensory data obtained from wearable sensor devices.

Overall, the research aims to contribute to advancements in healthcare technology by exploring the potential of the IoMT and addressing challenges to improve the quality of healthcare treatment and patient outcomes.

References

1. Abdellatif, A.A., Emam, A., Chiasserini, C.F., Mohamed, A., Jaoua, A., Ward, R., Edge-based compression and classification for smart healthcare systems: Concept, implementation and evaluation. *Expert Syst. Appl.*, 117, 1–14, 2019.
2. Liang, X., Zhao, J., Shetty, S., Liu, J., Li, D., Integrating blockchain for data sharing and collaboration in mobile healthcare applications, in: *2017 IEEE 28th Annual International Symposium on Personal, Indoor, and Mobile Radio Communications (PIMRC)*, pp. 1–5, October 2017.
3. Adeniyi, E.A., Ogundokun, R.O., Awotunde, J.B., Lomt-based wearable body sensors network healthcare monitoring system, in: *IOT in Healthcare and Ambient Assisted Living*, pp. 103–121, Springer, 2021. https://link.springer.com/chapter/10.1007/978-981-15-9897-5_6
4. AbuKhousa, E., Mohamed, N., Al-Jaroodi, J., E-health cloud: Opportunities and challenges. *Future Internet*, 4, 621–645, 2012. https://doi.org/10.3390/fi4030621. URL: https://www.mdpi.com/1999-5903/4/3/621.
5. Alam, M.M., Malik, H., Khan, M.I., Pardy, T., Kuusik, A., Le Moullec, Y., A survey on the roles of communication technologies in IOT-based personalized healthcare applications. *IEEE Access*, 6, 36611–36631, 2018.
6. Dilsizian, S.E. and Siegel, E.L., Artificial intelligence in medicine and cardiac imaging: Harnessing big data and advanced computing to provide personalized medical diagnosis and treatment. *Curr. Cardiol. Rep.*, 16, 441, 2014.
7. Srivastava, J., Routray, S., Ahmad, S., Waris, M.M., Internet of medical things (IOMT)-based smart healthcare system: Trends and progress. *Comput. Intell. Neurosci.*, 2022, 7218113, Jul. 16, 2022. doi: 10.1155/2022/7218113. PMID: 35880061; PMCID: PMC9308524.
8. Vishnu, S., Ramson, S.R.J., Jegan, R., Internet of medical things (IOMT)-An overview. *2020 5th International Conference on Devices, Circuits and Systems (ICDCS)*, Coimbatore, India, pp. 101–104, 2020, doi: 10.1109/ICDCS48716.2020.243558.
9. Ashfaq, Z., Rafay, A., Mumtaz, R., Zaidi, S.M.H., Saleem, H., Zaidi, S.A.R., Mumtaz, S., Haque, A., A review of enabling technologies for internet of medical things (IOMT) ecosystem. *Ain Shams Eng. J.*, 13, 4, 2090–4479, 2022.
10. He, Y., Aliyu, A., Evans, M., Luo, C., Health care cybersecurity challenges and solutions under the climate of COVID-19: Scoping review. *J. Med. Internet Res.*, 23, 4, e21747, 2021.

11. Abdulqader, T., Saatchi, R., Elphick, H., Respiration measurement in a simulated setting incorporating the internet of things. *Technologies*, 9, 2, 30, 2021.

12. Jayaraj, I., Shanmugam, B., Azam, S., Samy, G., A systematic review of radio frequency threats in IOMT. *J. Sens. Actuator Netw.*, 11, 4, 62, 2022.

13. Koohang, A., Sargent, C., Nord, J., Paliszkiewicz, J., Internet of things (IOT): From awareness to continued use. *Int. J. Inf. Manage.*, 62, 102442, 2022.

14. Yadav, S.P. and Yadav, S., Fusion of medical images in wavelet domain: a discrete mathematical model. *Ing. Solidaria Universidad Cooperativa Colombia-UCC*, 14, 25, 1–11, 2018. https://doi.org/10.16925/.v14i0.2236.

15. Joyia, G., Liaqat, R., Farooq, A., Rehman, S., Internet of medical things (IOMT): Applications, benefits and future challenges in healthcare domain. *J. Commun.*, 12, 240–247, 2017, doi: 10.12720/jcm.12.4.240-247.

16. Rayan, R., Tsagkaris, C., Iryna, R., The internet of things for healthcare: Applications, selected cases and challenges, 2021, doi: 10.1007/978-981-15-9897-5_1. https://www.jocm.us/index.php?m=content&c=index&a=show&catid=175&id=1103

17. Razdan, S. and Sharma, S., Internet of medical things (IOMT): Overview, emerging technologies, and case studies. *IETE Tech. Rev.*, 39, 4, 775–788, 2022. DOI: 10.1080/02564602.2021.1927863.

18. Yadav, S.P., Bhati, B.S., Mahato, D.P., Kumar, S., Federated learning for IOT applications, in: *EAI/Springer Innovations in Communication and Computing*, Springer International Publishing, 2022, https://doi.org/10.1007/978-3-030-85559-8.

19. Thimbleby, H., Technology and Healthcare in future. *J. Public Health Res.*, 2, 3, 160–167, 2013.

20. White Paper, *Internet of Things Strategic Research Roadmap*, Antoine de SaintExupery, September 15, 2009.

21. Dey, N., Hassanien, A.E., Bhatt, C., Ashour, A., Satapathy, S.C., *Internet of Things and Big Data Analytics Toward Next-Generation Intelligence*, pp. 3–20, Springer, 2018.

22. Dey, N., Ashour, A.S., Borra, S. (Eds.), *Classification in BioApps: Automation of Decision Making*, p. 26, Springer, 2017.

23. Tan, L. and Wang, N., Future internet: The internet of things. *3rd International Conference on Advanced Computer Theory and Engineering*, vol. 5, pp. 376–380, 2010.

24. Mewada, S., Saroliya, A., Chandramouli, N., Rajasanthosh Kumar, T., Lakshmi, M., Suma Christal Mary, S., Jayakumar, M., Smart diagnostic expert system for defect in forging process by using machine learning process. *J. Nanomater.*, 2022, Article ID 2567194, 8, 2022. https://doi.org/10.1155/2022/2567194.

25. Wu, M., Lu, T.J., Ling, F.Y., Sun, J., Du, H.Y., Research on the architecture of Internet of Things. *3rd International Conference on Advanced Computer Theory and Engineering*, vol. 5, pp. 484–487, 2010.

26. Pandikumar, S. and Vetrivel, R.S., Internet of things-based architecture of web and smart home interface using GSM. *Int. J. Innov. Res. Sci. Eng. Technol.*, 3, 3, 1721–1727, 2014.

27. Gómez, J., Huete, J.F., Hoyos, O., Perez, L., Grigori, D., Interaction system based on internet of things as support for education. *Proc. Comput. Sci.*, 21, 132–139, 2013.

28. Botterman, M., Internet of Things: An early reality of the future Internet, in: *Meeting at EU*, Prague, 2009.

29. Sharma, M. and Siddiqui, A., RFID based mobiles: Next generation applications, in: *2nd IEEE Int. Conf. Inf. Manag. Eng*, Chengdu, China, pp. 523–526, 2010.

30. Ziegler, J. and Urbas, L., Advanced interaction metaphors for RFID-tagged physical artefacts, in: *IEEE Int. Conf. RFID-Technologies Appl.*, Sitges, Spain, pp. 73–80, 2011.

31. Pandikumar, S. and Vetrivel, R.S., Internet of things-based architecture of web and smart home interface using GSM. *Int. J. Adv. Comput. Sci. Technol.*, 3, 3, 1721–1727, 2014.

32. Dimitrov, D.V., Medical internet of things and big data in healthcare. *Healthc. Inform. Res.*, 22, 3, 156–163, 2016.

33. Patel, S., Park, H., Bonato, P., Chan, L., Rodgers, M., A review of wearable sensors and systems with application in rehabilitation. *J. Neuroeng. Rehabil.*, 9, 21, 2012.

34. Yu, L., Lu, Y., Zhu, X., Smart hospital based on internet of things. *J. Netw.*, 7, 10, 1654–1667, 2012.

2

Fuzzy-Based IoMT System Design Challenges

Ramakrishna Kolikipogu[1]*, Shivaputra[2] and Makarand Upadhyaya[3]

[1]Department of Information Technology, Chaitanya Bharathi Institute of Technology (A), Hyderabad, India
[2]Department of Electronics and Communication Engineering, Dr. Ambedkar Institute of Technology, Bengaluru, India
[3]Department of Marketing, University of Bahrain, College of Business, Bahrain

Abstract

The desire for 24/7 Internet access to information is increased due to the rapid advancement of technology. With the help of the Internet of Things (IoT), intelligent items can be a key component of the omnipresent architecture. The organization experiences a decrease in expenses and workload as a result of inter-object communication. The industry is currently facing trouble integrating the Internet of Medical Things (IoMT) into its facilities. It is important to evaluate and solve these problems that are not only a time-consuming process but also need financial resources. It has applications in all industries, including medicine and healthcare. The writers of this study looked into several aspects of IoMT. This method aims to evaluate the relative significance of the elements causing the aforementioned problems. Fuzzy logic and MCDM techniques are used to achieve this. It would be beneficial for businesses to maximize productivity by lessening costs. After careful consideration and interaction with experts, the primary criteria and sub-criteria are decided. This inquiry aims to point out standards and constraints that prevent the widespread use of this method. Our research will enable to identify 19 criteria that the industry should prioritize in the evolution of the IoMT that speeds up adoption by reducing the time and financial hardship with the aid of this study.

Keywords: Pervasive framework, Internet of Medical Things (IoMT), fuzzy logic, multicriteria of decision-making

*Corresponding author: krkrishna.cse@gmail.com

Satya Prakash Yadav, Sudesh Yadav, Pethuru Raj Chelliah and Victor Hugo C. de Albuquerque (eds.)
Advances in Fuzzy-Based Internet of Medical Things (IoMT), (25–38) © 2024 Scrivener Publishing LLC

2.1   Introduction

Exceeding today's creative power, computing technology instantaneously soars [1]. The Internet of Things (IoT) is one of the top-ranking technologies, and soon, everything will be connected to it. It will develop its own space where everything will be controlled and transmitted through the Internet with the aid of sensors and radio frequency identification (RFID) [2]. The gadgets will design their ecosystem. The tremendous data results will be effectively saved, refined, and revealed for easy understanding [3, 4]. The virtual infrastructure for visualization platforms and utility computing acknowledgment to cloud computing [5], which integrates device monitoring [6, 7], storage device integration [8], client delivery [9, 10], analytics tools [11], and visualization [12, 13]. Users and organizations will be able to access applications on demand and from any location, to cloud computing [14]. Healthcare is one of the most significant Internet of Things (IoT) applications. In this project, a health-monitoring gadget is constructed to track and maintain human health statuses, including heart rate, temperature, and air quality, using available and affordable sensors [15].

A fuzzy logic strategy is adopted. The idea of the fuzzy logic method was introduced by Lotfi Zadeh [16]. The truth values of this logic range between any two real integers, 0 and 2. The partial truth idea is handled by fuzzy logic, where the truth value can range from fully faulty to completely true [17].

2.1.1   Multiple Criteria Analysis

Multiple criteria analysis identifies optimal choices from a range of alternatives with distinct attributes. They are often opposing one another and utilizing a decision matrix. This facilitates and supports the process of decision-making in situations where intricate criteria are involved. The method of multi-criteria decision-making (MCDM) consists of the identification of distinct criteria and sub-criteria, followed by the evaluation, selection, and prioritization of available alternatives. Numerous multi-criteria decision-making techniques have been examined in the literature review. The decision-making tool is highly advanced and incorporates both quantitative and qualitative factors [18, 19].

As shown in Figure 2.1, the topic of multi-criteria decision-making comprises a variety of techniques, and these techniques are currently used to address issues concerning the IoT [20, 21].

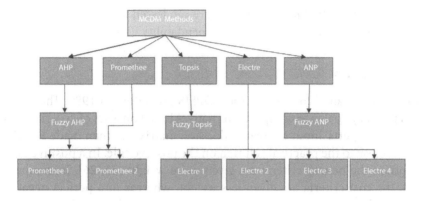

Figure 2.1 Comprises a variety of techniques are provided.

This article used a composition of AHP and TOPSIS and combined them to assess difficulties associated with the IoT. Create conditions and sub-criteria to compare the table to determine the weight requirement. Finally, conclude the grid matrix to mark the options [22, 23].

2.1.2   AHP Methods

Thomas Saaty, a famous mathematician, developed AHP for complex judgments and made work easier for various sectors to prioritize different options. It is an effective method for resolving difficult and unstructured problems. The problematic scenario is consistently broken down into minor issues and arranged into hierarchical tiers in AHP. Some criteria, sub-criteria, are alternatives represented at each level of the hierarchical structure. Each possibility is synthesized and ranked or prioritized to arrive at the ideal answer. The AHP is a weighting-based multi-criteria analysis methodology where each criterion denotes its relative relevance. AHP is used in engineering, healthcare, finance, and education. In AHP, the initial weighting methodology is utilized where each measure is compared to the other criteria by assigning values. There are several areas where the AHP's initial version might be improved. While pointing out the shortcomings of AHP, Chen and Yang [24] also noted that it is only used for precise information, that judgments are made utilizing an unbalanced scale, it is unable to account for the uncertainty intrinsic in human opinions, it produces imprecise rankings, and that the end decision solely depends on the idea of experts. Several scholars combined AHP with fuzzy set theory to eliminate the inconsistencies in the AHP. To determine the weights in 1986, Buckley [25] employed fuzzy trapezoidal numbers. Applying the ambiguous analytic hierarchy procedure can lessen the biases of the assessors, improve validity, and increase dependability [24].

2.1.3 Topics

Yoon and Hwang [26] created the TOPSIS procedure in 1980. The method's primary goal is to compare alternatives based on a set of criteria. They gathered experts' input to create a decision matrix and then made a choice that is close to the practical solution on the positive side. In a positive ideal solution, the benefit criteria are given more weight [25, 26]. In comparison, the cost criteria are given less weight, whereas in a perfect negative answer, the cost criteria are given more weightage while the benefit criteria are given less weightage [27]. The conclusion is, based on the requirements, the positive ideal solution offers the best values, and vice versa. A complete survey can be read by readers who are more interested in learning about TOPSIS. Fuzzy TOPSIS is similar to classical TOPSIS in Chen's methodology. Numerous studies have been carried out using fuzzy logic with TOPSIS for the IoT.

2.2 TOPSIS Method

Problems associated with the Internet of Medical Things (IoMT) in world mid-size industries are evaluated in this study. The goal of the investigation is to determine the obstacles to the adoption and implementation of the IoMT by analyzing and defining its significance. The factors need special consideration to be highlighted. Discussions with IoMT advisers and pertinent organization stakeholders and standards are created. This analysis is used in micro and mid-sized businesses (SMEs) open to utilizing IoMT services as a record. Specialists are engaged for this expert input on the criterion evaluation. There are three decision-makers questioned by the organization. These decision-makers refer to the Internet for medical-related information. The decision-makers have dealt with information about the IoMT-related literature and have faced similar difficulties. The study is being hampered by a smaller number of decision-makers. The authors use the literature analysis to validate the perfection of the assessment to address this article's provoking lack of assessments. Three decision-makers evaluated the IoMT utilizing fuzzy-based methodologies. The decision-makers evaluated fuzzy-based pairwise comparisons on matrices independently. Following that, these judgments are combined using fuzzy aggregation equations.

2.2.1   Medical IoT Challenge

Medical-related topics are investigated via the Internet as part of a thorough methodical literature evaluation. The same problem examined in the literature review is also the subject of our investigation, and it also establishes the criteria and methods that the study's author utilized. The comprehensive literature evaluation at each research branch is essential and is still developing. The IoT concept is not new, but due to its dynamic expansion, particularly in the healthcare industry, it is evolving rapidly. This study was initially tested with small- and medium-sized businesses. Before assessing, decision-makers and specialists first analyze the organizational structure. The decision-makers researched the ideas from this article's literature study and on Internet medical things. Experts established survey goals and revised and finalized their recommended conditions and sub-criteria of the IoT issues while considering the previous research on relevant themes. With specialists and industry stakeholders, the criteria's validity and authenticity are examined thoroughly before the evaluation process begins.

The pairwise comparison matrix must then be created, and the real numbers must be converted into fuzzy numbers. In Figure 2.2, Fuzzy triangular numbers are employed to achieve this, as seen below.

Information on a particular aspect of TFIS numbers (TrFNs), TFNs, AHP (Analytic Hierarchy Process), TOPSIS (Technique for Order of

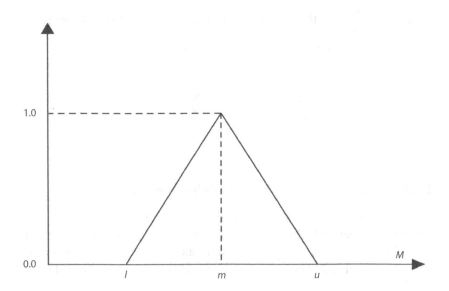

Figure 2.2 Fuzzy triangular number.

Preference by Similarity to Ideal Solution), or FTMF (I presume Fuzzy Topsis Multi-Factor), among other things. Equation 2.1 formulates FTMF, and (L, M, u) for cross-reference.

$$\mu(M) = \begin{cases} 0 \\ (X-L)(M-L) \\ 0 \end{cases} \tag{2.1}$$

$$M_{gi}^1, M_{gi}^2 \ldots\ldots, M_{gi}^m, i = 1,2,3\ldots\ldots n \tag{2.2}$$

2.2.2   Fuzzy Analytic Hierarchy Process

Calculate the weights method, fuzzy synthetic concerning object by utilizing the given equation:

$$S_i = \sum_{j-1}^{m} Mj = 0 \tag{2.3}$$

To obtain $\sum_{j-1}^{m} Mj$, the fuzzy addition formula applies to m extent method by using the equation:

$$\sum_{j-1}^{m} Mj = \left[\sum_{i=1}^{m} m \ \sum_{j=1}^{m} mM_{ji}^j \right] \tag{2.4}$$

2.2.3   Calculating of Local and Global Weights

The general local weight is determined once the consequences of the criteria have been defined. The difference in the pairwise matrix will be created for each sub-criterion, and the local weights of the sub-criteria determine Equations 2.1 to 2.2. The values of the weights must be multiplied by the local consequences of the sub-criteria to ascertain the global importance of the criteria. The entire process of calculating the general and global weight of the criteria is done by the FIS system. Values entered on the ruler are displayed in the weighted values column. The weighting of measures concerning other criteria in the same criteria folder is shown in the local weights column. One will always be the sum of the local weights of all the requirements found in a single criteria folder. Each criterion's weight concerning the top of the tree is displayed in the global and global weight and international weights both depict how a slice of a pie corresponding to a criteria folder is divided up among its sub-criteria. Decision-maker weights can be accessed from the model menu. This shows a table with relevant weight paradigm criteria in the rows and the decision-makers in the model's columns. Each row's values are normalized, and each row's weights add up to 1.

2.2.4   Fuzzy TOPSIS Technique

The fuzzy TOPSIS technique is introduced in the study's fourth stage to examine the options depending on criteria established by the murky analytic hierarchy process. To create a TOPSIS method decision, this approach takes advantage of linguistic variables.

$$\widehat{B} = [r]m *_n$$

2.3   Results and Discussion

The proposed methodology can be used for installing the IoMT by the organization to assess the difficulties it will face in actual use. There are four choices, 20 sub-criteria, and five criteria in this IoMT problem. The planned company is small- to medium-sized business. In-depth interviews with three (IoMT) specialists and business stakeholders are undertaken. Prior to interviewing the specialist, a linguistic scale is established based on ambiguous triangular numbers and discussed with them [refer Fig. 2.3]. The bulk of the IoMT experts approached by the authors declined to help them because of their own and their employers' restrictions. After the language scale is approved, a discussion with the experts about the criteria and sub-criteria will be taken. It is important to note that the expert personally visited every IoMT specialist and had a discussion with them about the above topics. It is important to note that the experts'

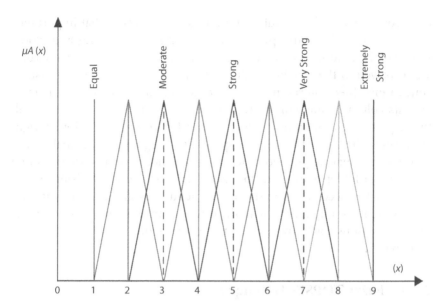

Figure 2.3 Linguistic triangular numbers.

names and the names of their organizations are excluded from this article in order to respect their right to privacy. The experts provided the finalized recommended criteria and linguistic scale, along with instructions on how to input their contribution into the paired matrix. The writers suggested this fuzzy methodology after creating a pairwise matrix, and the outcomes are displayed in Table 2.1. The four options were chosen by the writers as a sample for evaluation and ranking. The experts then ranked each possibility after considering the TOPSIS parameters, providing their assessments of each. In Table 2.2, the aggregated matrix is displayed.

The fuzzy hierarchy method and TOPSIS method are coupled to produce the greatest results to overcome defects in both processes. The suggested

Table 2.1 Each criterion on weight.

(C1)	(C2)	(C3)	(C4)	(C5)
282	242	213	134	129

Table 2.2 Fuzzy decision matrix.

Sub-criteria alternative	S1	S2	S3	S4	S5	S6	S7
Alternative 1	(5, 7,9)	(3,7,9)	(3,5,7)	(3,6,9)	(1,6,9)	(1,5,9)	(3,7,9)
Alternative 2	(1, 6, 9)	(1,6,9)	(5,7,9)	(1,6,9)	(1, 4, 9)	(1,3,7)	(1, 6, 9)
Alternative 3	(5,8,9)	(1,6,9)	(5,8,9)	(5,7,9)	(5,7,9)	(1,6,9)	(3, 6, 9)
Alternative 4	(5, 8, 9)	(3,5,7)	(1,2,5)	(1,4,7)	(1, 6, 9)	(3,6,9)	(1,5,9)

method for solving the difficulties related to the IoMT is numerically illustrated below.

Defining the study's objectives and aims is as follows:

Step 1. Research goals in this instance are to assess and rank the difficulties incorporated, identify the most pressing issues, and take timely action to reduce costs.

Step 2: The most crucial step in this study is to finalize the standards to be used to assess and rank substitutes. These specifics are developed and covered in the preceding section.

Step 3: A variety of linguistic substitutes throughout the literature study. These measures had been created with the nature of the issue in mind. In this study, employ Saaty's scale and TFNs.

FIS numbers and scale values, FIS-based dual comparison matrix as shown in Tables 2.3 and 2.4.

Table 2.3 FIS numbers and scale.

Scale (0–1)	Evaluation	FIS scale	Reciprocal
1	Equal important (EI)	(1, 1, 1)	(1, 1, 1)
3	Moderate important (MI)	(1, 3, 5)	(1/5, 1/3, 1)
5	Strong important (SI)	(3, 5, 7)	(1/7, 1/5, 1/3)

Table 2.4 FIS-based dual comparison matrix.

Criterion	C-1	C-2	C-3	C-4	C-5
C-1	(1, 1, 0)	(3, 5, 0)	(1, 3, 0)	(1, 3, 0)	(1, 1, 0)
C-2	(17,15,13)	(1, 1, 0)	(3, 5, 0)	(1, 3, 0)	(1, 1, 0)
C-3	(15, 13, 0)	(17, 15, 3)	(1, 1, 0)	(5, 7, 0)	(13, 13, 13)
C-4	(15, 13, 1)	(15, 13, 1)	(9,7, 5)	(0, 1, 0)	(1, 3, 0)
C-5	(0, 1, 2)	(1, 0, 2)	(3, 3, 0)	(1, 0, 1)	(0, 1, 1)

2.4 Conclusion

The decision to operate in a complicated network environment becomes a critical technological and operational choice on the net. This work employs techniques to handle the IoMT for the first time. The weights of the TOPSIS criteria can be determined by applying fuzzy set theory in conjunction with AHP, which will help to lessen the uncertainties and worries that continue to be a barrier in finding IoT, provocation, particularly in healthcare. For two-way differentiation and the grid analysis, we include fuzzy variables and skillful judgment, which is relied upon, and realistically affected the ultimate decision-making process. The suggested method consists of four divisions, each of which is autonomous to modify its result for the subsequent phase. This study is related to the IoMT and looks at Pakistani minor and mid-sized businesses. The condition related to the Internet of Medical Things needs to be evaluated by experts in that field. All legal issues including cost need to be examined as they relate to the challenges posed by the Internet of Medical Things. Twenty different criteria are divided into four options. The significance of the criterion is calculated using the fuzzy method. The research findings led to the conclusion that data, legal concerns, and the cost should all be taken into consideration by the industry before embracing the Internet of Medical Things. The aggregate TOPSIS weight criteria are calculated using the fuzzy approach, and the prime four conditions are regular affairs (12.5%), secrecy (10.5%), data use (10.5%), and real-time processing (8.5%). Recent comparison and earlier studies are encouraged. For the upcoming work, various criteria and standards can also be taken into account.

References

1. Atiew, S., Usman, M., Chaudhry, S.A., Bashir, A.K., Jolfaei, A., Srivastava, G., Fuzzy-in-the-loop-driven low-cost and secure biometric user access to server. *IEEE Trans. Reliab.*, 70, 3, 2020. https://e-space.mmu.ac.uk/626645/7/2020-IEEE%20TRL-%20Fuzzy-in-the-Loop%20Driven%20Low%20Cost%20and%20Secure%20e.pdf

2. Almogren, A., Mohiuddin, I., Din, I.U., Almajed, H., Guizani, N., FTM-IoMT: Fuzzy-based trust management for preventing sybil attacks in internet of medical things. *IEEE Internet Things J.*, 4485–4497, 1–17, 2021.

3. Al-Turjman, F., Nawaz, M.H., Ulusar, U.D., Intelligence in the internet of medical things era: A systematic review of current and future trends. *Comput. Commun.*, 150, 644–660, 2020.

4. Jeyavel, J., Parameswaran, T., Mannan, J.M., Hariharan, U., Security vulnerabilities and intelligent solutions for iomt systems, in: *Internet of Medical Things: Remote Healthcare Systems and Applications*, pp. 175–194, 2021.

5. Panja, S., Chattopadhyay, A.K., Nag, A., Singh, J.P., Fuzzy-logic-based IoMT framework for COVID19 patient monitoring. *Comput. Ind. Eng.*, 176, 108941, 2023.

6. Singh, N. and Das, A.K., Energy-efficient fuzzy data offloading for IoMT. *Comput. Netw.*, 213, 109127, 2022.

7. Jaaz, Z.A., Ansari, M.D., JosephNg, P.S., Gheni, H.M., Optimization technique based on cluster head selection algorithm for 5G-enabled IoMT smart healthcare framework for industry. *Paladyn J. Behav. Robotics*, 13, 1, 99–109, 2022.

8. Kumar, P., Gupta, G.P., Tripathi, R., An ensemble learning and fog-cloud architecture-driven cyber-attack detection framework for IoMT networks. *Comput. Commun.*, 166, 110–124, 2021.

9. Tariq, M., II, Mian, N.A., Sohail, A., Alyas, T., Ahmad, R., Evaluation of the challenges in the Internet of medical things with multicriteria decision making (AHP and TOPSIS) to overcome its obstruction under fuzzy environment. *Mob. Inf. Syst.*, 2020, 1–19, 2020.

10. Alattas, K. and Wu, Q., A framework to evaluate the barriers for adopting the internet of medical things using the extended generalized TODIM method under the hesitant fuzzy environment. *Appl. Intell.*, 52, 12, 13345–63, Sep. 2022.

11. Yuan, X., Chen, J., Zhang, K., Wu, Y., Yang, T., A stable AI-based binary and multiple class heart disease prediction model for IoMT. *IEEE Trans. Industr. Inform.*, 18, 3, 2032–2040, 2021.

12. Zanbouri, K., Al-Khafaji, H.M., Navimipour, N.J., Yalçın, Ş., A new fog-based transmission scheduler on the Internet of multimedia things using a fuzzy-based quantum genetic algorithm. *IEEE MultiMedia*, 1–14, Feb. 28, 2023.

13. Yadav, S.P., Blockchain security, in: *Blockchain Security in Cloud Computing. EAI/Springer Innovations in Communication and Computing*, K. Baalamurugan, S.R. Kumar, A. Kumar, V. Kumar, S. Padmanaban, (Eds.), Springer, Cham, 2022, https://doi.org/10.1007/978-3-030-70501-5_1.

14. Pujahari, R.M., Yadav, S.P., Khan, R., Intelligent farming system through weather forecast support and crop production, in: *Application of Machine Learning in Agriculture*, 8, 2, pp. 113–130, 214–219, Elsevier, 2022, https://doi.org/10.1016/b978-0-323-90550-3.00009-6.

15. Fiaidhi, J. and Mohammed, S., Internet of medical things (IOMT) standards and security challenges, *An Adaptive Intrusion Detection System in the Internet of Medical Things Using Fuzzy-Based Learning, Sensors*, 23, 9247, 1–19, 2023. https://doi.org/10.3390/s23229247 https://www.mdpi.com/journal/sensors

16. Praveen, R. and Pabitha, P., A secure lightweight fuzzy embedder based user authentication scheme for internet of medical things applications. *J. Intell. Fuzzy Syst., (Preprint)*, 1–20, 1–36, 2023.

17. Dhotre, V.A. *et al.*, Big data analytics using MapReduce for education system. *Linguist. Antverp.*, 3130–3138, 1–20, 2021.

18. Yao, Y.C., Wu, H.T., Shu, L.F., Lu, C.Y., Developing a multifunctional heating pad based on fuzzy-edge computations and IoMT approach. *J. Internet Technol.*, 23, 7, 1519–1525, 2022.

19. Ur Rasool, R., Ahmad, H.F., Rafique, W., Qayyum, A., Qadir, J., Security and privacy of internet of medical things: A contemporary review in the age of surveillance, botnets, and adversarial ML. *J. Netw. Comput. Appl.*, 103332, 1–23, 2022.

20. Ravi, V., Pham, T.D., Alazab, M., Attention-based multidimensional deep learning approach for cross-architecture IoMT malware detection and classification in healthcare cyber-physical systems. *IEEE Trans. Comput. Soc. Syst.*, 1–12, 2022.

21. Dong, X. *et al.*, Secure chaff-less fuzzy vault for face identification systems. *ACM Trans. Multimidia Comput. Commun. Appl.*, 17, 3, 1–22, 2021.

22. Chakraborty, C. and Kishor, A., Real-time cloud-based patient-centric monitoring using computational health systems. *IEEE Trans. Comput. Soc. Syst.*, 9, 6, 1613–1623, 2022.

23. Sodhro, A.H. and Zahid, N., AI-enabled framework for fog computing driven e-healthcare applications. *Sensors*, 21, 23, 8039, 2021.

24. Aslam, B., Javed, A.R., Chakraborty, C., Nebhen, J., Raqib, S., Rizwan, M., Blockchain and ANFIS empowered IoMT application for privacy preserved contact tracing in COVID-19 pandemic. *Pers. Ubiquitous Comput.*, 1–17, 1–24, 2021.

25. Pirbhulal, S., Wu, W., Li, G., A biometric security model for wearable healthcare, in: *2018 IEEE International Conference on Data Mining Workshops (ICDMW)*, IEEE, pp. 136–143, November 2018.

26. Hassanien, A.E., Dey, N., Borra, S. (Eds.), *Medical Big Data and Internet of Medical Things: Advances, Challenges and Applications*, 356 pp, Imprint CRC Press, Boca Raton, 2018.

27. Silva, A.F. and Tavakoli, M., Domiciliary hospitalization through wearable biomonitoring patches: Recent advances, technical challenges, and the relation to COVID-19. *Sensors*, 20, 23, 6835, 2020.

3

Development and Implementation of a Fuzzy Logic-Based Framework for the Internet of Medical Things (IoMT)

Santosh Reddy P.[1]*, Mamatha A.[2], Akshatha Kamath[2], Sreelatha P. K.[3], Santosh Y. N.[4] and Pallavi C. V.[1]

[1]Department of Computer Science & Engineering, B.N.M Institute of Technology, Bangalore, India
[2]Department of Computer Science & Engineering, Ramaiah Institute of Technology, Bangalore, India
[3]Department of Computer Science & Engineering, Presidency University, Bangalore, India
[4]Department of Information Science & Engineering, Sai Vidya Institute of Technology, Bangalore, India

Abstract

The growth of remote sensors and worn-out technologies revolutionized health status. Massive amounts of health data, often unstructured and diverse, are produced by the widespread sensors and health devices. Many methods are established to safeguard the sharing of private information. However, fuzzy logic systems are used to organize and verify health data. Their energy reserves impact the reliability, accuracy, and responsiveness of wireless sensors and devices. To make proper medical diagnoses and decisions, it is necessary to use techniques such as categorization, noise reduction, and precise health data interoperability. The difficulties associated with crude medical information and administrative data can be mitigated using a fuzzy logic system and related algorithms. Fuzzy logic depends on artificial intelligence (AI) networks and enhancement methods. The healthcare-related application and framework can be improved by testing the information to improve accuracy; the current study reviews a variety of works that incorporate these systems and algorithms to do so. The present study outlines a novel technique in topic modeling, known as fuzzy latent semantic analysis (FLSA), which incorporates a fuzzy perspective. The fuzzy latent semantic analysis

*Corresponding author: santoshreddy@bnmit.in

Satya Prakash Yadav, Sudesh Yadav, Pethuru Raj Chelliah and Victor Hugo C. de Albuquerque (eds.)
Advances in Fuzzy-Based Internet of Medical Things (IoMT), (39–58) © 2024 Scrivener Publishing LLC

has the capability to address the problem of redundancy in health and medical datasets and introduces a novel approach for determining the number of topics. Future studies should focus on increasing the reasoning component's flexibility by integrating new features into the existing cloud infrastructure and testing new machine-learning approaches.

Keywords: Fuzzy logic, data sharing, neural networks, FLSA

3.1   Introduction

There are significant opportunities to enhance clinical outcomes and patient satisfaction, decrease healthcare costs, and impact population health as artificial intelligence (AI) matures in enhancing healthcare. When it comes to keeping servers online around the clock [1, 2], the contents and assets of large corporations often need a helping hand, AI health-checking tasks must follow certain guidelines for clearing stored data. These tasks cannot handle long-pending resource deletion. More doctors need to be increased to meet the need of society, where the population is growing and new diseases are appearing. In the artificial neural network (ANN), neuro-fuzzy is a hybrid approach that combines AI with fuzzy logic [3]. "Fuzzy logic" has an infinite valued reason that depends on human decision-making where non-numerical information may be expressed as a set of mathematical terms [4]. This method may recognize, manipulate, describe, interpret, and use data and information. The following sets of Mamdani rules underpin the operation of fuzzy models.

(a)   Convert all input values to fuzzy membership.
(b)   To calculate the fuzzy output functions, it is necessary to carry out all relevant rules in the rule-based system.
(c)   Converting fuzzy values into crisp values is called defuzzification.

The fuzzy model system operates through the process of fuzzification, which involves the use of layered structures. Fuzzification refers to transforming a numerical input system into fuzzy sets characterized by varying degrees of membership. The fuzzy sets are represented using linguistic terms. The observation lies within the range of 0 and 1. Membership in a fuzzy group is determined by the degree to which an element satisfies the set's membership function. Specifically, a membership function gives a degree of membership to each element in the universe of discourse, and a value of 0 indicates full non-membership in the fuzzy set associated with that membership function; whereas if the value is between 0 and 1, it belongs to the fuzzy set to some degree. The graphical representation of fuzzy sets is commonly depicted through triangle and trapezoid curves. The graph displays the gradient at points where there is a variation in the values. The apex is situated at a numerical value of 1, and as the value diminishes, the gradient exhibits a sigmoidal trend. The comparative analysis between Boolean and fuzzy logic systems is presented in Figure 3.1.

Fuzzy logic algorithms have been applied in managing medical data, decision-making, and safety protocols [5]. The advent of WBAN devices has simplified regular monitoring and medical management owing to the swift advancements in wireless communication and sensor technology. The primary limitations of WBAN sensors pertain to the imprecision and inaccuracies associated with data sensing and exchange, mainly when operating under conditions of low usage of power. Evaluating efficacy models and systems based on fuzzy logic is a crucial aspect of performance analysis.

Chronic illnesses, neurodegenerative disorders like glaucoma and Parkinson's disease, and carcinogenic tumors like blood cancer and breast and lung cancer are only a few examples where adaptive neuro-fuzzy models may be used and give applicable detection models. Some instruments, including computer-aided diagnosis (CAD), which physicians and medical professionals widely use, may help with the early identification and treatment of many disorders. The CAD is used before making life-or-death decisions on the care of patients. There are two main components to the CAD system's operation: feature extraction and categorization. Decision trees, random forests, support vector machines (SVMs), and adaptive neuro-fuzzy inference systems (ANFISs) are some of the most often used classifiers in computer-aided design (CAD) systems. M-GSO, a glow worm optimization technique variant, may help with this. The differential evolution (DE) method is used to enhance the performance of the M-GSO algorithm.

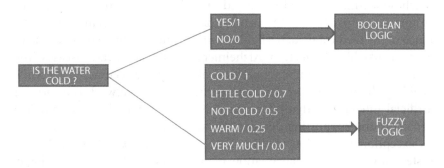

Figure 3.1 Difference between fuzzy systems and Boolean.

The result is compared with those obtained using the classic ANFIS model, the genetic algorithm, the ANFIS, the lion optimization method, the ANFIS differential evolution algorithm, and several other algorithms to demonstrate the superiority of the DE approach.

A range of neurological disorders can be identified, including neuromuscular disorder, epilepsy, autism, cognitive impairment, brain tumor, ADHD, and stroke. Specific neurological issues are considered congenital, during the prenatal period. Additional complications may occur due to tumors, degenerative conditions, traumatic injuries, infections, and structural abnormalities. Neurological impairment arises from damage to the nervous system regardless of the origin. The degree of impairment of communication, vision, hearing, and sensation is contingent upon the site of the injury. Neurological disorders, including but not limited to Parkinson's disease, Alzheimer's disease, brain tumors, epilepsy, dementia, memory loss, and stroke, are prevalent among individuals of all ages. These conditions are often associated with depression, anxiety, and other nervous system-related ailments. As per the World Health Organization (WHO), a significant proportion of the global population is afflicted by neurological diseases, leading to a surge in mortality and morbidity rates.

However, it is widely acknowledged that diagnosing neurological disorders poses a significant challenge due to the intricate nature of diagnostic protocols involved. Modern censoring equipment enables early diagnosis and accurate management of chronic diseases. Numerous researchers are currently studying neurological disorders by implementing artificial intelligence, specifically, deep learning techniques, to achieve precise diagnosis and effective treatment. The utilization of computing systems is crucial in the realm of medical diagnosis and treatment based on various AI technologies; the neuro-fuzzy method is widely recognized and utilized for its efficacy in disease classification and detection. This system reduces the workload of the workers. In brief, the neuro-fuzzy system represents a machine learning method enhanced by utilizing machine learning algorithms. The utilization of the neuro-fuzzy system is a paramount importance in the medical field, particularly in the timely diagnosis of persistent ailments like blood infection, Alzheimer's disease, and heart diseases. The neuro-fuzzy system exhibits superior proficiency and accuracy levels while enabling the information. Fojnica's artificial neural network is a form of artificial intelligence that offers capabilities for comprehending physical problems and supporting decision-making in critical scenarios owing to its exceptional precision in disease detection. The execution of the NF system involves the amalgamation of neural networks and fuzzy logic, which results in enhanced accuracy and performance. The artificial neural network operates through a layered structure comprising an input, hidden, and output layer. Artificial neural networks are designed to emulate the human brain's functionality. They are also utilized in developing artificial animal brains for pattern recognition.

In many contexts, a fuzzy logic differential application might be helpful as shown in Figure 3.2. Early detection and healing of diabetic foot ulcers are done in many ways in which NFS is essential. Practitioners use several fuzzy logic systems and algorithms in managing health information and decision-making. The advent of WBAN sensor devices facilitates real-time observing health management more accessible. Evaluating the efficacy of models and systems built using fuzzy logic is crucial.

The proliferation of WBAN sensors and wearable devices has increased exponentially, which is attributed to the development of wireless communication technology and the industrial revolution. Massive amounts of diverse unorganized data are being produced. Many suggested theories and methods for data interpretation, categorization, and analysis have been proposed, but they need to be more consistent and reliable. Fuzzy logic has

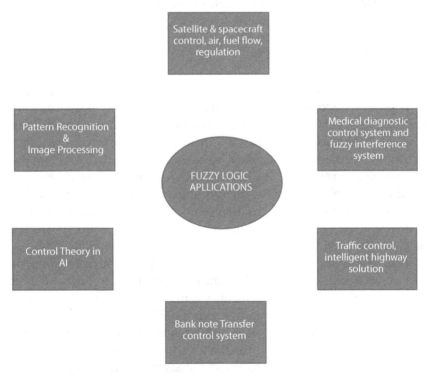

Figure 3.2 Fuzzy logic—different applications.

been successfully used in many healthcare settings, including electronic health records, mobile health applications, and hospital administration. The suggested approach has real-world implications for people with heart disease and diabetes.

Wireless body area network system has played an important role in real-time and health management more accessible. This is due in the part of discharging elderly patients and in part to the development of the WBAN sensor system. Uncertainty in data sensing and sharing while operating on low power consumption are significant limitations of WBAN sensors. Evaluating the efficacy of models and systems built using fuzzy logic is crucial.

One further case is the remote monitoring and discharging of elderly patients from hospital care. The fuzzy model helps in various purposes, including the automation of health history, the administration of security-critical applications, improved patient prognosis and forecasting, precise diagnosis, and the efficient support of medical professionals, scientists, and researchers.

A thorough study shows that this system in the healthcare application needs improvement. This is what inspired the author to discuss how fuzzy logic impacts the KPIs of a health data management architecture.

3.2   Literature Review

A proposed framework for the secure distribution of health records aims to ensure safe access control and privacy of electronic healthcare data (EHD). Implementing blockchain technology will eliminate the need for a reliable data storage intermediary. The framework employs a technique known as searchable key attribute-based encryption (ABE) to attain precise access control [1–3]. The present authors comprehensively examine the divergent objectives of accessibility and security of electronic medical records. They also analyze the nontechnical and technical components that comprise a viable security resolution [4]. The contention posits that an electronic medical record, coupled with appropriate policy guidelines and contemporary technology, may provide superior security compared to a conventional paper record [5]. The present study introduces MedRec, a decentralized record management system that utilizes blockchain technology to manage electronic health records (EHRs). The system provides patients with an all-inclusive and unalterable record and convenient access to their medical data throughout various healthcare providers and treatment locations [6–8]. The present study on survey research examines multiple text mining techniques, subdisciplines, and domains of application, encompassing the scholarly works published from 2010 to 2022. The document's structure is predicated upon delineating subtasks, utilizing various text-mining methodologies and techniques, and contextualizing potential application scenarios [9–11]. According to the classifications above of Web mining, this study examines these methods. These methods fall into three categories: fuzzy Web use mining, fuzzy Web content mining, or fuzzy Web structure mining [12]. Design a system that can analyze the word sequences produced by voice recognition systems by learning the fuzzy semantic links between the ideas represented by words from a linguistic corpus [13]. To be more specific, the system will be able to make predictions about the words that a voice recognition system missed [14]. For sentence-level similarity-based text summarization, we suggest using fuzzy rough sets. The representation of textual data is inherently shaky due to their intrinsic ambiguity, imprecision, and incompleteness [15–17]. It uses word patterns to describe both high-level and low-level aspects. Words are organized into groups, and their relative importance is adjusted depending on how often they appear in the text and other factors [18]. Using the big data paradigm, this study describes an automated fuzzification approach that allows finding connections and patterns in the weather and sensor data that may be retrieved from an indoor office environment [19]. One hundred twenty publications covering the many tasks and applications of opinion mining during the previous decade are summarized in this overview, which depicts the various uses of fuzzy logic [20]. The load frequency control (LFC) issue has been an important topic in designing and operating electrical power systems. LFC systems commonly employ uncomplicated proportional-integral (PI) controllers in practical applications. The findings indicate that the fuzzy logic controller exhibits adaptability and has been effectively implemented for power system stabilization control [21]. The objective of load frequency control is to manage and regulate the power balance in a two-area interconnected reheat thermal power system. The authors have considered the generation rate constraint (GRC) as a factor in their approach. The verification of system parametric uncertainties is conducted through the simultaneous alteration of parameters from their normal values [22]. A fuzzy logic controller, often known as an FLC, is being used with the intention of improving video quality by outperforming conventional controllers. FLC is utilized to demonstrate the response in various network scenarios, such as Internet cross-traffic or the occupation of video streams on an Internet protocol (IP) network [23]. Implementing fuzzy logic control (FLC) yielded a significant enhancement in performance, surpassing that of Type-1 FLC by an order of magnitude. A novel control methodology is proposed, employing a type-fuzzy neural network and adaptive filter to regulate non-linear uncertain systems. This approach is detailed in their published work [24]. The second-order feedforward neural network (FNN) system possesses the capacity for universal approximation, enabling it to discern nonlinear dynamic systems. The control scheme comprises a PD-type adaptive FNN controller and a prefilter [25]. Using type-2 fuzzy logic and sliding mode control (SMC), we offer a unique, robust crank angular speed control scheme for a four-bar mechanism. This system uses DC motors. An SMC approach is the foundation of the suggested controller. Using streamlined interval fuzzy sets, its real-time functionality is improved. Adopting a trade-off approach between the manipulator's position and the actuators' internal stability and employing computationally cheap input signals independent of the noisy torque and acceleration signals further improve the control scheme's efficiency. The topic of preventative care for mining equipment is explored. Using min-max composition, fuzzy logic, and the notion of fuzzy sets, they provide a model for assessing the probability of failure in technological systems. The likelihood, frequency, and impact of potential dangers are assessed. Language factors are provided as risk indicators. The model was used to determine how likely it was that individual belt conveyor parts would break under the extreme working conditions of a coal mine. Compared to conventional logic-based general-purpose controllers or processors like PID controllers, a fuzz-based controller may provide more accurate and efficient outcomes in a shorter time. The fuzzy logic-based controller is built via a systematic expert-guided process. Previous research in fuzzy natural logic and fuzzy transform proposes three unique soft computing software systems. Some SNP finding techniques provide inconsistent results. To address this, a fuzzy logic-based inference system for decision-making is presented. A fuzzy controller neural network reduces washing machine water and utility use. Fuzzy logic, the basis for the neural network used to operate the washing machine, has been the subject of many studies of neuronal networks and the training procedure it employs.

3.3   The Integration of a Fuzzy Logic System

A thorough study algorithm is diabetic sensorimotor polyneuropathy (DSPN) diabetic sensor engine to gather information on foot ulcers and complications in diabetic patients. Through this approach, the authors could propose precise values for accuracy, specificity, and sensitivity.

Distal symmetric polyneuropathy is a prevalent severe complication of diabetes that damages multiple components of the nervous system. This condition may result in inadequate treatment and can damage the nervous system. Approximately half of diabetic patients experience symptoms of peripheral nervous system impairment, although the manifestation of these symptoms can vary among individuals.

Consequently, it is classified as a chronic ailment due to its potentially lethal nature and propensity to manifest surreptitiously. Identifying this ailment poses a considerable challenge, prompting numerous scholars to dedicate their efforts toward enhancing the intelligent system within the healthcare industry. The researchers endeavored to ascertain how they could effectively scrutinize the intricacies of diabetic patients. Among the various options explored, the CCM system was particularly noteworthy for its precise identification of diabetic sensorimotor polyneuropathy. Nevertheless, this approach is considerably costly, rendering it arduous to procure in conventional medical facilities. During the early stages of diabetic sensorimotor polyneuropathy, patients are typically assessed using screening tests like the neuropathy disability score (NDS) and Michigan neuropathy screening instrument (MNSI). These tests evaluate various factors like vibrations, temperature, and loss of sensation to provide a real-time assessment of the patient's condition. The diagnostic techniques employed involve the utilization of artificial intelligence. The fuzzy inference system (FIS) is widely utilized in decision-making methodology and is renowned for its simplicity and popularity. Its effectiveness stems from its ability to predict future states based on current conditions. The model's performance parameter is recorded and utilizes muscle activity and EMG to assess the severity level.

Figure 3.3 explains the overview of fuzzy logic systems. The role of MIoTs in the medical domain is of significant importance. The implementation of this approach contributes to the enhancement of the healthcare system by reducing hospital visits and costs that are deemed unnecessary. The performance of wearable devices and gadgets, such as smartphones, iPhones, smart bands, bright clothes, and smart houses with smart beds, floors, and toilet seats, equipped with various sensors, enables MIoTs to accurately monitor patients' real-time condition. These sensors can detect and analyze data from daily routine activities. The information collected by these devices is transmitted to medical personnel through a cloud network, enabling doctors and other healthcare professionals to identify the patient's condition and initiate appropriate treatment and medication. The MIoTs consist of three fundamental layers, namely, the perception, network, and

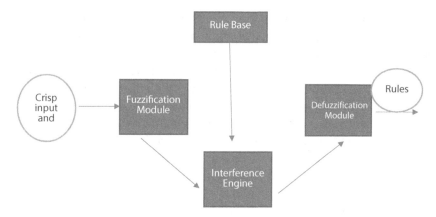

Figure 3.3 Overview of the fuzzy logic system.

application layers. The initial one is capable of gathering comprehensive data through a variety of methodologies and devices. The second layer in the communication protocol stack facilitates the transmission of the gathered data from the devices to the cloud system. This transmission is achieved through either cordless or wired connections.

Cordless connectivity in healthcare benefits patients. However, this has notable limitations, one of which is the issue of security. This issue may be attributed to the inadequate strength of the wireless connection and the lack of encryption functionalities, thereby facilitating unauthorized access to the data by malevolent actors. Implementing algorithms and hybrid deep learning techniques like fuzzy logic systems can effectively address security complexities. The adaptive neuro-fuzzy inference system (ANFIS) is utilized for enhancing and identifying security parameters. The suitability of fuzzy logic systems to secure data can be attributed to their flexible and versatile capabilities. The classified data are subsequently categorized into two classes, with 0 representing positive and 1 representing negative. The results indicate that the NB classifier exhibits a sensitivity of 0.730 and a specificity of 0.332.

On the other hand, the KNN classifier achieves the highest accuracy of 0.974%. The X-axis of the figure represents the classifiers utilized, while the Y-axis represents the number of classified instances. It can be asserted that the support vector machine exhibits superior classification performance when compared to the other four classifiers. The utilization of ANFIS parameters has been observed to address security concerns.

3.4   Fuzzy Latent Semantic Analysis

The Internet of Things (IoT) significantly contributes to preserving health-related data within corporate settings. The abundance of textual documentation, including medical and electronic health records, poses a challenge in locating pertinent health-related information. The implementation of an automated storage system may alleviate this issue. There exist several automation techniques in the market. However, it is imperative to identify the most optimal and user-friendly approaches. Among the available methods, fuzzy latent semantic analysis (FLSA) has been deemed the optimal approach for automated storage. This particular approach is widely recognized for its high quality and high performance. The NSF has identified a significant challenge to secure the storage of data. This challenge necessitates the collection of digital storage, electronic documentation, appropriate surfing, organization, searching, and indexing. The bag-of-words (BOW) approach is the second most commonly utilized technique for digital sorting, shown in Figure 3.4. This approach is used in computer vision. This process entails compiling lexical and syntactic elements found within electronic texts.

Textual analysis approaches are integrated into a topic modeling approach that uses object documentation and feature frequency as inputs. The topic modeling approach uses a word-to-document metric transformation. While the topic modeling approach has shown to be helpful, there is room for improvement; the FLSA model showed superior performance in nonredundant and redundant settings.

This approach involves treating each cluster as a distinct topic and representing documents as fuzzy clusters. The system operates utilizing a spectrum of fuzzy logic comprising seven precise steps. Investigating the

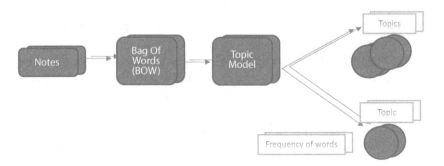

Figure 3.4 Overview of BOW.

similarities and differences between fuzzy latent semantic analysis and other modelling approaches, including the LDA-T dataset. Warped Gibbs sampling is deemed the most appropriate approach. Based on the presented figure, it can be inferred that the FLSA approach exhibits superior performance compared to the LDA method. This can be attributed to its ability to maintain stability even with increased topics, prevent negative issues, and effectively handle discrete and nonstop data.

Implementing an innovative medical system connected to a mobile app enables the effective monitoring of a patient's health condition. Patient-observing devices gather medical and other pertinent health information, which can then be transmitted to a cloud or physician platform through the smartphone's data connection. Implementing remote patient monitoring for individuals with heart failure resulted in significant improvement. The (IoT) application can gather and transmit various health metrics including but not limited to heart beat rate, oxygen saturation and blood glucose levels, body weight, and electrocardiograms. The information above is stored in a cloud-based system. It can be retrieved by authorized personnel, including physicians, insurance providers, collaborating healthcare organizations, or external consultants, without regard to geographical location, time constraints, or device limitations. Implementing an Internet of Things based on a health monitoring method has enabled the instantaneous monitoring of patients regardless of their geographical location.

The paradigm change brought about by WBAN sensors and wireless devices in health monitoring has been spectacular. There are benefits to hiding data management processes in this way. The information collected by these sensors and gadgets is massive and varied. Type 1 fuzzy logic systems, widely used in existing healthcare systems and frameworks, are a significant source of inconsistency and ambiguity in sensor data. To these data management problems, the data fusion strategy uses type 2 fuzzy logic and the Dempster–Shafer theory to retrieve accurate information. Heterogeneous, frequently inaccurate, and misleading indications result from data collected by multiple sensors worn by the patient and data collected by sensors worn by others near the patient.

Consequently, the amalgamation of data originating from multiple sources, such as nodes and sensors, is imperative to enhance service quality and ensures the delivery outcome precisely. The accuracy of information fusion techniques, such as artificial intelligence-based, probability-based, evidence-based fusion, and fuzzy logic-based decisions of type 1, may be compromised, dealing with large volumes of data. The utilization of type 2 fuzzy logic has been deemed appropriate for decision-making processes involving datasets characterized by high uncertainty. The fusion model under consideration operates through a bifurcated approach. In the first phase, T2FL processes the patient data obtained from the sensors to extract an accurate membership value. The DST, or Dempster–Shafer theory, amalgamates the inferences acquired from various nodes or sensors during the second phase. The deduced information is transmitted to the medical practitioners and the patient for evaluation and examination. The study has conducted a comparative analysis of the proposed methodology with similar models, and the results are reported accurately. The fusion methodology under consideration has been executed on a pair of datasets. The proposed model exhibits superior performance over the existing model, as evidenced by a comparative analysis of their F1 scores.

Combining fuzzy logic and machine learning, a similar method creates a system to retrieve medical information from electronic health data. An aging population, a steady decline in the quality of medical services, and skyrocketing treatment costs have all contributed to the need for this system, designed with those challenges in mind. The innovative method is used to analyze the vast quantities of data found in electronic healthcare records via machine learning. An accurate picture of the patient's health may be gleaned from the e-HCRs if they are integrated into developing an intelligent conclusion support system, providing evidence-based pharmaceutical service and improving decision-making. e-HCR incorporates disparate pieces of evidence-based data needed to provide optimal care. There are two main categories for e-HCR information: organized and unstructured. The suggested network employs the fuzzy interference system to make decisions in real time while considering human expertise. The FIS's predicting and decision-making abilities have been cross-validated using the k-fold technique.

3.5   Fuzzy in Healthcare

The dynamic time slot technique based on fuzzy logic was introduced. This fuzzy allocation-based method in health care information management for WBAN sensors and wearable devices is able to achieve reliable communication, enhanced overall performance, and essential minimal cost energy-based data packet routing. Real-time monitoring of crucial physiological signals is made possible by WBAN sensors and wireless devices, but their small-sized battery and network access limit their performance. Increase in body movement are big difficulties in the WBAN network on the grounds that the sensors are intended for basic application where unfortunate help and execution can be shocking for patients and medical experts. Inefficient data transmission technologies like IEEE and MAC protocols are accessible for use in a WBAN network. A heuristic hybrid time slot fuzzy allocation mechanism has been included in the WBAN to facilitate communication between nodes and the network coordinator. In sensors and wearable devices, 50 patients are monitored in real time through the suggested algorithm. The model under consideration exhibits superior performance compared to other models of similar nature.

A framework based on CNN and fuzzy logic has demonstrated efficacy in forecasting risk and seriousness through interconnected recommendation methods in the healthcare domain. CNN utilizes a comprehensive disease classification mechanism by analyzing data from WBAN sensors. Incorporating a fuzzy inference system facilitates the computation of both the level of risk and seriousness of conditions in a patient. The exchange of medical reports and recommendations that are based on evidence is subsequently followed. The utilization of HRS messages in response to the COVID-19 pandemic has gained widespread popularity worldwide. Various human resource systems (HRSs) can be utilized to propose conditional logical data and make decisions based on personal and contextual factors. Many human resource systems need help with reliability, dependability, and quality issues. The amalgamation of fuzzy logic and deep learning can augment the quality of service provided by human resource systems. The proposed model employs a fuzzy logic type 2 inference system (T2FLIS). Figure 3.5 describes the IoT-based healthcare system using the fuzzy system. There is a growing need for computational technologies, information storage, and digital data processing. The proliferation of mobile applications, particularly in the health sector, can be attributed to several factors, including the affordability of Internet access, rapid technological advancements, and the availability of numerous applications that facilitate daily activities. Of particular significance are applications that aid in identifying chronic and general illnesses, which are designed to operate efficiently on mobile devices with minimal power consumption. These applications include electronic patient records (EPRs), which are computational records that store large amounts of data related to individual patients, including their medical history, current condition, and potential symptoms.

By leveraging these records, healthcare professionals can easily identify symptoms and develop effective patient treatment plans. The utilization of e-working has increased activity among medical personnel compared to previous periods. Internet of Things devices, including clinics, hospitals, and mobile devices, are increasingly prevalent in healthcare settings. These

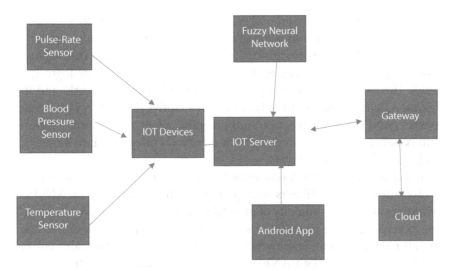

Figure 3.5 IoT-based health care system using the fuzzy system.

devices can monitor chronic conditions like eclampsia, hemolysis, low platelet count (HELLP) syndrome and elevated liver enzymes. In situations where patients cannot physically visit hospitals, such as in the case of pregnant women, telemedicine is a critical tool for managing severe conditions. Telemedicine has the potential to reduce unnecessary visits and alleviate discomfort, and its implementation can be facilitated through the use of algorithms. Because it may be challenging to detect HELLP syndrome in its earliest stages, it is occasionally responsible for losing a pregnant woman's life.

Women with preeclampsia (pregnancy-induced hypertension) often exhibit this condition's vital diagnostic signs, including low platelet counts and hemolytic anemia. WHO estimates that between 0.2% and 0.6% of women worldwide have HELLP syndrome, affecting approximately 7% of pregnant women with preeclampsia. Until today, the causes of this condition have been mysterious. Laboratory testing is the foundation of medical diagnosis. Applying fuzzy logic algorithms and others may simplify the process of syndrome diagnosis. Compared to other algorithms, the radial basis function (RBF) network seems excessively effective. The chart demonstrates that RBF and fuzzy neural techniques have a higher actual positive rate than other approaches because of the unpredictability behavior that reduces dependability.

Big data analysis algorithms can enhance decision-making capabilities by considering the five Vs. Integrating big data with AI and neural network systems can yield significant outcomes. One limitation of artificial neural networks is their ability to solely process discrete inputs, rendering them incapable of effectively processing large-scale linguistic data. The Sugeno-like fuzzy system (SFZ) is a well-defined concept within fuzzy logic systems. This particular system operates within a linear framework, and its output is determined, commonly called the adaptive neural fuzzy inference system (ANFIS). The subject exhibits favorable attributes, including robust and versatile characteristics that can be effectively integrated into linguistic and numerical methodologies.

Regarding engineering, economics, transportation, and—most importantly—medicine, ANFIS is indispensable. The complexity of ANFIS's working system, the difficulty of managing significant amounts of computing expense, and the problem of addressing issues with a high dimension are all obstacles to its employment. To alleviate these issues, alternative methods, such as a BSO-ANFIS algorithm, a novel combination of the ANFIS algorithm and the beetle swarm optimization (BSO) algorithm, are used. BAS and MA are integrated with Particle Swarm Optimization (PSO) techniques to create an algorithm that can identify common ailments and assess large amounts of healthcare data. When compared to competing algorithms, BAS's simplicity stands out. It is possible that BSO, an amalgam of the BAS and PSO algorithms, represents a novel combination of algorithms. Common illnesses may also be diagnosed using modified Crow search algorithms (MCSAs).

The ANFIS algorithm utilizes autogram analysis as input data for diagnostic purposes. Numerous studies conducted by medical professionals have demonstrated the efficacy of using simultaneous aided diagnosis models (SADMs) through algorithmic technology, which can significantly facilitate the process of disease diagnosis. To establish the superiority of the algorithm in question, it was subjected to a comparative analysis with other algorithms, namely, the support vector machine and artificial neural network. The focus of this analysis has been on the treatment of hyperlipemia, a condition characterized by elevated levels of lipids in the bloodstream. Empirical evidence suggests that the SADM approach yields precise disease detection outcomes. However, certain limitations have been observed, such as its susceptibility to high sensitivity leading to reduced accuracy. This approach operates on the foundation of machine learning. The performance of different algorithms in improving heart disease outcomes is compared. According to the findings, it can be inferred that BSO-ANFIS outperforms the other methods in accuracy and precision. Specifically, BSO-ANFIS exhibits accuracy and precision values, notably higher than the other methods. The detection of multiple diseases has been made possible using advanced algorithms in this domain.

The fuzzy logic methodology is ubiquitous across various domains to enhance operational efficacy. One such application pertains to the real-time tracking of the conductivity of goat's milk within the healthcare sector. Consuming healthy milk is advantageous for promoting good health, as it is free from disease and remains uncontaminated by microorganisms. Microbial attacks have a significant impact on the quantity and quality of milk. Here exist diverse categories of parasitic ailments, bacterial, viral, and protozoal that impact milk production and its derivatives. Intramammary infection (IMI) is a prevalent ailment of the mammary glands in dairy goats, which has a detrimental impact on the quality and quantity of milk produced. Currently, goat milk is widely recognized for its significant contribution to the healthcare industry. Several studies have suggested that it is particularly advantageous for individuals with low blood cell counts, thus necessitating enhanced attention and care. Intramammary infection is attributed to the high somatic cell count (SCC) quantity. Incorporating SCC is a prevalent technique utilized to enhance milk production. However, a substantial increase in these cells can lead to mammary gland infections in cows and ruminants.

The harmful effects on human health are attributed to the abundance of somatic cells in the bloodstream, albeit indirectly. This variety of milk harbors many pathogens that can infiltrate the human body. The microorganisms in question are responsible for the proteolysis of dairy products such as cheese and curd. This process is crucial for maintaining ion balance within the human body, making early detection of these microbes necessary. Electrolytic conductivity is utilized to ensure proper balancing of anions and cations. This parameter has been effectively implemented. The milk's electrical conductivity is assessed through conductimetry, a technique utilized in the goat group. The detection of superior milk quality is achieved through a comparative analysis of milk readings obtained from intrinsic variations in animals and previous milk samples. A fuzzy logic system is an easy and effective method for facilitating the evolution of unique animal forms. This approach minimizes mathematical calculations in translating qualitative data into quantitative data. In particular, it allows for analyzing somatic cell counts across various dairy milk types. To attain more accuracy and precision in results, try using a fuzzy logic system. According to the results, using fuzzy logic models to assess the health of dairy goats has helped make important decisions about the animals' future.

3.6   Conclusion

This paper discusses health data uncertainty management challenges. Doctors need precise data to diagnose and cure. Power sources limit wireless body area network sensors, wearable devices, data, and transmission. As energy runs out, information detection and communication become more precise. This prevents doctors from diagnosing and treating accurately. It highlights the complexity of the decision-making process, which involves both logical and intuitive components. Fuzzy logic-based frameworks and artificial intelligence are utilized in healthcare to manage data that exhibit high levels of heterogeneity, uncertainty, and noise, which exceed acceptable thresholds. While the application of fuzzy logic in health data management has shown promise, its complete potential has yet to be realized. Nevertheless, it has proven to be a valuable tool in aiding decision-making processes. The domain of health information has recently seen a surge in interest from researchers due to the advancements made in fuzzy logic models and algorithms, which have piqued their curiosity regarding its full potential. A comprehensive assessment of the current state of health data management is necessary to identify gaps and unexplored areas. However, there appears to be a need for more rigorous and foundational analyses in this domain, which underscores the need for greater dissemination of research findings to the broader public. The realm of control systems is a topic of interest. The current work provides a comprehensive overview of the most recent era. By identifying gaps and uncharted territory, this review work paves the way for further study of fuzzy logic in health data management, aiming to improve management and service quality.

References

1. Vyas, S., Gupta, S., Bhargava, D., Boddu, R., Fuzzy logic system implementation on the performance parameters of health data management frameworks. *J. Healthc. Eng.*, 2022, 9382322. PMID: 35449858; PMCID: PMC9018188, Apr. 12, 2022.
2. Ali, S.E., Tariq, N., Khan, F.A., Ashraf, M., Abdul, W., Saleem, K., BFT-IoMT: A blockchain-based trust mechanism to mitigate sybil attack using fuzzy logic in the internet of medical things. *Sensors,* 23, 4265, 2023. https://doi.org/10.3390/s23094265.
3. Shahariar Parvez, A.H.M. *et al.*, The role of AI, fuzzy logic system in computational biology and bioinformatics, in: *Data Science for Effective Healthcare*

Systems, pp. 133–148, Chapman and Hall/CRC, 2022. https://www.science-direct.com/science/article/pii/S0360835222009299

4. Elhoseny, M. *et al.*, Effective features to classify ovarian cancer data in internet of medical things. *Comput. Netw.,* 159, 147–156, 2019.

5. Rashed, B.M. and Popescu, N., Performance investigation for medical image evaluation and diagnosis using machine-learning and deep-learning techniques. *Computation,* 11, 3, 63, 2023.

6. Pajila, P.J.B., Julie, E.G., Robinson, Y.H., FBDR-fuzzy based ddos attack detection and recovery mechanism for wireless sensor networks. *Wirel. Pers. Commun.,* 2023, 1–31, Article ID 9816424, 2022. https://doi.org/10.1155/2023/9816424

7. Verma, H. *et al.*, Introduction to computational methods, in: *Computational Intelligence Aided Systems for Healthcare,* p. 1, 2023.

8. Kumar, K. *et al.*, A deep learning approach for kidney disease recognition and prediction through image processing. *Appl. Sci.,* 13, 6, 3621, 2023.

9. Baba, A., Flying robots for a smarter life, 2023. *arXiv preprint arXiv:2303. 12044.* https://www.mdpi.com/1424-8220/23

10. Kaushal, C. *et al.*, A framework for interactive medical image segmentation using optimized swarm intelligence with convolutional neural networks. *Comput. Intell. Neurosci.,* 2022, 1–12, 2022.

11. Mitra, A. *et al.*, Everything you wanted to know about smart agriculture, 2022. *arXiv preprint arXiv:2201.04754.*

12. Arora, D., Sharma, A., Agarwal, B.K., Forecasting disclosure of cardiovascular disease using machine learning. *2022 International Conference on Augmented Intelligence and Sustainable Systems (ICAISS),* IEEE, 2022.

13. Kasture, K. and Shende, P., Amalgamation of artificial intelligence with nanoscience for biomedical applications. *Arch. Comput. Methods Eng.,* 1–19, 2023.

14. Garse, S. *et al.*, Cancer diagnosis using artificial intelligence (AI) and internet of things (IoT), in: *Revolutionizing Healthcare Through Artificial Intelligence and Internet of Things Applications,* pp. 50–71, IGI Global, 2023.

15. Mishra, J. and Tiwari, M., Detection of heart disease utilising a feature fusion technique and machine learning-augmented classification. *SN Comput. Sci.,* 3, 5, 406, 2022.

16. Yazici, İ., Shayea, I., Din, J., A survey of applications of artificial intelligence and machine learning in future mobile networks-enabled systems. *Eng. Sci. Technol. Int. J.,* 44, 101455, 2023.

17. Singh, C. *et al.*, Applied machine tool data condition to predictive smart maintenance by using artificial intelligence, in: *Cognitive Computing and Intelligent IoT: 5th International Conference, ICETCE 2022,* Jaipur, India, February 4–5, 2022, Revised Selected Papers. Cham, Springer International Publishing, Emerging Technologies in Computer Engineering, 2022.

18. Yadav, S.P. and Yadav, S., Mathematical implementation of fusion of medical images in continuous wavelet domain. *J. Advanced Res. Dynamical And Control System*, 10, 10, 45–54, 2019.

19. Veerabaku, M.G. *et al.*, Intelligent Bi-LSTM with architecture optimization for heart disease prediction in WBAN through optimal channel selection and feature selection. *Biomedicines*, 11, 4, 1167, 2023.

20. Yadav, H., Singh, S., Mishra, K.K., Srivastava, S., Naruka, M.S., Yadav, S.P., Brain tumor detection with MRI images, in: *2022 International Conference on Computational Intelligence and Sustainable Engineering Solutions (CISES)*. *2022 International Conference on Computational Intelligence and Sustainable Engineering Solutions (CISES)*, IEEE, 2022, https://doi.org/10.1109/cises54857.2022.9844387.

21. Peta, J. and Koppu, S., An IoT-based framework and ensemble optimized deep maxout network model for breast cancer classification. *Electronics*, 11, 24, 4137, 2022.

22. Ahlawat, P. and Rana, C., A comprehensive insight on machine learning enabled internet of things recommender systems (IoTRS). *2021 3rd International Conference on Advances in Computing, Communication Control and Networking (ICAC3N)*, IEEE, 2021.

23. Chowdhary, C.L. *et al.*, Past, present and future of gene feature selection for breast cancer classification–A survey. *Int. J. Eng. Syst. Model. Simul.*, 13, 2, 140–153, 2022.

24. Melarkode, N. *et al.*, AI-powered diagnosis of skin cancer: A contemporary review, open challenges and future research directions. *Cancers*, 15, 4, 1183, 2023.

25. Razzaq, M.A., Unobtrusive complex human activity recognition, 2021.

4

Detecting Healthcare Issues Using a Neuro-Fuzzy Classifier

D. Saravanan¹*, R. Parthiban², G. Arunkumar³, D. Suganthi⁴, Revathi R.⁵ and U. Palani⁶

¹*Department of Computer Science and Engineering, Sathyabama Institute of Science and Technology, Chennai, India*
²*Department of Computer Science and Engineering, IFET College of Engineering, Villupuram, India*
³*Department of Computer Science & Engineering, Madanapalle Institute of Technology & Science, Madanapalle, Andhra Pradesh, India*
⁴*Department of Computer Science, Saveetha College of Liberal Arts and Sciences, SIMATS, Thandalam, Chennai, India*
⁵*Department of Computer Science, Karpagam Academy of Higher Education, Coimbatore, India*
⁶*Department of ECE, IFET College of Engineering, Villupuram, India*

Abstract

In the healthcare industry, the use of medical imaging for diagnosis, treatment planning, and monitoring disease development is increasing. In reality, medical imaging handles data that have a solid structural character and include ambiguous, lost, vague, complimentary, conflicting, redundant, contradictory, and distorted information. The understanding of any image often involves the similarity of the content retrieved from the image using presto red models. The development of fuzzy pattern recognition-based medical imaging, which aids in resolving diagnostic and visualization problems in medicine, has drawn more attention. Medical imaging is continuously subject to flaws, some of which may cause segmentation mistakes. The efficiency of various contrast-enhancing strategies is evaluated using visual quality, CII, and computation time. Several low-contrast color photos were used to compare multiple methods. On the basis of the performance analysis, argue that the recommended fuzzy logic and a histogram-based solution are

---

*Corresponding author: saranmds@gmail.com

Satya Prakash Yadav, Sudesh Yadav, Pethuru Raj Chelliah and Victor Hugo C. de Albuquerque (eds.)
Advances in Fuzzy-Based Internet of Medical Things (IoMT), (59–74) © 2024 Scrivener Publishing LLC

suitable for contrast-enhancing low-contrast color images and fuzzy logic-based homomorphic filtering.

Keywords: Medical diagnosis imaging, fuzzy logic, homomorphic filtering, analysis, healthcare services

4.1 Introduction

The goal of image enhancement is to make an image look better visually or to offer a better transform representation for upcoming automated image processing. Numerous concepts, including real-world photography, satellite images, aerial photographs, and medical images, suffer from inadequate contrast and noise. The image enhancement procedures that increase images' quality (clarity) for human viewing are one of the most crucial steps in medical image detection and analysis. Enhancement procedures include removing blurriness and noise, boosting contrast, and highlighting details. Here, suggest a quick and effective fuzzy and histogram-based automatic contrast improvement methodology for low-contrast color photos and grayscale image contrast enhancement technique and compare these methods with the current methods. The average picture intensity value M and the contrast intensification parameter K are the essential foundations for the fuzzy and histogram-based technique. The suggested method stretches only the V component of the HSV color space while keeping the H and S chromatic information intact. The logarithmic transform and fuzzy membership functions are used in the homomorphic filtering with fuzzy logic technique to produce an approach to image improvement that is simple to understand. By doing away with the necessity for forward and inverse Fourier transforms as well as image-dependent filter kernels, this approach lowers the computational complexity. By separating the light and reflectance components, the log transform utilized here raises the reflectance component, hence raising the contrast of the image. The log-transformed image is subjected to fuzzy logic, and the enhanced image is produced by applying the exponential operation afterward. The ratio of signal-to-noise and entropy calculation are performed to analyze statistical properties of the proposed system contrast improvement index (CII). When compared to the current Figure 4.1, these two methods require significantly less computational time to execute.

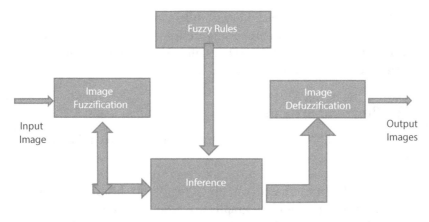

Figure 4.1 Fuzzy image processing.

4.1.1 Processing of the Medical Image

The field of image processing encompasses a range of imaging modalities and medical image processing techniques, which are implemented through diverse methodologies. This facilitates the generation of multiple medical image modalities that undergo processing via medical image processing techniques. Medical images undergo processing, from which useful information is extracted. Subsequent to obtaining these data, an analysis is generated to facilitate the identification of the visual representations and the anticipation of ailments. Medical image processing facilitates the disclosure, diagnosis, and investigation of various conditions, as well as the study of typical anatomy and physiology, by researchers, students, scientists, doctors, and other professionals. The healthcare sector necessitates well-organized and methodical databases and data retrieval systems in response to the increasing volume of patient information databases. The aforementioned requirements can be readily fulfilled through the utilization of suitable medical image processing methodologies. Medical imaging modalities such as magnetic resonance imaging (MRI), computed tomography (CT), and ultrasound imaging are commonly utilized in clinical settings. Medical image processing involves the manipulation of diverse medical images generated by a range of medical imaging modalities. Various imaging modalities such as X-ray, radiography, and magnetic resonance imaging employ these methodologies to generate their respective images. Subsequently, medical images undergo a series of techniques such as image augmentation, preprocessing, restoration, registration, postprocessing, segmentation, and 2D/3D visualization. Segmentation of images is a crucial element of computer-aided design.

4.1.2 Proposed Systems

Here, two distinct fuzzy logic-based picture-enhancing techniques are presented and contrasted.

1. An algorithm based on fuzzy logic and histograms for improving color photographs with poor contrast.
2. Homomorphic filtering for low-contrast image enhancement using fuzzy logic.

4.1.3 Histogram-Based Method

The three components of the suggested method for enhancing low-contrast color photographs are fuzzification, membership function modification, and defuzzification. The proposed method is only meant to enhance dimly lit and low-contrast color photographs. The suggested system's block diagram is shown in Figure 4.2.

4.1.4 Stages of Image Enhancement

During fuzzification, the input pixel values are converted into gray-level values, transforming the initial scalar value into a fuzzy value. The initial step involves the conversion of the input color image to the HSV (hue saturation value) color space, which is utilized to retain the chromatic data present in the picture. The HSV color model facilitates the separation of intensity components from color-carrying information in a given color image. The HSV model is a suitable instrument for creating image-processing algorithms that rely on uncomplicated and user-friendly color characterizations. In the HSV color model, the hue component represents the dominant wavelength of light perceived by the observer, while the saturation component denotes the degree of color purity. The value or element of intensity, on the other hand, refers to the amount of black or white mixed with a given hue.

Once the HSV image model has been acquired, it is possible to recover the particular hue, saturation, and value components. The proposed

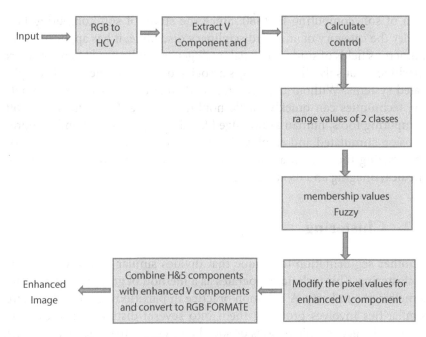

Figure 4.2 Logic diagram and HBM.

methodology utilizes a fuzzy-based approach whereby solely the value (V) component is extracted and subsequently employed for all fuzzy operations.

4.1.5 Soft Computer Techniques

In applications based on digital image processing, soft computing methods or tools are very helpful for various goals, such as classification, sample training, and optimization. These tools are employed in addition to diverse approaches and algorithms to improve performance. Soft computing techniques include artificial neural networks, neural networks (NNs), fuzzy logic (FL), and genetic algorithms (GAs). Applying the proper procedures with soft computing techniques can address realistic world problems like interpreting an image, locating the damaged area in breast scans, etc. Good tolerance of uncertainty and impropriety can be accomplished to neural networks' learning and training capabilities as well as those of other soft computing tools. Many applications, including pattern recognition and clustering performance optimization, use soft computing approaches. Basically, fuzzy logic was introduced in the middle of the 1970s and the idea of soft computing in 1980. Since the study of soft computing falls under the category of an interdisciplinary discipline, it has applications in numerous fields of study. Artificial intelligence can be used to create smart machines that solve the challenges associated with nonlinear and complicated systems. Without the need for mathematical models, soft computing techniques can quickly tackle nonlinear issues. Computers and soft computing tools, human knowledge like identity, cognition, and comprehension stimulated and employed. The idea of fuzzy logic is essential for minimizing the level of ambiguity in numerous forms of data, including medical imaging and its attributes.

4.2   Clustering

Another segmentation technique that divides similar sections of objects is clustering. This technique operates as a method of grouping by utilizing a metric of similarity. A common practice in partitioning areas that share similarities involves grouping them into several distinct parts. Clusters refer to the geographic regions or social collectives that emerge as a result of certain factors or characteristics.

Clustering refers to the procedure of creating clusters. Clustering techniques utilize distinct metrics, such as distance, to generate diverse clusters or groups. Clustering is considered an unsupervised classification method due to the lack of available information about the data set prior to the clustering process. In a multidimensional space, patterns or groups are organized as vectors into coherent groups based on similarity, while dissimilar groups are separated into distinct vectors. Clustering techniques are extensively employed in various computer applications, remote sensing, medical imaging-based applications, and satellite applications.

4.2.1   K-Means Clustering

The most widely studied and applied clustering approach in the literature is k-means clustering. Moreover, this is an unsupervised technology that aids in the first segmentation of MRI and other medical pictures of the human body and the brain. According to a literature review, there are numerous local minima in locations with similar brightness in the photographs. As the initial segmentation, the coarse sections are smoothed. Because of its simplicity and comparatively low computing cost, K-means clustering is used. The method can be used to segment medical photos and other biomedical images because of the method's low computing complexity.

The k-means clustering approach is what this method is called because it chooses K for k clusters as the number of mean values to employ in its implementation. Regions of MRI brain imaging typically show bone, soft tissue, and fat as a result.

The complete data set is divided into K clusters, and the data points are randomly assigned to the collections, resulting in a fixed number of data points for each group. The Euclidean distance between a data point and the cluster mean is determined for every cluster. If an information point is far from its collection, choosing from the nearest set can be done; otherwise, if it is near its own location, it can stay in its group. Up until there are no more clusters that need to be confirmed, this process is repeated. A "database" is an ordered collection of computer-stored and accessible data. Databases store, retrieve, update, and manage massive volumes of data effectively. The diagnosis center's radiologists helped with this. The 2,046 × 1,214 24-bit RGB pictures were the first format used to store the database images. The colour photos were transformed into 12-bit grayscale pictures with 266 × 276 and 513 × 303 dimensions, respectively, after going through a conversion procedure. Due to the increased dimensionality, the segmentation was performed using the algorithms on grayscale images rather than directly on RGB images. The processing time requirements for RGB pictures are also very high. Results for 08 MRI images (MRIa to MRIi) are shown. The values of the pixels corresponding to the tumor's region are increased after optimization. The entire area is determined by deducting the segmented area location from the territory of the tumor region. The joined approach addressed the excessive segmentation problem and other limitations of the conservative watershed algorithm. It was advantageous when oversegmentation was less. Comparison of k-means optimized and comparison K-means grouping system as shown in Table 4.1.

Table 4.1 The grouping method.

Test image	Total area image	Group of k-means	Tumor-area–use optimized k- means cluster
MRI	75146	1522	1347
MRI	53237	573	793
MRI	65536	1659	2024
MRI	65536	729	932

4.2.2   C-Means Clustering

Techniques particularly are used to reduce the degree of uncertainty. To reduce the cost function of the dissimilarity measure, a cluster center is found in each of the c-fuzzy groups formed by the division of the set of n-vectors into groups. Medical image segmentation and tumor extraction were performed on images taken from brain MRIs. The field of tumor detection is relatively young, since current research contributions' robustness and best performance are frequently questioned. Several results were obtained on an experimental basis using the same algorithms. This method includes standard k-means and c-means clustering approaches that are applied to MRI brain images for tumor identification.

Additionally, k-means and c-means algorithms' optimization was created.

The implementation was carried out using the high-performance program MATLAB. Superior segmentation outcomes are achieved after optimizing a genetic algorithm. A refined iteration of the c-means clustering algorithm was implemented on magnetic resonance imaging brain scans. The efficacy of the strategy was assessed in conjunction with the methodologies. The optimized clustering approach yields a notably greater degree of segmentation than the conventional clustering algorithm.

Moreover, the issue of superfluous segmentation becomes relatively less significant. The tumor region can be effectively retrieved by utilizing the edges of the segmented areas. Table 4.2 compares the k-means and c-means clustering techniques following optimization.

As demonstrated, optimized c-means perform better than the optimized k-means technique due to a better-segmented region and the level of the detected area in c-means clustering.

Table 4.2 Comparison of c-means and k-means clusters.

Test image	Total image (values)	Area using C-means cluster (values)	Area-use - optimized C- means cluster (values)
MRI	75146	1522	1347
MRI	53237	573	793
MRI	65536	1659	2024
MRI	65536	729	932

Table 4.3 Search-time comparison.

Test image	K-means clustering time minimization by varying the number of iterations (in Sec.)	Time savings from using a larger number of C-means iterations (Sec.)
MRI	73.539(106)	1.9880(106)
MRI	53.129(98)	2.0650(100)
MRI	70.912(104)	3.2190(105)
MRI	72.245(105)	4.1350(106)

Table 4.3 indicates a further comparison made between the optimized c-means and k-means algorithms regarding search time. As a result, the fuzzy-based means clustering approach is more effective than the optimized k-means clustering algorithm.

4.3   Fuzzy Clustering

Using fuzzy-based clustering, it is possible to group data objects into homogeneous categories or clusters that are as similar and consistent as possible. As items vary across different classes, it is important to distinguish their differences. To differentiate the classes, many similarity metrics, including centroid, connectedness, density, and intensity, are frequently used. The information set is divided into multiple unique groups via hard or conventional clustering by avoiding fuzzy logic, in which each information point belongs to accurately one group. Accurately refers to the assignment of data points to clusters is done with a high degree of precision. The data fragments in fuzzy-based clustering could be a part of multiple clusters. The relationship of the data items is shown by the degree to which they are members of the various clusters or by the membership function. An object may belong to several classes depending on varying degrees or memberships, which is the basic concept of fuzzy clustering. In general, a suitable heuristic method is used to establish the membership function. The important objective of grouping is to divide a given set of data items into groups, which represent subsets or groupings. Homogeneity determines the degree of similarity between two locations before segmenting them. Applications like pattern recognition, data analysis, and image segmentation gain a lot from fuzzy clustering.

Segmentation using clustering techniques is achieved by transforming each pixel into a point in an n-dimensional feature space defined by the vector of its feature values.

It is possible to resolve the problem, which is a general pattern recognition problem, by segmenting the feature space into various clusters.

Each observation or set of data's n quantifiable variables is grouped into an n-dimensional column. The group of N is represented by the vector and a R k k nk T k n = 1 1 1.

Z. a. k. N. k. = = |, ..., 1 2 3 provides the observations, which are denoted by N.

4.3.1   C-Means Fuzzy Clustering

Assigning every sample to a cluster based on cluster membership, fuzzy c-means (FCM) clustering is one of the most used approaches for fuzzy clustering. The FCM method employs iterative minimization to generate candidate prototypes that adequately meet the objective function, ultimately leading to the creation of the optimal fuzzy c-partition. All input samples are considered for establishing a cluster hub, with each example's contribution weighted according to its membership values. The distance from the center of the relevant cluster is used to quantify the importance of each class. The effect of weak membership values is mitigated by the weight factor m.

Samples with low membership values have less effect as m increases in significance. Iterative minimization, simulated annealing, and evolutionary algorithms may all be used to address the nonlinear optimization issue that the c-means method's illustration of minimization depicts. The fuzzy c-means (FCM) algorithm, which uses a straightforward iteration of the initial requirements for stationary points, has emerged as the most often used approach. Data in the fuzzy c-means approach may share membership coefficients with two or more clusters. This process is already in motion. The first fuzzy cluster centers are decided upon once the fuzzy partition matrix has been generated. Figure out where the clusters should go. At each repetition, the objective work is minimized, where cluster centers and membership grades are updated. The difference in the improvement of the target function between the two most recent iterations is less than the required minimum. A fuzziness coefficient is selected; this might be any positive real number larger than 1.

The steps in the fuzzy c-means (FCM) algorithm are as follows:

1. Read the input image, select the repetitions, decide on the image size, calculate the distance, and combine the required dimensions;

2. Start the repetition by identifying significant information components by comparing them with pixel value;
3. To produce significant data items for prospective distance estimates;
4. Stop iterating when there is no longer any probability of identification.
5. There are two types of clustering: soft clustering, sometimes referred to as fuzzy clustering, and hard clustering, where every object is either a cluster or not.
6. Each object partially fits into each cluster.
7. Since the characteristics of the clusters found by various techniques differ substantially, few clustering models are consequently built.

4.3.2 Neuro-Fuzzy Model

A neuro-fuzzy method used to group images into clusters with related spectral characteristics is called FCM clustering. It uses the membership function computed using the spectral domain distance between pixels and cluster centers. An essential feature that can be used to help label the pixels in an image is their high spatial correlation. The enumeration of membership functions of neighboring clusters centered on a pixel in the spatial domain is a crucial aspect of cluster distribution statistics. The membership function incorporates these particulars after their weighting. Employing matching clusters generated by FCM cluster is a characteristic feature of the SIFT. The initiation process is commenced. The process of identifying registration parameters and components that correspond to significant features both the reference and target images involves extraction of said images as shown in Figure 4.3. Fuzzy c-means (FCM) is used in a feature space that stays the same after rotation and scaling of rotation to find reliable clusters. The analysis of each pixel involves the examination of its intensity value, position, typical neighborhood intensity, and variance from the eight adjacent pixels.

4.4 Fuzzy Based on Image Fusion

To create a composite image that is more informative and more suited for computer processing or visual perception, a technique called "image fusion" combines data from two or more embodiments. This has several applications in medicine. It utilizes, among other things, machine vision,

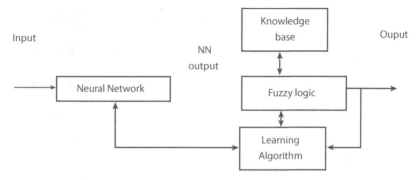

Figure 4.3 A neuro-fuzzy model.

Table 4.4 Entropy and PSNR for accuracy.

Segmentation	Entropy	PSNR (database)
Watershed algorithm	1.012	3.60
k-means cluster	1.372	3.70
FCM	1.768	3.60

biometrics, navigation, remote sensing, and the military. Fuzzy logic is developed for multi-sensor image fusion, which combines pictures from many sensors to enable visualization outcomes. Fuzzy radial basis function neural networks are utilized for auto-adaptive image fusion. Image defuzzification, image fuzzification, and modification of membership values using appropriate fuzzy rules are all techniques used to produce clear or accurate results (Table 4.4).

4.5   Neuro Techniques

Soft computing methods, such as those based on neural networks and fuzzy logic, have been considered. The efficiency gains from using genetic algorithms were also taken into account. They are trying to improve and maximize things. NFC techniques combine neural networks, fuzzy logic, and genetic algorithms to produce a hybrid system that is more effective than any of the components used alone. While neural networks and fuzzy logic have their uses and limitations, hybrid systems will combine the best of both worlds. Neuro-fuzzy methods, hybrid systems that overcome component limits to perform better, are exceptional in all ways and find applications in process control, financial trading, engineering design, cognitive science, and medical diagnostics, where intelligent hybrid systems are becoming more popular. By combining the strengths of fuzzy logic with neuro-fuzzy systems, a hybrid intelligent system with reasoning capabilities close to those of humans may be created. At its core, an NFS is a learned fuzzy method, which may have been inspired by the concept of a neural network and its associated learning algorithm. The learning process only makes little adjustments to the underlying fuzzy system, which only influences data in a small area.

4.6   Results of Fuzzy Logic

A compilation of medical MRIs, comprising mammograms and images of MRI scans. Calculations for sensitivity, specificity, and accuracy are presented in Table 4.2, and Figure 4.3 displays the outcomes of applying three distinct segmentation techniques—the watershed algorithm, k-means, and FCM—to the same input image. PSNR and entropy values were calculated and are shown in the table. These findings speak for themselves.

4.7   Conclusion

Medical imaging has a wide range of applications, and medical image processing is currently a popular application area for digital picture processing. An overview of medical picture processing has been given, together with information on its requirements and challenges. There have been numerous advancements in this area of study, but soft computing approaches remain the best option to tackle issues like robustness, accuracy, and result validation. Many people are curious about the potential of fuzzy logic in the field of medical image processing. Both neuro-fuzzy systems and iterative fuzzy logic provide satisfactory outcomes. The following is a summary of the work's learning objective:

- ❖ Soft computing can be very beneficial in resolving challenging issues with medical imaging systems;
- ❖ The most crucial step in processing medical images is picture segmentation, which can be made more accessible by using the right soft computing technologies;

❖ The use of the genetic algorithm as an optimization soft computing tool allows for the appropriate detection of tumors and other anomalies as well as improved localization.

❖ Tumor identification becomes more accurate with the use of fuzzy-based techniques, which have been supported by actual findings and a comparison with other clustering approaches. FCM methods give the most promising results among existing clustering methods. Another crucial technique is k-means clustering.

❖ FCM also aids in overcoming the typical clustering algorithm's sensitivity to noise.

Medical image processing using fuzzy logic has great promise for healthcare and computer-assisted diagnosis. However, accurate instruments are needed for maximum improvement and far better results. When it comes to performance, the genetic algorithm can be compared to other optimization techniques like differential equations and bacterial foraging, as well as the outcomes of fuzzy-based methodologies used to create medical devices.

Bibliography

Yang, Y., Que, Y., Huang, S., Lin, P., Multimodal sensor medical image fusion based on type-2 fuzzy logic in NSCT domain. *IEEE Sens. J.*, 16, 10, 3735–45, Feb. 23, 2016.

Teng, J., Wang, S., Zhang, J., Wang, X., Neuro-fuzzy logic based fusion algorithm of medical images, in: *2010 3rd International Congress on Image and Signal Processing*, vol. 4, IEEE, pp. 1552–1556, 2010.

Barro, S. and Marín, R. (Eds.), *Fuzzy logic in Medicine*, vol. 83, Springer Science & Business Media, 2001. https://www.hindawi.com/journals/mpe/2021/5854966/

Khan, A., Li, J.-P., Shaikh, R.A., Medical image processing using fuzzy logic, in: *2015 12th International Computer Conference on Wavelet Active Media Technology and Information Processing (ICCWAMTIP)*, IEEE, pp. 163–167, 2015.

Teng, J. *et al.*, Fusion algorithm of medical images based on fuzzy logic. *2010 Seventh International Conference on Fuzzy Systems and Knowledge Discovery*, vol. 2, IEEE, 2010.

Tsai, D.-Y., Lee, Y., Sekiya, M., Ohkubo, M., Medical image classification using genetic-algorithm based fuzzy-logic approach. *J. Electron. Imaging*, 13, 4, 780–788, 2004.

Jayachandran, A. and Dhanasekaran, R., Multi class brain tumor classification of MRI images using hybrid structure descriptor and fuzzy logic based RBF kernel SVM. *Iran. J. Fuzzy Syst.*, 14, 3, 41–54, Jun. 29, 2017.

Chauhan, N. and Choi, B.J., Denoising approaches using fuzzy logic and convolutional autoencoders for human brain MRI image. *Int. J. Fuzzy Log. Intell. Syst.*, 19, 3, 135–139, 2019.

Ozsahin, D.U., Uzun, B., Ozsahin, I., Mustapha, M.T., Musa, M.S., Fuzzy logic in medicine, in: *Biomedical Signal Processing and Artificial Intelligence in Healthcare*, pp. 153–182, Academic Press, 2020.

Nguyen, T.M. and Wu, Q.J., A fuzzy logic model based Markov random field for medical image segmentation. *Evol. Syst.*, 4, 171–181, 2013.

Costin, H. and Rotariu, C., Medical image analysis and representation using a fuzzy and rule-based hybrid approach. *Int. J. Comput. Commun.*, 1, 156–162, 2006.

Yuvaraja, T. and Sabeenian, R.S., Performance analysis of medical image security using steganography based on fuzzy logic. *Cluster Comput.*, 22, 3285–3291, 2019.

Kaur, J., Saxena, J., Shah, J., Fahad, Yadav, S.P., Facial emotion recognition, in: *2022 International Conference on Computational Intelligence and Sustainable Engineering Solutions (CISES)*, IEEE, 2022, https://doi.org/10.1109/cises54857.2022.9844366.

Alawad, A.M., Rahman, F.D.A., Khalifa, O.O., Malek, N.A., Fuzzy logic based edge detection method for image processing. *Int. J. Electr. Comput. Eng.*, 8, 3, 1863, 2018.

Ahmmed, R., Rahman, M.A., Hossain, M.F., Fuzzy logic based algorithm to classify tumor categories with position from brain MRI images, in: *2017 3rd International Conference on Electrical Information and Communication Technology (EICT)*, IEEE, pp. 1–6, Dec. 7, 2017.

Patro, P., Azhagumurugan, R., Sathya, R., Kumar, K., Kumar, T.R., Babu, M.V.S., A hybrid approach estimates the real-time health state of a bearing by accelerated degradation tests, Machine learning. *2021 Second International Conference on Smart Technologies in Computing, Electrical and Electronics (ICSTCEE)*, Bengaluru, India, pp. 1–9, 2021, doi: 10.1109/ICSTCEE54422.2021.9708591.

Javed, U., Riaz, M.M., Ghafoor, A., Cheema, T.A., Local features and Takagi-Sugeno fuzzy logic based medical image segmentation. *Radioengineering*, 22, 4, 1091–1097, 2013.

Vashisht, V., Pandey, A.K., Yadav, S.P., Speech recognition using machine learning. *IEIE Trans. Smart Process. Comput. Institute Electron. Engineers Korea*, 10, 3, 233–239, 2021. https://doi.org/10.5573/ieiespc.2021.10.3.233.

Shivlal, M., Saroliya, A., Chandramouli, N., Rajasanthosh Kumar, T., Lakshmi, M., Suma Christal Mary, S., Jayakumar, Mani, Smart diagnostic expert system for defect in forging process by using machine learning process. *J. Nanomater.*, 2022, Article ID 2567194, 8, 2022. https://doi.org/10.1155/2022/2567194. https://www.ncbi.nlm.nih.gov/pmc/articles/PMC8659829/

Torres, A. and Nieto, J.J., Fuzzy logic in medicine and bioinformatics. *J. Biomed. Biotechnol.*, 20062006.

Haq, I., Anwar, S., Shah, K., Khan, M.T., Shah, S.A., Fuzzy logic based edge detection in smooth and noisy clinical images. *PloS One*, 10, 9, e0138712, 2015.

Ping, W. *et al.*, A multi-scale enhancement method to medical images based on fuzzy logic. *TENCON 2006-2006 IEEE Region 10 Conference*, IEEE, 2006.

Sinha, G.R., Fuzzy-based medical image processing, in: *Fuzzy Expert Systems for Disease Diagnosis*, pp. 45–61, IGI Global, 2015.

Arnal, J. and Súcar, L., Fast method based on fuzzy logic for gaussian-impulsive noise reduction in CT medical images. *Mathematics*, 10, 19, 3652, 2022.

Dey, N., Ashour, A.S., Shi, F., Balas, V.E.E., *Soft Computing Based Medical Image Analysis*, Academic Press, 2018.

Hata, Y. *et al.*, A survey of fuzzy logic in medical and health technology. *World Automation Congress 2012*, IEEE, 2012.

Development of the Fuzzy Logic System for Monitoring of Patient Health

Norma Ramírez-Asís[1]*, Ursula Lezameta-Blas[2], Anil Kumar Bisht[3], G. Arunkumar[4], Jose Rodriguez-Kong[5] and D. Saravanan[6]

[1]Hospital Uldarico Rocca Fernandez, Lima, Perú
[2]Universidad Nacional Santiago Antúnez de Mayolo, Huaraz, Peru
[3]Department of CS&IT, MJP Rohilkhand University, Bareilly, Uttar Pradesh, India
[4]Department of Computer Science & Engineering, Madanapalle Institute of Technology & Science, Madanapalle, Andhra Pradesh, India
[5]Universidad Señor de Sipán, Chiclayo, Peru
[6]Department of Computer Science and Engineering, Sathyabama Institute of Science and Technology, Chennai, India

Abstract

Rising healthcare expenses are a big issue for many people and governments. The high expense of the conventional hospital-based monitoring and care method has prompted researchers to look for cheaper alternatives. One way involves sending mobile equipment to patients' houses for remote monitoring and diagnosis. Enhancing the VLSI system by utilizing a single embedded chip for computation. Cell phone and Wi-Fi connection are used to improve the current framework and mobile-based health monitoring system. One of the promising options that might be used in future healthcare systems is radio frequency identification (RFID) technology. Vital sign sensors, such as those for measuring temperature, blood pressure (BP), heartbeat, sugar level, and oxygen level in the blood, may be incorporated into RFID tags for use in patient identification and monitoring. A mobile RFID-based healthcare system is proposed here, along with its design, implementation, and testing. The system includes portable wireless data acquisition equipment for vital signs and a fuzzy logic algorithm for continuous monitoring and assessment of patient health. The patient's condition is diagnosed using a set of fuzzy criteria based on his or her body temperature, blood pressure, heartbeat, oxygen level, and breathing per minute. The system is measured against the current gold standard

*Corresponding author: elva.ramirez@essalud.gob.pe

Satya Prakash Yadav, Sudesh Yadav, Pethuru Raj Chelliah and Victor Hugo C. de Albuquerque (eds.)
Advances in Fuzzy-Based Internet of Medical Things (IoMT), (75–92) © 2024 Scrivener Publishing LLC

in the industry, the Modified Early Warning Score (MEWS), to see how well it performs. The proposed system is superior to the MEWS system in several tests, demonstrating the efficacy of this fuzzy logic technique.

Keywords: Mobile monitoring system, RFID technology, fuzzy logic system

5.1   Introduction

The escalating medical care expenses and the surging requests for health services have caused significant apprehension in developed nations regarding the aging and expanding population. An increasing aging population has been consistently observed over the past few decades. Elderly individuals have experienced a 3-fold increase within the past half century, and it is projected to undergo another 3-fold increase within the subsequent 50 years. Figure 5.1 depicts a comparative analysis of the growth rates of older people and the total population, revealing a notable surge in the former.

Healthcare for millions of individuals worldwide has improved due to the incorporation of computer platforms and wireless communication technology. It has improved the organization of healthcare services, patient records, and medical inventory. Indoor patient monitoring still requires

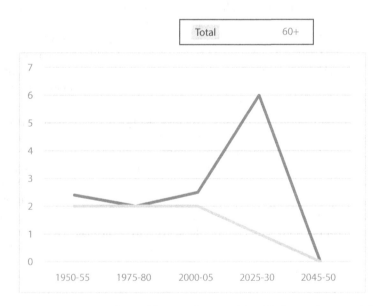

Figure 5.1 Comparative analysis of the growth rates of the elderly population and the total population.

a significant time commitment from nurses, increases costs, and strains hospitals' scarce resources.

The safety, cost, and quality of healthcare have all begun to feel the effects of patients' health data becoming standard practice. Rapid technological advancements are being made in creating, transmitting, storing, and managing patients' health records. Because of technological advances in health information management, patients and carers will have 24/7 electronic access to their data. These advantages can only be attained via patient-centered electronic health information, necessitating a foundational infrastructure that any provider, health plan, or delivery system does not constrain. Departments, clinical wards, surgeries, and labs have separate hospital medical information systems. The hospital's primary information system may house its database, although radiology may have its application system. Integrating patient medical records and picture files is of utmost importance, since it facilitates sharing patients' vital signs and health data across various healthcare practitioners, which is necessary for prompt and correct diagnosis and treatment.

5.2   Literature Review

Vital signs, such as an electrocardiogram (ECG), may be monitored using a patient monitoring system, a network of sensors, and other diagnostic equipment [1]. Life-threatening conditions, critical physiological states, and chronic disorders, including diabetes [2] and high blood pressure, need such systems. Improved wireless video monitoring reduces healthcare resource utilization owing to cost-effectiveness. After WWII, new technologies emerged, creating a wide variety of monitoring methods [3]. Various patient monitoring systems, both wired and wireless, are now on the market.

On the other hand, wireless technologies are expanding in popularity because of their portability, small size, durability, low cost, and simple installation. Researching the newest and most popular system. Several reports of wireless patient monitoring devices are in the literature [4]. Bluetooth, Zigbee, Wi-Fi, and radio frequency identification (RFID) are examples of systems that use short-range communication protocols. GPRS and WiMAX are two examples of networks that combine short- and far-reaching protocols [5]. As detailed in the cited article, a framework has been developed to record and communicate with the concerned patient's EKG, heartbeat, and body weight using Bluetooth connectivity and Zigbee technologies [6]. The approach utilizes an electrocardiogram, a pulse, and a body weight wireless sensor trio to simplify cardiovascular monitoring. A single 16-bit RISC processor receives sensor data, formats them, and sends them to a Zigbee base wirelessly gateway [7]. The Zigbee gateway transfers information to a computer for processing and storage using a Bluetooth transmitter.

The gateway that has been designed exhibits a considerable physical footprint. However, it lacks provisions for ensuring the security and privacy of the Internet connectivity and has a limited array of connectivity [8]. SpO_2, heartbeat, body temperature, and respiration rate are the four vital indicators monitored by another wireless device for psychiatric patients [9]. Two portable data acquisition devices plus a CMS make up the whole system. The SpO_2 reading is taken by one of the data-gathering devices and sent to the CMS via Bluetooth. The second one uses Bluetooth to transmit data about the user's heartbeat, body temperature, and breathing rate to a central server [10]. The raw data sent by the wireless acquisition modules required the creation of a software suite for analysis. The collected signals are visually presented for use in medical diagnosis. The technology was evaluated by using healthy subjects in a controlled environment. The system is challenging to transport because of its large size and lack of network connectivity [11]. This system comprises a portable data acquisition (DAQ) device and a server. The electronic cardiogram (ECG) sensor, processing module, and transceiver include the DAQ unit. Two electrodes on the patient's chest read the electrocardiogram signal [12]. The process module (PM) comprises an analog-to-digital converter (ADC), a control microcontroller, and a signal purification circuit. The ECG signal is acquired, processed, and framed. After being formatted, the ECG signal is sent to the server through a Bluetooth module [13]. The server extracts the ECG signal and sends it to the doctor's PC screen for analysis and diagnosis. The system had no central repository for patients' demographic and medical background information. It is important to note that the DAQ unit has three distinct parts [14]. It also does one-on-one monitoring of patients. Monitoring a patient's electrocardiogram (ECG), body mass index (BMI), mobility tracking, and snoring detection with the use of a wireless local area network [15]. An electrocardiogram is recorded using a textile electrode fastened to the patient's sheet. Four compression-type load cells mounted to the bed's legs measure and track the patient's weight and motion throughout the night. Finally, nighttime breathing in patients is diagnosed using an electret condenser microphone and an RMS-to-DC conversion [16]. To do this, a small data processing device was developed. The microprocessor, Bluetooth module, and battery are the three primary parts. A wireless local area network (WLAN) was used to link the

Bluetooth server to the home server, and personal digital assistants (PDAs) were put in each room to enable WLAN [17]. Patients can only be watched when in bed and can only sleep in that position. The employment of wristbands bearing barcodes is a prevalent method for patient surveillance in medical facilities. RFID tags have the potential to replace barcodes [18] due to their extended read range, increased storage capacity, and ability to operate without a direct line of sight. The utilization of body-matched tags, specifically suspended patch-type, has been suggested to promptly monitor and locate patients in a clinical setting [19]. A recent study has documented the use of an implantable RFID chip to store patient data and monitor their whereabouts.

A study in reference [20] details the design of an RFID tag intended for remote human monitoring, specifically for operation on the human body. This particular label can be affixed to belts, collars, or waistbands. By simulating human cognitive processes in complicated situations and precisely completing repeated activities that people are ill-suited to, fuzzy algorithms have potential to enhance the clinician-related performance. Fuzzy logic has been used before in medicine [21]. The creator used fuzzy logic to create an AI system. An implantable glucose monitor was employed in this system. The sensor data were utilized to adjust the insulin infusion rate to test if it could handle reactions to typical "inputs" such as daily insulin, meals, and exercise. Researchers discovered a significant discrepancy (approximately 10%) between anticipated and actual blood glucose levels. In another research effort, an internal blood glucose monitoring device was developed [22]. Using a sophisticated fuzzy logic algorithm, the device tracked sugar levels and made necessary to adjusting by insulin or regular medicine. Noimanee *et al.* [23] investigated the potential of a combination of an insulin and fuzzy algorithm to serve as a patient's artificial pancreas. So far, some problems with FL systems have been identified, such as instances when the systems' performance does not equal that of humans. This is usually due to insufficient programming (an expert diabetologist still needs to specify the principles by which an expert system should operate) [24]. Medical control systems benefit significantly from fuzzy logic, since the parameters involved often have an extensive range that might result in varied diagnoses; for instance, one doctor may consider a patient unwell while another may deem him or her extremely ill. High performance and dependability may be achieved by well-planned hardware and software architecture [25]. Multiple input sensors are used in such a system to track metrics like glucose levels in the blood. The obtained information will be compared to one another to regulate insulin administration. Because of this fail-safe, the system is more reliable [26].

5.3   Fuzzy Logic System in Healthcare

Fuzzy logic is a type of logic that falls under the category of many-valued logic. It pertains to the process of reasoning that is not strictly fixed or precise but is characterized by an element of approximation. Fuzzy logic variables possess a degree of truth that varies between 0 and 1, as evidenced by sources. The statement above pertains to using a rule-based algorithm known as "fuzzy logic" to conclude. This conclusion is based on linguistic variables employed to create membership functions (MFs), which may or may not possess overlapping boundaries. The input provided to the rule-based system may exhibit binary values, such as affirmative or harmful, or numerical values ranging from 0 to 1, allowing for a range of potential deals. The algorithm systematically examines the input values and produces an output decision that indicates the current state of the object(s) being monitored.

Algorithms based on fuzzy logic have demonstrated the capacity to enhance clinicians' performance by emulating human cognitive processes in intricate scenarios and effectively carrying out monotonous tasks that could be better suited for humans. Prior research has utilized fuzzy logic in the domain of patient care. The development of an artificial intelligence system using fuzzy logic was undertaken—the method above employed a blood glucose sensor implanted within the subject. The data obtained from the sensor were utilized to modify the insulin infusion rate to assess its ability to manage reactions to typical stimuli such as routine insulin administration, dietary intake, and physical activity. A general average percentage error of more than 11% was found between the estimated and measured blood glucose levels. A therapeutically viable device using an internal blood sugar monitoring mechanism has been developed in recent research—expert fuzzy logic program altered the insulin dosage based on glucose monitoring data. The study examined how people with diabetes may use an insulin pump and fuzzy logic technologies to create a kind of artificial pancreas. The stated restrictions relate to situations when FL systems underperform relative to human levels, often resulting from inefficient programming. It is important to remember that a savvy diabetologist is still needed when programming behavioral guidelines into an expert system. Because the variables involved generally have an extensive range, which can result in varied diagnoses, fuzzy logic is a highly ideal method to use in medical control systems. It is not uncommon for doctors to have vastly different assessments of the same patient. A customized system design that encompasses both hardware and software components has the potential to offer a superior level of functionality and dependability. This type of system implementation employs a variety of input sensors to monitor essential physiological indicators including but not limited to blood glucose levels. The data gathered will be subjected to comparative analysis to regulate insulin dosage. The presence of redundancy within the system results in a reduction of errors.

Fuzzy logic is used in blood glucose monitoring as shown in Figure 5.2. From the author's point of view, the fuzzy logic technique is used to develop decision-based support to enrich glycemia in diabetic patients. The procedure considers the kind of sustenance consumed by individuals, the blood glucose levels before eating, and the body's resistance to insulin. The findings exhibited a high degree of promise. The system successfully recommended the optimal insulin dosage before a meal.

The use of FL in intensive care unit medical decision-making is only one example of the many medical applications of fuzzy logic. The inputs used were MAP and HOU or the amount of urine passed per hour. The intravenous fluid rate (IFR) is adjusted when new data become available. A diagnostic method with practical application was developed. The inputs of Protein, Red blood cells, Lymph cell, Neutrophils, and Eosinophils are processed via a fuzzifier, implication engine, instruction base, and defuzzification to provide Unvarying, Hemorrhage, and Brain Tumor as possible outputs. MATLAB Simulink was used to build the rule-based engine. The results of the simulation agree with the calculated consequences of the strategy. The results of this research could help doctors detect brain illnesses more quickly and accurately.

A monitoring and diagnostic alarm system utilizing fuzzy logic was devised to identify important occurrences during anesthesia delivery. The system searches the complete database of head and neck cancer patients

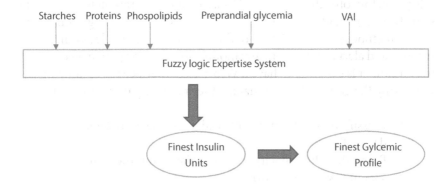

Figure 5.2 Utilization of fuzzy logic in blood glucose monitoring.

and produces a patient record that displays the treatment plan of another patient with similar symptoms. This record is a recommended starting point for generating a new treatment plan. The utilized methodology involved the implementation of case-based reasoning, which had been executed through the utilization of fuzzy IF-THEN rules to search the patient database.

5.4   Proposed Design

A system design that meets functional and nonfunctional objectives such as reliability, scalability, security, cheap cost, and low power consumption is essential. In this section, the necessary features and characteristics of the proposed system are outlined. All of the design's attention will be focused on meeting those criteria.

The process of delineating the system requirements facilitates the designers in making more informed decisions regarding the selection of components and resource optimization. The present study concerns the establishment of system requirements for a wireless monitoring system, encompassing both the structures and facilities that the organization should offer and the restrictions it must adhere to. The subsequent segment delineates the practical and nonfunctional requisites of the proposed method.

A. Functional Requirements

The practical demands of the system are what determine the system's capacity to complete tasks. "A condition requires a purpose that a system or integral must be able to complete." Applicable requirements stipulate a software project's expected features and capabilities. The primary objectives of this project involve the use of RFID-based gauges to remotely collect vital signs from a patient, assess the patient's state of health using a fuzzy reasoning method, keep the history of the patient's health in electronic health records, and alert caregivers to any modifications to the patient's condition. In addition, it is essential to have a Web-based interface for organizing and visualizing the gathered sensor data. Other necessary functions include:

1. Classifying the locations of readers inside a predetermined data collection
2. Possessing the capacity to collect data from individual sensors in a wireless network
3. Activities related to registration include:

I. Employee Registration

Each employee needs his or her log-on to the monitoring system. Every employee has his or her own unique ID number and log-on credentials. Your initial and last name, as well as your contact number, are all we need to get started.

II. Patient Registration

Patient registration is a crucial step in the healthcare process, as it involves the creation of a comprehensive patient profile stored in a database. This information is essential for effective patient management and care delivery. It is imperative to document the personal details of patients, including assigning them a unique patient ID and identification tags for temperature, blood pressure, SpO_2, and blood sugar. They must be allocated to a specific staff member.

III. Patient Deletion

Patient profile, billing, and discharging are all tasks that should be under the staff's purview.

IV. Removing Access for Employees

Employees who are not supposed to have access to the system should not be able to use it.

V. Authentication

The system allowed only authorized personnel to log on, track, and monitor patients.

VI. Gathering Vital Signs of Patients

The process of obtaining vital signs of patients through RFID sensors can be accomplished through a variety of methods, such as:

i. **Retrieving Information from Temperature-Measuring Wristbands**
   Our inventory comprises wristbands equipped with radio frequency identification technology and integrated with temperature sensors. To read multiple tags concurrently, it is imperative to own a reader that has multi-tag interpretation capabilities.

ii. **Retrieval of Data from the Blood Pressure Meter**
   In addition, the system is required to interpret frames received from an RFID tag that is linked to a plasma pressure-related sensor.

    iii. **Retrieval of Statistics from Blood Glucose-Monitoring Devices**
The system is required to process frames received from an RFID tag that is linked to a blood glucose sensor.

    iv. **The Process of Retrieving Information from SpO$_2$ Meters Through Reading**
The system is required to interpret frames that are transmitted from an RFID tag that is linked to a SpO$_2$ sensor.

VII. The Process of Retaining Information Electronically
The acquisition of all data is deemed crucial and necessary for patient monitoring. Data must be consistently and persistently stored within a database to achieve this. The data above are intended to be utilized within the scheme's fuzzy logic engine outline to display patients regularly.

VIII. Presenting Data

    i. **Presenting the Data of Patients**
Healthcare professionals can access personal information and data collected from patients. The preferences of the users will vary in the presentation of data. The end users can select their preferred platform for accessing the collected patient data through either the Web-based or desktop application. Additionally, they will be able to specify the duration of the monitoring period. The process of patient selection involves the input of a unique patient identifier. The personnel can access the patients' vital signs, including their temperature, BP, SpO$_2$, heartbeat, and blood glucose levels.

    ii. **Presenting Personnel Information**
Staff members must have access to the personal information of their colleagues, such as telephone numbers, in the event of unforeseen circumstances. The process of staff member selection involves choosing an individual from a comprehensive roster containing all staff members' names and identification numbers (SIDs).

    iii. **Notifying Workers**
If there is an unexpected change in a patient's information, the staff will get a text message picked up. The patient's condition may be classified as "normal," "low risk," or "high risk" by the use of the fuzzy logic engine.

B. Nonfunctional Requirements

The limits and limitations of a product's implementation are described by its nonfunctional needs. In this paper, it is necessary to explore the following nonfunctional requirements:

- **Accessibility**
  The requirement for a Web-based interface to transmit information to consumers is driven by the dispersed structure of transmission lines. Accessible through a Web browser, these interfaces eliminate the need to download and install any additional software in order to see data and are therefore universally accessible.

- **Scalability**
  To increase the system's scalability in terms of the number of users it can support, a Web-based instrument was used to visualize the activities of wireless sensor networks. Moreover, the system exhibits scalability to accommodate supplementary patients. According to research, a reader has the capacity to read and comprehend up to 100 tags at the same time. The system can accommodate multiple readers.

- **The Necessary Specifications for Ensuring the Safety and Protection of a System or Entity**
  In order to maintain the safety and security of the system, it is necessary for the users, regardless of whether they are a clinician or a nurse, to input a legitimate log-on and password each time they seek to gain entry to the system. This action is implemented with the purpose of safeguarding the confidentiality between medical practitioners and their patients. The updating of information is contingent upon the fulfillment of appropriate security prerequisites. Typically, the updating of information is not feasible, as healthcare professionals do not manually input data. Rather, the data are transmitted from RFID tags to a reader and subsequently relayed to clients.

- **Standards for Software Usability**
  The interface of the system must be intuitive and uncomplicated. The system should not be too complicated for any physicians or nurses to utilize.

- **Safety**
  It is important that the system does not interact with or crash into any other nearby systems. The importance of data backup cannot be overstated.
- **Necessities of Operation**
  The durability and battery life of products are of paramount importance.

5.5   Overall System Architecture

According to the aforementioned specifications, the wireless monitoring system under consideration ought to comprise five primary structural components.

The patient is equipped with sensor modules that make up the mobile data-gathering module. Real-time monitoring of temperature, BP, heartbeat, SpO$_2$, and sugar level is possible with the sensor units. Using RFID and wireless access points, critical data on vital signs may be sent wirelessly to an essential intensive care computer. The mobile announcement network component will then use this information. The proposed system architecture may be expanded to include more patients and more monitoring locations. There may be many sensor units per monitoring zone. With the help of automated monitoring, many patients may be cared for by a small number of medical professionals. The suggested system's block diagram is shown in Figure 5.3.

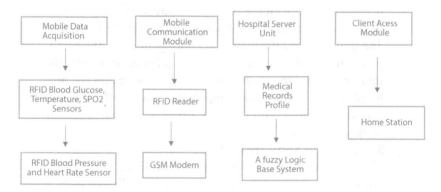

Figure 5.3 Proposed architecture.

A. Software Architecture

Figure 5.4 provides a high-level overview of the system's software architecture and the components that make it up. Five main parts form the mobile patient monitoring system (MPMS). When put together, the parts ensure that the system functions smoothly and reliably. The data acquisition unit (DAQ) API, the MySQL Database Manager, the MATLAB code for fuzzy logic, the GUI, the C# code, and the HTML code for the Web application are all part of the whole. All five components of the program work together to form the MPMS. Following the construction of the system, tests were conducted to verify the robustness, reliability, etc., of the finalized framework. Indoor office conditions were used for the testing of the system.

B. DAQ and API

The DAQ API lets the reader, so you can get the data needed and see them on the API interface. It is the interface that system operators use to manage and monitor the system from the front end. It has a variety of screens that let doctors keep tabs on their patients' health. Summit Co.'s API (a program needed to interface with the reader) was the basis for implementing the API. Summit Co. supplied the RFID equipment. Code modifications and additions were made to accommodate the system's needs better. The C#-based API provides authorized users access to real-time patient information. Functions include:

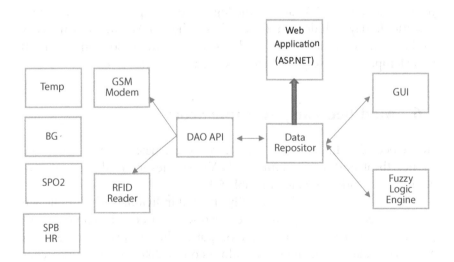

Figure 5.4 High-level software architecture system.

(a)   Determining the tag type;

(b)   Extracting the body temperature, BP, SpO_2, diabetes, and heartbeat values from an RFID reader;

(c)   Determining the related patient from the tag ID;

(d)   Adjusting the health indicator values to align with the newly structured table structures in the database;

(e)   Filling up the table with the vitals; and

(f)   Setting off a warning signal in the event of any deviations.

C. System *Database Manager*

The SDBM is in charge of building and updating a database including all relevant patient and staff information, including vital signs. For each patient added to the system, the SDBM generates a log file containing the time and date the file was created. Each log file is automatically updated in real time to prevent significant data loss in the case of a system crash. The GUI sends the SDBM a packet comprising all of the patient information gathered in response to the current patient inquiry. The SDBM analyzes the information and writes it to the proper patient record. The SDBM also processes data requests made via the GUI. When a user requests a patient's medical history, the SDBM obtains the data and sends them to the user interface (UI) for presentation. In response to this query, the SDBM will bring the entire database into memory and then deliver its contents to the user interface. When user interface users remove patient log files and folders, they utilize the SDBM. When an administrator deletes a patient from the database, the SDBM deletes the log file for that patient and any subdirectories it may include from the database. The RFID reader transmits data to the database, which stores readings from many sensors, including BP, body temperature, oxygen-related issues, and diabetes level.

5.6   Modified Early Warning Score

At the bedside, clinicians use the MEWS to evaluate patients' conditions. BP, heartbeat, body temperature, and AVPU values are the different parameters in this work (tabulated in Table 5.1).

It is possible to identify medically afflicted individuals who might benefit from receiving comprehensive treatment. To do this, compare each patient's blood pressure and urine output to their respective norms. The MEWS was authorized in hospital admissions in 2002. In 2015, researchers looked at the usefulness of MEWS as a screening tool for prompting early assessment and hospital or ICU admission to determine its effectiveness in

Table 5.1 Parameters of MEWS.

MEWS	+3.0	+2.0	+1.0	0.0	+1.0	+2.0	+3.0
BP	<70	71-79	80-99	100-199		>201	
Heartbeat		<45	46-55	56-100	100-110	110-135	>135
Respiratory		<8.9		9-13.9	14.9-20	22-29	>30
Body temperature		<37	37.1-38	38.1-40	38.1-38.5	>38.5	
AVPU/GCS score	<9	9-13	14	A/15	V/Confused	P	U

AVPU, Alert, Value, Pain, Unresponsive; GCS, Glasgow Coma Scale.

identifying people at risk. The MEWS has emerged as the standard of care for patients receiving treatment outside of an emergency department. Data analysis of all sick patients may lead to the Early Warning Score (EWS), a humble grading system. This approach has the potential to identify patients whose health is quickly deteriorating and who thus need immediate medical intervention. The MEWS might help screen patients and keep tabs on their health while on the road. Patients whose health is failing consistently might benefit from using the MEWS.

Each number in the table represents a score between the indicated ranges. Patient statistics for each structure is compared with the MEWS database, and a score between 0 and 3 is determined depending on the agreement between the two. Each criterion's value is added together to get the final MEWS. If the patient's score is 0, everything is OK; if it is between 1 and 5, the scenario is considered low risk; and if it is 5 or more, intensive care unit admission is warranted. Several MEWS features were used to calculate the score in this investigation. Systolic blood pressure, heart rate, oxygen saturation, core body temperature, and blood sugar levels are some of the parameters that have been studied. It was shown in the year 2000 that medical patients who would benefit from intensive care could be identified using a MEWS. To do this, compare each patient's blood pressure and urine output to their respective norms. The MEWS was validated in hospital admissions in 2001. In 2006, scientists examined MEWS to see whether it was beneficial as a screening tool for encouraging early evaluation and hospital or ICU admission. The MEWS has become the gold standard for patient assessment in nonemergency care settings. The EWS is a straightforward scoring system that may be determined by analyzing data from all ill patients. Patients whose health is rapidly deteriorating and who need emergency medical attention may be detected using this method. The Modified Early Warning Score might be helpful in screening patients and monitoring their condition while in travel. Individuals whose health steadily worsens might benefit from the MEWS.

5.7   Conclusion

The main work of the current development is a universal healthcare platform that uses RFID technology and is suitable for use in both homes and hospitals. This system monitors the patients using the mobile and even keeps track of their vitals. A diagnostic method based on fuzzy logic techniques is included in the platform to improve it further. The system enhances healthcare personnel's proficiency in monitoring patients' vital signs across diverse settings, including medical facilities and home environments. The services above encompass monitoring and alerting vital signs, Web-based monitoring applications, and clinical decision support based on established rules across various settings. The system aims to mitigate the potential for severe harm caused by delayed healthcare delivery by continuously monitoring patients in critical condition. The comprehensive system underwent testing on actual patients who were associated with the Rashid Centre for Diabetes and Research (RCDR) located in Ajman, United Arab Emirates. The findings suggest that the created fuzzy logic warning system exhibits superior performance compared to the MEWS system. Therefore, the result can serve as a valuable clinical instrument. Moreover, the design above has the potential to be expanded to encompass a wide range of medical fields and seamlessly integrated with various other hospital information systems. The proposed method is expected to enhance the quality and safety of medical services in the healthcare industry by integrating additional medical centers into the network.

References

1. Desa, United Nations Population Division, II. Magnitude and speed of population ageing, in: *World Population Ageing 1950-2050*, Population Division, Desa, United Nations, World Assembly on Ageing, 2002.
2. *Defining Key Health Information Technology Terms*, Department of Health & Human Services, Office of The National Coordinator for Health Information Technology, USA, April 28, 2008.

3. Berg, J., *Current and Future Possibilities of Medical Informatics*, Tromso University Norway, Spring, 2005.
4. Laguna, J., López, S., Fontecha, J., Fuentes, C., Hervás, R., De Ipiña, D.L., Villarreal, J.B.V., A proposal for mobile diabetes self-control: Towards a patient monitoring framework, in: *IWANN, LNCS 5518*, pp. 869–876, 2009.
5. Mcisaac, W.J., Tisler, A., Irvine, M.J., Saunders, A., Dunai, A., Rizo, C.A., Feig, D.S., Hamill, M., Trudel, M., Cafazzo, J.A., Logan, A.G., Mobile phone based remote patient monitoring system for management of hypertension in diabetic patients. *Am. J. Hypertens.*, 20, 942–948, 2007.
6. Polk, T., Hande, A., Bhatia, D., Walker, W., Remote blood pressure monitoring using a wireless sensor network, in: *IEEE Sixth Annual Emerging Information Technology Conference*, 2006.
7. Yan, Z., Shi, J., Kandachar, P., Freudenthal, A., Jiang, J., A mobile monitoring system of blood pressure for underserved in China by information and communication technology service. *IEEE Trans. Inf. Technol. Biomed.*, 14, 1–12, May 2010.
8. Benyo, B., Varady, P., Benyo, Z., Patient monitoring on industry standard fieldbus, in: *The First Joint BMES/EMBS Conference*, Atlanta, GA, USA, 1999.
9. Figueiredo, C.P., Mühle, C., Ruff, R., Mendes, P.M., Hoffmann, P., Becher, K., Design and realization of a wireless sensor gateway for health monitoring, in: *32nd Annual International Conference of The IEEE EMBS*, Buenos Aires, Argentina, August 31-September 4, 2010.
10. Blanckenberg, M.M., Scheffer, C., Rademeyer, A.J., Wireless physiological monitoring system f or psychiatric patients, in: *31st Annual International Conference of The IEEE EMBS*, Minneapolis, Minnesota, USA, September 2-6, 2009.
11. Rani, P., Verma, S., Yadav, S.P., Rai, B.K., Naruka, M.S., Kumar, D., Simulation of the lightweight blockchain technique based on privacy and security for healthcare data for the cloud system. *Int. J. E-Health Med. Commun. IGI Global*, 13, 4, 1–15, 2022. https://doi.org/10.4018/ijehmc.309436.
12. Choi, B.H., Seo, J.W., Sohn, R.H., Ryu, M.S., Yi, W., Park, K.S., Choi, J.M., A system for ubiquitous health monitoring in the bedroom via a bluetooth network and wireless lan, in: *26th Annual International Conference of The IEEE EMBS*, San Francisco, CA, USA, September 1-5, 2004.
13. Ekström, M., *Small Wireless ECG with Bluetooth™ Communication to A PDA*, Mälardalen University, Thesis, MSC, 2006.
14. Bai, Y.-W. and Yang, D.-C., Mobile blood-glucose monitoring of an integrated health information management system, in: *IEEE International Conference on Consumer Electronics (ICCE)*, 2012.
15. Cho, J., Choi, J., Nam, T., Park, J., *A Zigbee Network-Based Multi-Channel Heart Rate Monitoring System for Exercising Rehabilitation Patients*, IEEE, 2007.
16. Roffia, L., Lamberti, C., Salmon, T., Auteri, V., Zigbee-based wireless ECG minitor, in: *Computers in Cardiology*, 2007.

17. Vashisht, V., Pandey, A.K., Yadav, S.P., Speech recognition using machine learning. *IEIE Trans. Smart Process. Comput. Institute Electron. Engineers Korea*, 10, 3, 233–239, 2021. https://doi.org/10.5573/ieiespc.2021.10.3.233.

18. Chambers, D., Rotariu, C., Frehill, P., Using Zigbee to integratemedical devices, in: *29th Annual International Conference of The IEEE EMBS Cité Internationale*, Lyon, France, August 23-26, 2007.

19. Choi, J.S. and Zhou, M., *Performance Analysis of Zigbee-Based Body Sensor Networks*, IEEE, 2010.

20. Wood, A., Selavo, L., Cao, Q., Fang, L., Doan, T., He, Z., Stoleru, R., Lin, S., Stankovic, J.A., Virone, G., *An Advanced Wireless Sensor Network for Health Monitoring*, IEEE, 2005.

21. Sai Pavan, K.V., Deepthi, K., Saravanan, G., Rajasanthosh Kumar, T., Vinay, A.V., Improvement of delamination spread model to gauge a dynamic disappointment of interlaminar in covered composite materials to forecast of material debasement. *PalArch's J. Archaeol. Egypt/Egyptol.*, 17, 9, 6551–6562, 2020. Retrieved from https://archives.palarch.nl/index.php/jae/article/view/5214.

22. González-Parada, E., Alarcón-Collantes, V., Casilari-Pérez, E., Cano-García, J.M., A PDA-based portable wireless ECG monitor for medical personal area networks, in: *IEEE MELECON*, Benalmadena (Malaga), Spain, May 2006.

23. Noimanee, S., Khunja, P., Keawfoonrungsie, P., Noimanee, K., Medical consult-based system for diagnosis on WiMAX technology. *Int. J. Appl. Biomed. Eng.*, 3, 1, 2010.

24. Cheng, J.-C. and Yu, S.-N., A wireless physiological signal monitoring system with integrated bluetooth and WIFI technologies, in: *IEEE Engineering in Medicine and Biology 27th Annual Conference*, Shanghai, China, 2005.

25. Liu, C.S., Trappey, A.J.C., Trappey, C.V., Develop patient monitoring and support system using mobile communication and intelligent reasoning, in: *IEEE International Conference on Systems, Man, and Cybernetics*, San Antonio, TX, USA, October 2009.

26. Want, R., *An introduction to RFID technology*, Intel Research, IEEE Cs and IEEE Comsoc, 2006.

6

Management of Trust Between Patient and IoT Using Fuzzy Logic Theory

L. Rajeshkumar[1]*, J. Rachel Priya[2], Konatham Sumalatha[3],
G. Arunkumar[4], D. Suganthi[5] and D. Saravanan[6]

[1]*Department of MBA, St. Joseph's College of Engineering, OMR, Chennai, India*
[2]*Department of Business Administration, Madras Christian College, Chennai, India*
[3]*School of Computer Science and Engineering, VIT, Vellore, India*
[4]*Department of Computer Science & Engineering, Madanapalle Institute of Technology & Science, Madanapalle, India*
[5]*Department of Computer Science, Saveetha College of Liberal Arts and Sciences, SIMATS, Thandalam, Chennai, India*
[6]*Department of Computer Science and Engineering, Sathyabama Institute of Science and Technology, Chennai, India*

Abstract

The machine-to-machine revolution was created by the advent of the Internet of Things. Offering innovative services to various sectors. The potential constraints or capabilities of these diverse intelligent devices may give rise to the generation of confidential data and novel concerns pertaining to security, privacy, and technological assurance. In a manner that is spread out. The provision of a scalable decentralized trust management mechanism for the access control system serves to mitigate these issues. Trust-based security models have been found to be more efficacious than cryptography-based security in detecting and preventing a range of insider threats through the analysis of trust scores. The article titled "Scalable Trust Management (STM)" presents a thesis that employs a fuzzy approach and incorporates various factors such as experience and classification device to ascertain the precise value of the trust score. The capability device has taken into account the formulation of the rule. The simulation results obtained from NS2 demonstrate that the use of STM technology can effectively enhance the energy efficiency and scalability of heterogeneous networks.

Corresponding author: drrajeshmagt@gmail.com

Satya Prakash Yadav, Sudesh Yadav, Pethuru Raj Chelliah and Victor Hugo C. de Albuquerque (eds.)
Advances in Fuzzy-Based Internet of Medical Things (IoMT), (93–106) © 2024 Scrivener Publishing LLC

Keywords: TM, IoMT, communication of machine matters, fuzzy logic, STM

6.1 Introduction

For intelligent applications, numerous new wireless technologies have been developed. M2M or Internet of Things methods and technology are being adopted faster. Regarding the estimated number of linked devices, various associations have published estimates that range from 25 to 40 billion joined devices. M2M is the fantastic development of pervasive communication [1]. Numerous smart gadgets automatically communicate with one another either with or without human intervention. Multiple applications, including smart homes and intelligent e-health, are supported by M2M. An Internet of Things (IoT) subset is M2M [2, 3]. Bright things and smart devices can now connect through a network and offer a wide range of services to all people in the IoT universe [4, 5]. The security and privacy of data are two issues that IoT is dealing with as it delivers services. Security against multiple assaults can be provided through cryptography and authentication techniques. In the same context, a ton of research is being conducted. Strong cryptography and robust authentication lessen some safety concerns for IoT [6, 7]. This method is employed when nodes move information between themselves, and as such, they serve as the initial line of protection against outside threats. But internal attacks cannot be defended against by these algorithms and processes. Because the attacker already has all the necessary credentials because he is a system user, internal attacks can get around this authentication technique. Working on the idea of trust management is required to solve these issues [8, 9]. The Internet of Things network is a network that is dynamic with numerous nodes connecting and departing it regularly. Therefore, a flexible trust model is required, which calculates the active trust of various devices [10, 11].

Regarding resource security, trust management is the most crucial idea. The rule of managing trust varies depending on the situation; for instance, one can create trust mechanisms based on interactions and feedback [12]. Numerous theoretical and computational models have been recently proposed in the coming years. Nowadays, cloud service providers provide worthy trust management capabilities in apps [13, 14].

6.2   Scalable Trust Management

M2M communication is a subset of IoT. The scalability of the Internet of Things is a crucial factor in enabling the network to accommodate the connection of novel devices. The provision of services to newly or previously associated devices in the IoT network necessitates the implementation of an access control component [15, 16]. The implementation of dynamic access control necessitates the utilization of a trust calculation mechanism that is both scalable and dynamic in nature. Consequently, the proposed design provides a mechanism for computing trust dynamically among interconnected devices to meet this requirement [17, 18]. In the proposed approach, a Distributed Identifier (DID) it uniquely identifies each device in the network. Every gadget is classified as semi-expedient, expedient, or non-expedient by utilizing a fuzzy technique. FIS functions similarly to how people make decisions [19]. The suggested system used fuzzy logic in the Mamdani approach. Despite various confusing inputs, this approach offers smooth output control. Fuzzy logic, fuzzy inference, and defuzzification are all parts of the unclear logic process. Sharp input values are transformed into linguistic values by fuzzy logic. Fuzzy sets convert linguistic values like "Bad," "Average," and "Good" to actual values using membership functions. A crisp value is created from the defuzzification process's output. The inference engine computes fuzzy output functions by applying IF-ELSE rules. Although there are alternative defuzzification techniques, this system used the center of gravity (COG) technique to get a crisp output result. Machining productivity determines the volume of goods produced, with the most outstanding possible output being the logical objective. This study looked at performance indicators such as machining time (MT), dimensional accuracy (DA), kerf width (KW), and surface roughness (SR). Direct MT monitoring via the machine tool display is required for every machining process, i.e., the overall time needed to cut all geometric shapes.

Figure 6.1 depicts the M2M communication system's fuzzy-based trust score computation flow. This work aims to investigate the STM model and provide the access control framework with the trust score of each device to make access control decisions. This document does not cover the operation of the access control framework. The detailed operation will be provided in the following iteration of this paper.

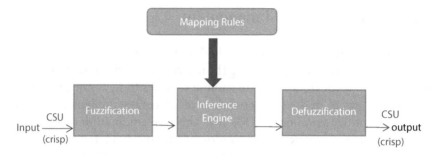

Figure 6.1 Architecture model of calculation system based on the trust score.

The following factors are taken into account in this study while calculating trust:

(a) Knowledge
(b) Suggestion
(c) Classification of devices

The following are detailed descriptions of how each parameter has been calculated:

6.2.1 Experience €

Devices A and B can be trusted based on their interactions' past performance, or Vk, where k is an integer between 1 and n. If the interaction is successful, Vk will be +1; if it fails, it will be -1. For some time now,

$$Ex_i = \sum_K n = 1v_K \Big/ \sum_K n = 1|v_K| \tag{6.1}$$

The experience calculated for the given time ti in Equation 6.1, where Exi:

$$E = \sum_{i=0} n\, Ex_i * g_i \tag{6.2}$$

E is the device's experience, determined using Equations 6.1 and 6.2, taking into account its prior experience.

There is a weight assigned to each experience that decreases as it gets older.

6.2.2   Recommendation (R)

The r-value found by adding the r values from 'N' A

In cases where there exist a total of n devices. The allocation of a weight, denoted as wi, is assigned to a device referred to as device. This advice is provided by the device in question B. r ∈ [-1,1]. wi∈ [0,1]

6.2.3   Device Classification (D)

Classification in three categories:

    i)   Expedient
    ii) Semi-expedient
    iii) Non-expedient

Classification of Parameters

Proximity	= {Excessive, Moderate, Shallow};
Environment	= {WLAN, 3G/4G}
Device Type (DT)	= {WSN, IP, RFID};
RSSI (RS)	= {High, Medium, Low};
Battery	= {Battery-operated, less battery}

For instance, "dp, ev, dt, Rs, " for an expedient device stands for "Excessive, 3G/4G, IP, High, Battery-operated. Device classification is mainly taken into account for parameters based on capacity. Each gadget has a unique ability for data processing. Trust is therefore calculated about the device's capabilities. As a result, guidelines for the fuzzy inference process are created. A Mamdani-type fuzzy rule-based model to categorize devices and assess trust is used. Two fuzzy logics were used: one for device categorization and the other for calculating trust scores, using imprecise values. When calculating the overall trust score of devices using two separate applications of fuzzy logic, which use hazy and imprecise values of dp, ev, DT, BT, and RS. The classification of devices and corresponding TD, TE, and TR scores indicating device trustworthiness. Table 6.1 lists the linguistic

Table 6.1 Linguistic values for D-P, E-V, D-T, R-S, B-T.

D-P	E-V	D-T	R-S	B-T	Crisp range	FIS numbers
Shallow	3g/4g	RFID	less	less battery	below -0.4	-1, -0.6, -0.2
Shallow	WiMAX	IP	Medium	battery-operated	-0.2 to 0.6	-0.2, 0.2, 0.6
Excessive	WLAN	WsN	High	AC power	above 0 to 6	0.6, 1, 1

Table 6.2 Linguistic values for Td, Te, Ti, and Tr.

Td	Te	Tr	Crisp range	Number of fuzzy
Non-Expedient	Bad	Negative	below 0-2	1, -0.6, -0.2
Semi-Expedient	Normal	Neutral	-0.2 to 0.7	0.2, 0.2, 0.6
Expedient	Better	High	above 0.5	0.6, 1, 1

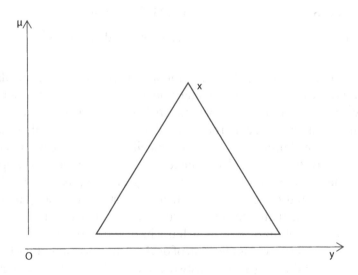

Figure 6.2 Function of device proximity (D-P).

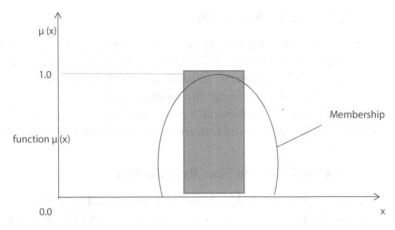

Figure 6.3 Function of environment (Ev).

values for the following categories: Device proximity, Environment, Device type, RSSI, and Battery. Table 6.2 shows the linguistic values for the trust score for Device categorization, Experience, and Recommendation. The membership functions of Device proximity, Environment, Device type, RSSI, Battery, Device categorization, Experience, and Recommendation are each represented in Figures 6.2 and 6.3.

For device classification and trust computation, the fuzzy rule will be applied in accordance with Figure 6.3. Each direction is represented by an IF-THEN connection in the Mamdani scheme, a kind of fuzzy relational model. The unclear logic-required conditional statements are written using the IF-THEN rules. Multiple IF-THEN rules are possible.

6.3   IoT Integration

Since its inception, the Internet of Things has given rise to intriguing applications like smart homes, smart cities, and intelligent health systems. The quality of life for humans is improved by automation and digitization technologies. The centralized administration system for data transfer and share calculation, however, is unreliable. The submission must deal with problems related to security, confidentiality, dependability, and scalability. In order to overcome issues with IoT applications, blockchain adds decentralized properties such as scalability, autonomy, stability, security, immutability, and trust. It also incorporates blockchain-conceptual domains that can profit from the IoT.

6.3.1   IoT Device Authentication

Traditionally, a central server is used for authentication. IoT device authentication is made possible by the blockchain-based smart contract as a distributed and peaceful multi-party authentication. IoT devices that require decentralized authentication can use the bubble trust technique. Smart contracts are developed using sophisticated programming languages and blockchain technology. IoT devices and conventional authorization are contrasted.

6.3.2   Confidentiality and Non-Repudiation

Every transaction is encrypted, and the block format is checked before it is included. The digital signature of each node depends on ECC, and a node that provides various contract privileges which are smart used to authenticate each node's hash address. Thus, blockchain technology maintains user privacy. In a blockchain system, non-repudiation is not possible, as a result of the fact that every node sends a message along with its digital signature. As a result, the sender's public key is used to validate and decrypt the transaction information. Nobody can deny that the later part of the deal did not favor them. In the registration process, every node receives a different identifying number that is stored in the blockchain and makes it difficult to forge a node. The phrase describes the use of authentication along with public key cryptography. Interference and rejection can be avoided with effective authentication.

6.3.3   Trust Management and Data Leakage

All information is digitally signed by the sender and safeguarded by cryptography. A digital ledger format is used to store all topics in network data forms. Therefore, a blockchain-based system cannot be subjected to a data leak or data transmission assault. As each node has a copy of the same transaction, they can all confirm any further transactions. All users are more confident in the nodes, since they are identified by a special key and their digital signature.

6.4   Approaches to Blockchain Solutions for IoT Applications

A blockchain design idea is an intelligent application based on the IoT. There are two types of blockchain architecture: authorized and unauthorized.

The IoT gadget has a peer fog linked to another intermediate system. These auxiliary nodes are connected and divided to serve computers and communication. To enhance multiphase calculations, define a single node during the decision-making process. As for the prerequisites for the application, creating a smart contract will be used on the blockchain platform. Presently, Ethereum and Hyperledger Fabric are the two most popular blockchain platforms. The output of an intelligent contract corresponds to the corresponding output of a self-executing program that is necessary. Innovative home monitoring systems can alert a responsible user in the case of a fire, much like the creation of several applications. Similar to intelligent healthcare systems, fog computing and smart contracts built on blockchains can be utilized to react to the data gathered instantly. If the incident is known, actions can be taken right away in some intelligent apps. The IoT systems will also be more dependable and safe, as the blockchain systems are tamper-proof, secure, immutable, and distributed.

6.5   Implementation and Result

Ethereum is a public, open-source, decentralized, hassle-free blockchain platform that allows for the running of computer programs on top of it. This eliminates the need for developers to build their own blockchain and enables them to program smart contracts using the solidity language. The blockchain's applications can communicate with decentralized apps (dApps), and a full network of interconnected applications will grow as they communicate with one another in the blockchain network. It is easier to operate the application since the Ethereum platform has a shorter blocking time than Bitcoin. Ethereum handles the blocking and recording of crypto currency transactions, and because it works quickly, transactions are completed more quickly. Without the consumer having to wait very long, Ethereum can manage a lot of Internet transactions.

6.5.1   Experimental Setup

A blockchain virtual network is built using a machine with an Intel Core i5-5200U CPU, running at 2.2 GHz, and 8 GB of Linux RAM, in order to set up Ethereum. A 10-user Ethereum network with a special hash ID for establishing communications has been built. Nodes can use the concept of signatures to transfer messages from one person to another using a unique identifier. An electronic message needs a digital signature to be controlled by someone else. Utilizing digital signatures has two advantages that prevent users from having their applications rejected: user identification verification and content verification. Due to the unique code that each document possesses, a digital signature is easily recognized. In a blockchain system, a message can be signed digitally by each node and sent, where other nodes can verify it with their own signatures.

6.5.2 Implementing Smart Contracts for IoT Solutions

The blockchain is made into little computer programs by intelligent contracts. The blockchain contains the smart contract's data. Therefore, its operation is entirely decentralized. No network member can take control of the asset using this technique.

6.5.3 Experimental Purposes for SCHIS (Smart Contract-Based Health Insurance System)

The Ethereum platform has been used to construct an infrastructure for verification and auditing. Additionally, the Internet of Things application in healthcare has been explored. The healthcare sector encompasses medical professionals, healthcare facilities, individuals seeking medical attention, and insurance providers. The smart contracts implemented by these organizations are meticulously coded and deployed on the blockchain network as shown in Figure 6.4. Upon fulfillment of the input prerequisites and submission of the message to the network, the initial smart contract of the patient is executed automatically in the given context as shown in Figure 6.5. Both the hospital and insurance company will deliver their

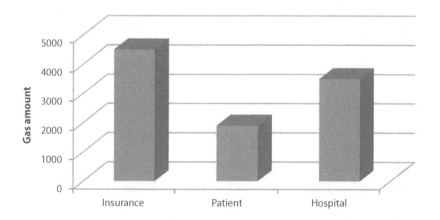

Figure 6.4 Various smart contracts of Ethereum network in the deployed state.

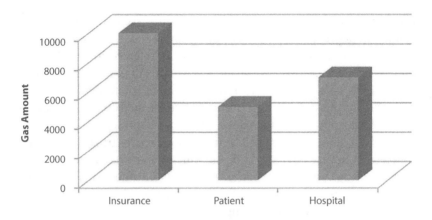

Figure 6.5 Various smart contracts of Ethereum network in the execution state.

respective presentations regarding the news. All subsequent occurrences shall be digitally documented and rendered accessible to all three blockchain network nodes. This system presents several security and privacy concerns, encompassing address space, authentication and authorization, secure communication, trust management, data authentication, integrity, and secure computing for Internet of Things devices.

The event will be triggered automatically if a blockchain network is deployed in a smart contract. It performs as smart contract execution and events corresponding to triggers. In order to avoid rejection, the digital signature is used along with the message when sending it.

6.6   Conclusion

The Internet of Things has been one of the most cutting-edge study areas in the past 10 years. The objective is to incorporate intelligent environmental monitoring, intelligent traffic management, and many other applications using the Internet of Things trust management into the architecture of an intellectual house. Numerous sensors, actuators, and intelligent devices enable the application to operate in real time. One of the most fascinating sectors is the one involving health insurance. The traditional insurance system needs help with trust management, requirement clarity, processing lags, and settlement challenges. In this post, we present a framework that uses blockchain technology to link all parties involved. The blockchain implementation was run on the Ethereum virtual machine. Quantify the significance of trust and express the human essence of this concept, computational approaches are used to identify six key factors: role and identity management, reputation, peer recommendation, operational cost, operational risk, and privacy. It is sometimes referred to as the Hexagon framework. Because this is a private blockchain, all units must first be registered. Each block in each block has a different functionality—thanks to the intelligent agreement. The results demonstrated that if less gas were consumed during the performance, the smart contract would activate. In this case, a digital signature will be used to boost user trust throughout the complete insurance payment process, which will be documented in a digital accounting system. Conveniences the establishment of a public blockchain environment in future to facilitate the users based on the network and enable multi-party computing.

References

1. Sun, C., Li, Q., Li, H., Shi, Y., Zhang, S., Guo, W., Patient cluster divergence based healthcare insurance fraudster detection. *IEEE Access*, 7, 14162–14170, 2018.
2. Kamienski, C., Kleinschmidt, J., Soininen, J.P., Kolehmainen, K., Roffia, L., Visoli, M., Maia, R.F., Fernandes, S., SWAMP: Smart water management platform overview and security challenges, in: *Proceedings of the 2018 48th Annual IEEE/IFIP International Conference on Dependable Systems and Networks Workshops (DSN-W)*, Luxembourg, pp. 49–50, June 25–28, 2018.
3. Hammi, M.T., Hammi, B., Bellot, P., Serrhrouchni, A., Bubbles of trust: A decentralized blockchain based authentication system for IoT. *Comput. Secur.*, 78, 126–142, September 2018. Blockchain cloud architecture for IoT. *IEEE Access*, 6, 115–124, February 2018.
4. Fotiou, N. and Polyzos, G.C., Smart contracts for the internet of things: Opportunities and challenges, in: *2018 IEEE European Conference on Networks and Communications (EuCNC)*, pp. 256–260, Ljubljana, Slovenia, 2018.
5. Almogren, A., Mohiuddin, I., Ud Din, I., Almajed, H., Guizani, N., Ftm-IoMT: Fuzzy-based trust management for preventing sybil attacks in internet of medical things. *IEEE Internet Things J.*, 8, 6, 4485–4497, 2020.
6. Jiang, Q., Zhou, X., Wang, R., Ding, W., Chu, Y., Tang, S., Jia, X., Xu, X., Intelligent monitoring for infectious diseases with fuzzy systems and edge computing: A survey. *Appl. Soft Comput.*, 21, 108835, Apr. 2022.
7. Farivar, F., Jolfaei, A., Manthouri, M., Haghighi, M.S., Application of fuzzy learning in IoT-enabled remote healthcare monitoring and control of anesthetic depth during surgery. *Inf. Sci.*, 2021, 21, 66, 1-11, 2023.

8. Kayes, A.S., Rahayu, W., Dillon, T., Chang, E., Han, J., Context-aware access control with imprecise context characterization for cloud-based data resources. *Future Gener. Comput. Syst.*, 93, 237-55, Apr. 1, 2019.

9. Ebrahimi, M., Haghighi, M.S., Jolfaei, A., Shamaeian, N., Tadayon, M.H., A secure and decentralized trust management scheme for smart health systems. *IEEE J. Biomed. Health Inform.*, 26, 5, 1961–1968, 2021.

10. Rahmani, M.K., II, Shuaib, M., Alam, S., Siddiqui, S.T., Ahmad, S., Bhatia, S., Mashat, A., Blockchain-based trust management framework for cloud computing-based internet of medical things (IoMT): A systematic review. *Comput. Intell. Neurosci.*, 2022, 1–12, 2022.

11. Yadav, S.P., Blockchain security, in: *Blockchain Security in Cloud Computing. EAI/Springer Innovations in Communication and Computing*, S.R. Kumar, A. Kumar, V. Kumar, S. Padmanaban (Eds.), Springer, Cham, 2022, https://doi.org/10.1007/978-3-030-70501-5_1.

12. Götzinger, M., Anzanpour, A., Azimi, I., TaheriNejad, N., Jantsch, A., Rahmani, A.M., Liljeberg, P., Confidence-enhanced early warning score based on fuzzy logic. *Mob. Netw. Appl.*, 2022, 27, 691–708, 1–18, 2019.

13. Shahbazi, Z. and Byun, Y.-C., A procedure for tracing supply chains for perishable food based on blockchain, machine learning and fuzzy logic. *Electronics*, 10, 1, 41, 2020.

14. Singh, C., Rao, M.S.S., Mahaboobjohn, Y.M., Kotaiah, B., Kumar, T.R., Applied machine tool data condition to predictive smart maintenance by using artificial intelligence, in: *Emerging Technologies in Computer Engineering: Cognitive Computing and Intelligent IoT. ICETCE 2022. Communications in Computer and Information Science*, vol. 1591 Springer, Cham, 2022, https://doi.org/10.1007/978-3-031-07012-9_49.

15. Mahalle, P., Thakre, P., Prasad, N., Prasad, R., *A Fuzzy Approach to Trust Based Access Control in Internet of Things*, pp. 1–5, 2013, doi: 10.1109/VITAE.2013.6617083.

16. Soleymani, M., Abapour, N., Taghizadeh, E., Siadat, S., Karkehabadi, R., Fuzzy rule-based trust management model for the security of cloud computing. *Math. Probl. Eng.*, 2021, Article ID 6629449, 14, 2021. https://doi.org/10.1155/2021/6629449.

17. Tyagi, H., Kumar, R., Kr Pandey, S., A detailed study on trust management techniques for security and privacy in IoT: Challenges, trends, and research directions. *High-Confid. Comput.*, 3, 2, 100127, ISSN 2667–2952, 2023. https://doi.org/10.1016/j.hcc.2023.100127. (https://www.sciencedirect.com/science/article/pii/S2667295223000259).

18. Bangui, H., Buhnova, B., Kusnirakova, D., Halasz, D., Trust management in social Internet of Things across domains. *Internet Things*, 23, 100833, ISSN 2542–6605, 2023. https://doi.org/10.1016/j.iot.2023.100833. (https://www.sciencedirect.com/science/article/pii/S2542660523001567).

19. Ruotsalainen, P., Blobel, B., Pohjolainen, S., Privacy and trust in eHealth: A fuzzy linguistic solution for calculating the merit of service. *J. Pers. Med.*, 12, 5, 657, Apr. 19, 2022. doi: 10.3390/jpm12050657. PMID: 35629080, PMCID: PMC9147882.

Improving the Efficiency of IoMT Using Fuzzy Logic Methods

K. Kiran Kumar[1]*, S. Sivakumar[2], Pramoda Patro[3] and RenuVij[4]

[1]*Chalapathi Institute of Technology, Mothadaka, Guntur, Andhra Pradesh, India*
[2]*Department of Electrical and Electronics Engineering, VelTech Rangarajan Dr Sagunthala R and D Institute of Science and Technology Avadi Chennai, Tamil Nadu, India*
[3]*Department of Engineering Mathematics, Koneru Lakshmaiah Education Foundation, Hyderabad, Telangana, India*
[4]*University School of Business, Department of AIT-MBA, Chandigarh University, Mohali, India*

Abstract

Among all industries, 20% are homes where home energy management systems have become more feasible with the introduction of smart appliances and clever sensors. When gauging the smart home's efficacy, it is important to strike a balance between energy efficiency and resident convenience. Up to 60% of a typical home's annual energy bill goes toward the operation of heating, ventilation, and air conditioning (HVAC) systems. Multiple studies have shown that reducing energy usage is the primary motivation for using fuzzy logic systems in conjunction with other methods. However, user convenience is typically compromised while using such methods. In this research, the fuzzy inference system (FIS) takes humidity into account both the current temperature and the user's preferred setting to keep the thermostat at an optimal level. Furthermore, utilize the variation in interior room temperature as feedback for the suggested fuzzy inference system to optimize energy usage. Determining each rule's parameters in FIS takes more time and introduces more room for human mistakes as the number of rules grows. Suggested the use of combinatorial methods for the automatic generation of rule basis. Also, Sugeno FIS and Mamdani FIS are used to analyze the effectiveness of the offered methods. The suggested solution utilizes adaptive algorithms and smart sensors to keep the user's preferred temperature constant. The suggested

*Corresponding author: kommineni.kiran11@gmail.com

Satya Prakash Yadav, Sudesh Yadav, Pethuru Raj Chelliah and Victor Hugo C. de Albuquerque (eds.)
Advances in Fuzzy-Based Internet of Medical Things (IoMT), (107–120) © 2024 Scrivener Publishing LLC

FIS system may be implemented in an Internet of Things (IoT) operating system like RIOT, since it makes use of sensors and needs little in the way of memory and computing resources. The suggested method has been shown via simulation to result in a 2.5% decrease in energy use.

Keywords: RIOT, Mamdani FIS, Sugeno FIS, HVAC systems, home energy management

7.1   Introduction

In the last several decades, controlling energy usage has become an increasingly pressing issue. The residential sector is the third greatest liveliness user behind industrial and transportation sectors and ahead of the commercial sector. Approximately 20% and 15% of total energy used in the United States and Canada are attributable to the residential sector, respectively. With a growing global population comes a growing need for power, which is predicted to rise by 24% by 2035. Heating, ventilation, and air conditioning (HVAC) systems account for over half of all home energy usage, making that an important factor. Peak-hour power demands are mostly attributable to HVAC equipment. The smart home's HEMS plays a crucial role in managing energy consumption by increasing the efficiency, dependability, and conservation of energy use. Utilities and smart grids have established many programs to incentivize energy consumers to engage in load management strategies. The success of such endeavors, however, is often found to rely heavily on the approval and engagement of users. The adoption of programmable thermostats, electric water heaters, etc., may help promote demand response and user interaction. HEMS adjust their schedules or reduce their workloads in response to the fluctuating costs. With the proliferation of Internet connectivity, embedded devices, and smart sensors, the Internet of Things (IoT) has shown its worth in the quest to reduce energy use. The operating system is the software layer between applications and the computer's hardware. When the Internet of Things is considered, the operating system must take into consideration new constraints on memory, space, power, and processing speed. The variety of IoT devices and networks has led to the development of several operating systems. The HEMS has gone a long way, but it still has a way to go before it is really energy-efficient, user-friendly, cost-effective, and has a low peak-to-average ratio (PAR). The level of user comfort is influenced by various environmental factors, such as indoor and outdoor temperatures, humidity levels, and light levels, among others. Hence, it is imperative to consider supplementary factors that have a direct impact on the user to effectively exploit the benefits of demand response incentives while ensuring user convenience. Prior studies failed to consider the objective of preserving consumer thermal comfort while simultaneously reducing energy consumption. However, our proposed methodology addresses this issue. By utilizing a humidity parameter, it is possible to ascertain the ideal thermostat settings that are not only comfortable for occupants but also energy-efficient. The difficulty in evaluating HVAC energy consumption across all possible input parameter permutations stems from the requirement of defining a substantial number of rules in a fuzzy inference system (FIS) rule base. The present study proposes a methodology to enhance the convenience of defining rules by utilizing permutations of input parameters within the membership function. The fuzzy inference system under consideration incorporates a feedback mechanism that enables real-time monitoring of the ambient temperature within the premises, thereby facilitating precise regulation of the fire's functioning. The proposed system in this research necessitates a reduced amount of memory (approximately 2 kB) for the examination of directions in the FIS rule ignoble. The proposed fuzzy controller exhibits reduced energy consumption, rendering it a viable functional component for household-level integration through the utilization of RIOT. The subsequent sections of the document are organized as follows: The second section presents a classification and tabular representation of the current state-of-the-art research. The third section offers an in-depth explanation of the problem at hand. The fourth section outlines a system model that is based on the fuzzy logic system. The fifth section deliberates on the results of the simulation. Finally, the sixth section presents a summary and conclusion. Table 7.1 enumerates the variables and abbreviations employed in this study.

Table 7.1 Nomenclature.

Variables	Description
FIS	Fuzzy interference system
PCT	Programmable communication thermostat
OCC	Occupancy fuzzy input parameter
ISP	Thermostat set point fuzzy input parameter

7.2   Related to Work

Researchers working with HEMS have discovered that electric load may be split into two camps: those managed by a thermostat and those controlled by a human operator. Thermostats are used to regulate the operation of loads such as HVAC systems. The majority of the peak demand at such times comes from HVAC units. Energy usage may be reduced by load shedding and scheduling of certain appliances. Scheduling and load shedding of various household appliances are only one topic covered by the literature.

7.2.1   Fuzzy Interface System for DSM

The RTP required an HVAC control method. A dynamic demand response controller (DDRC) assesses power pricing at 15-minute intervals and adjusts the thermostat set point to the user's preference. Energy Plus merged the home model with MATLAB-implemented DDRC. The suggested technique uses a tight temperature maintenance range without considering user choice. In this, fuzzy logic rule-based algorithms and wireless sensors were integrated. MATLAB simulated a wireless thermostat. The suggested system reduced thermostat set points in real time based on external things like demand in load and to improve heating/cooling energy efficiency. Demand response, energy usage, and occupant comfort are performance measures. The center of gravity (CoG) approach defuses parameters using triangle membership functions. The output parameter determines load reduction, whereas the defuzzied value shows how much a set point may shift after being established. The goal of this research is to reduce energy use and increase indoor comfort; however, the opposite occurred.

Users often fail to account for inflation when using predefined parameters according to the literature. Initiatives using wireless sensors, fuzzy logic, and the smart grid created an autonomous thermostat. Supervised fuzzy logic learning (SFLL) was utilized to lower the thermostat set point based on outside temperature, power price, and claim. The autonomous thermostat has Economy and Comfort settings. Mamdani FIS lets the thermostat manage all power price rates. Since the research was done in Canada, the suggested system is cold country-specific. DDRC monitors power pricing at 15-minute intervals and changes the control set point rendering to the user's preferences. MATLAB implemented DDRC and

Energy Plus integrated the home model. Since they did not consider user desire, the suggested solution uses a small temperature maintenance range.

Wireless sensors were integrated with a fuzzy logic rule-based system. A wireless programmable thermostat was modeled in MATLAB. Energy usage, demand response participation, and occupant comfort are performance measures. Defuzzification uses the center of gravity approach and triangular membership functions of parameters. This study sought to minimize energy usage and improve interior temperature at the expense of user comfort.

7.3 Problem Formulation

Uncertainty due to ambiguous language notions gives birth to the concept of "fuzziness." There is a lack of clarity on how to quantify user happiness in HEMS. If, for example, a user's thermal comfort is described as "cold" in everyday speech, have no way of knowing exactly how chilly it is. The physical amounts of the actual method are represented by mathematical models in conventional controllers. Fuzzy logic controllers (FLCs) take in and spit out actual variables through a nonlinear mapping. As a result, they have been discovered to be useful in simulating the complex dynamics of HVAC systems. The FLC is preferable to traditional controllers, since it

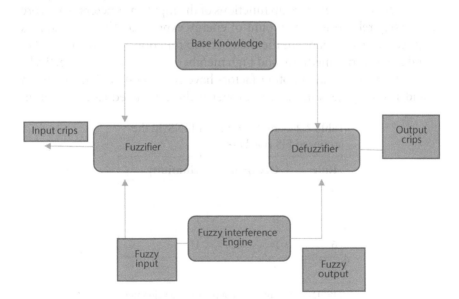

Figure 7.1 Conceptual diagram of the FIS.

does not need mathematical modeling. The FLC system's conceptual diagram is seen in Figure 7.1.

7.4   System Model Implementation

Parameters that have a direct impact on residential buildings' energy usage and occupant comfort have been taken into account in this suggested method. Indoor temperature (Tempindoor), outside temperature (Tempotron), user density (Occ), and humidity (H) are examples of these variables.

In the suggested method, the input and output variables' membership functions are explained by using a trapezoidal membership function. The system's only output is the amount of energy used. The study's parameters—temperature, set points, price, and humidity—are better characterized by a trapezoidal membership function rather than a triangular one, despite the triangle membership function's ease of use. Thus, the simplicity of these straight-line membership functions is an advantage.

7.5   Performance Evaluation

Exertion level is inversely proportional to score. It recommends removing the total value from all membership variables.In order to prevent a combinatorial explosion of IF-THEN rules, included in an energy consumption parameter, to the membership functions of the input parameters. The score is inversely related to the amount of energy expended. The total value is assigned to each variable in the membership function. Assign values of 0, 1, and 2 to the low, medium, and high membership functions, respectively. Except for Occupancy, all other factors have continuous weights between -1 and 1. Using the commutative property, the automated rule generation

Table 7.2 Sample of rule DEFINS[a] in the proposed FIS rule base.

Rule	Occupant	Humidity
2	A	L
4	P	L
6	P	H
8	A	L

[a]DEFINS - it is related to a relevant development or a specialized field, to get the latest information.

method generates a Score by summing the masses of the membership functions of the input limitations, which may be combined in any sequence. The results of one such automated rule development process are shown in Table 7.2 as examples of FIS rules. To facilitate the input and output of the proposed FIS, define and condense the following membership functions:

7.6   Results

This section simulates the suggested schemes. A tiny room's 2-kW heater is used to test the FIS's feedback loop, while a residential building's 10-kW HVAC is used to test the humidity parameter. Initializing of set points based on temperature and relative values. The presence of dampness increased consumer comfort. This section explains how to add a feedback loop to the Sugeno FIS decreases energy consumption. Cities that employ FLCs may reduce their energy use. Figure 7.2 depicts the simulated daily and monthly energy consumption for approaches with and without humidity as an input parameter, demonstrating the effect of including a feedback loop. The fuzzy rule basis with a feedback loop activates the current situation every 5 minutes.

Figure 7.3 shows a similar pattern. Sugeno FIS without a feedback loop consumes 16.43 kWh per day, whereas, with a loop, it consumes 3.31 kWh. This boosts the efficacy of the suggested FIS to minimize energy usage.

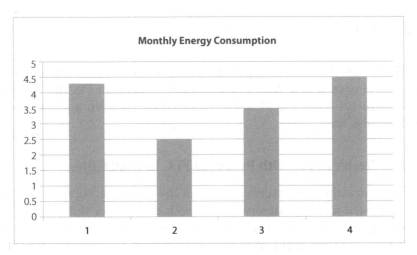

Figure 7.2 Monthly energy consumption 1.

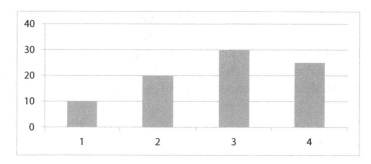

Figure 7.3 Monthly energy consumption 2.

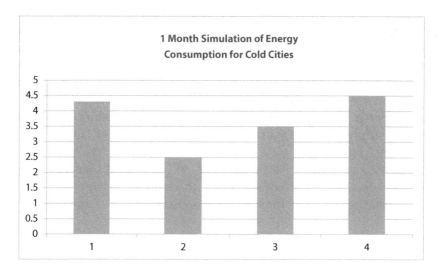

Figure 7.4 One-month simulation of energy for cold cities.

Figure 7.4 shows the suggested FIS beats the existing approach in monthly energy usage. With a feedback loop, Mamdani FIS and Sugeno FIS utilize 101 kWh and 99 kWh compared to 501 kWh and 493 kWh without one, respectively.

7.6.1   Result of FIS with Proposed FLC in Cold Cities

This part examines the assessment of cold city energy consumption, since the suggested method extensively deals with climate. For this purpose of assessing cold cities, the user occupancy schedule and ToU prices have not changed. Data from frigid cities were utilized to determine values for outside and interior temperatures, relative humidity, and thermostat settings.

Figure 7.4 shows the simulation of cold city energy use over a month using Sugeno FIS and Mamdani with and without the humidity parameter. Using ISPs, energy utilization may be reduced while still providing the appropriate degree of consumer comfort. Although chilly cities use more energy than warm ones, the suggested approach nonetheless manages to reduce that number, proving the scheme's superior efficiency over its predecessors.

Mamdani FIS consumes 2.5 kWh and Sugeno FIS uses 2 kWh per month without humidity; both increase to 298 kWh and 2,922 kWh, respectively, with humidity. Without humidity, the Mamdani FIS is 19% more efficient while the Sugeno FIS is 20% more efficient at using energy.

7.6.2   FLC Proposed Cost in Cold Cities

Figure 7.5 displays the daily energy expenses for the Mamdani FIS without humidity ($11.19), the Sugeno FIS ($10.20), and the planned M FIS with humidity ($9.42) and ($9.30). The addition of humidity to the Mamdani FIS decreases utility costs by 16.44%, whereas adding humidity to the Sugeno FIS decreases costs by 17.33%. Monthly usage was compared to present approaches and to tactics advised for chilly cities. According to Mamdani FIS, the cost per month of humidity factors in $282.87, whereas the monthly cost of Sugeno FIS is $279.17. The monthly expenses for the

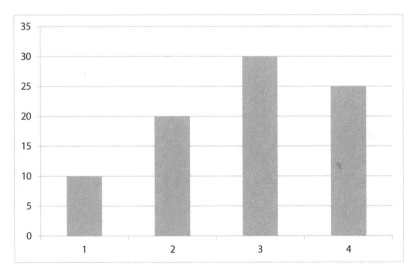

Figure 7.5 Daily cost for energy utilization in cold cities.

Mamdani FIS without humidity are \$335.75, while the Sugeno FIS without humidity are \$337.76, demonstrating better efficiency.

7.6.3   Proposed FIS Using PAR

When comparing and observing the effects of reducing energy usage, the mean value of peak-to-average ratio is an essential metric to keep in mind. Scheduling appliances may help enhance PAR by moving load away from peak times and into off-peak times. Figure 7.6 displays the chilly cities' PAR values. It is easy to observe that the efficiency of Mamdani FIS with humidity is 12% and of Sugeno FIS with humidity is just 10% when the simulation was repeated in warm cities; no significant savings were seen. The planned FLC acts in this way, since its primary goal is to reduce power usage. The suggested FLC has the added benefit of increasing the PAR in chilly cities.

7.6.4   Maintaining the Proposed FIS

The suggested FLC operated within a temperature range where the user reported feeling most comfortable for a given relative humidity. It was

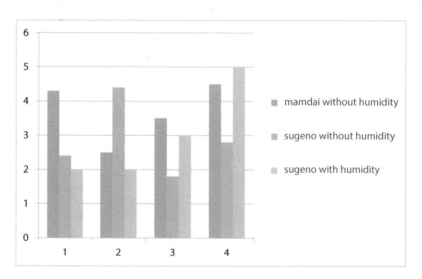

Figure 7.6 Peak-to-average ratio (PAR) of cold cities.

found that earlier methods often compromised user convenience. For warmer places, we may choose higher set points and for cold cities, lower ones. Therefore, it can be claimed that knowing the relative humidity helps save energy usage and keeps people comfortable.

7.7 Discussion

The energy consumption might be decreased by attaching a feedback loop to FIS with input parameters of interior temperature and pricing charge. The worst-case simulation showed that the suggested strategy may cut energy use by 50%. Temperature, humidity, metabolic rate, and other factors affect user thermal comfort. Temperature, humidity, and occupancy sensors are offered. A humidity parameter was added to the FIS to improve thermal comfort and energy efficiency. FIS rules are based on input parameter membership functions. Increase the value to create more fuzzy rule basis rules. Combinatorics gives consequents to the antecedents of imprecise rules based on human intuition. The suggested method to minimize energy usage by 28% was validated using 1-month MATLAB simulations. User comfort was maintained while reducing power costs by 24%. Mamdani FIS with humidity beats the current approaches. The operating nature of fuzzy inference systems is what causes performance differences. Cold city settings match Sugeno FIS's complexity better than hot city scenarios. Due to its simplicity, Mamdani excels in hot cities. The suggested approach may be implemented in IoT operating systems using smart sensors and appliances. The reported measurements are subjected to a combination of the abovementioned methods, and the findings are input into a fuzzy logic system, which is then tasked with deducing the level of hazard associated with a given occurrence. Decisions in uncertain situations, such as those seen in dynamic settings or while defining membership functions, may be made with the help of the type-2 fuzzy logic system that has been presented. Simulations conducted using real-world context data demonstrate the effectiveness of the suggested method. Present techniques are capable of early detection of phenomena to minimize the occurrence of false positive.

In the forthcoming research, endeavors entail the formulation of an adaptation mechanism that is congruent with environmental attributes. The mechanism of adaptation will be discussed.

7.8   Conclusion

This study proposes an FIS with minimal memory, computing power, and real-time capabilities. FIS may be incorporated into RIOT, a networked IoT operating system for low-power devices with memory limits. More input parameters to account for actual circumstances and determine energy usage might enhance the proposed study. To conserve energy and preserve user comfort, the suggested system might be expanded to accommodate additional domestic appliances. Future work should autonomously collect sensor data on temperature and humidity and set the thermostat without human input. This system might also adjust to user schedules. Renewable energy is entering the energy management system due to global warming and fossil fuel depletion. This study might include renewable energy's consequences. This technology may be linked to a microgrid by applying the same fuzzy controller to several dwellings. This technology may be combined with cloud or fog computing as data from many houses grow. Big data analysis may be applied to the smart grid component to enhance scalability due to an increase in system data while dealing with a high number of residential structures. Future research should build the suggested system on an IoT networked platform as it may be implemented in the IoT operating system.

Bibliography

Ullah, I., Youn, H.Y., Han, Y.H., Integration of type-2 fuzzy logic and Dempster–Shafer theory for accurate inference of IoT-based health-care system. *Future Gener. Comput. Syst.*, 124, 369–380, 2021.

Dhiman, N. and Sharma, M.K., IoMT Tsukamoto type-2 fuzzy expert system in medical diagnostic, Volume 213, 109127, 4 August 2022.

Kolomvatsos, K., Anagnostopoulos, C., Hadjiefthymiades, S., Data fusion and type-2 fuzzy inference in contextual data stream monitoring. *IEEE Trans. Syst. Man Cybern. Syst.*, 47, 8, 1839–1853, 2016.

Yuan, X. *et al.*, A stable AI-based binary and multiple class heart disease prediction model for IoMT. *IEEE Trans. Industr. Inform.*, 18, 3, 2032–2040, 2021.

De Miguel, L. *et al.*, Extension of restricted equivalence functions and similarity measures for type-2 fuzzy sets. *IEEE Trans. Fuzzy Syst.*, 30, 9, 4005–4016, 2021.

Chakraborty, A. *et al.*, A framework of intelligent mental health monitoring in smart cities and societies. *IETE J. Res.*, 1–14, 2023. https://www.mdpi.com/1424-8220/23/9/4265

Yang, L. *et al.*, Generative adversarial learning for trusted and secure clustering in industrial wireless sensor networks. *IEEE Trans. Ind. Electron.*, 1–22, 2022.

Rodríguez-Rodríguez, I., Rodríguez, J.V., Campo-Valera, M., Applications of the internet of medical things to type 1 diabetes mellitus. *Electronics*, 12, 3, 756, 2023.

Singh, C., Rao, M.S.S., Mahaboobjohn, Y.M., Kotaiah, B., Kumar, T.R., Applied machine tool data condition to predictive smart maintenance by using artificial intelligence, in: *Emerging Technologies in Computer Engineering: Cognitive Computing and Intelligent IoT. ICETCE 2022. Communications in Computer and Information Science*, vol. 1591 Springer, Cham, 2022, https://doi.org/10.1007/978-3-031-07012-9_49.

Sachdeva, P., Shukla, R., Sahani, A., A review on artificial pancreas and regenerative medicine used in the management of type 1 diabetes mellitus. *J. Med. Eng. Technol.*, 46, 8, 693–702, 2022.

Rocca, J., *GA Optimized Fuzzy Logic Controller for the Dissolved Oxygen Concentration in a Wastewater Bioreactor*, Diss. University of Guelph, 2012.

Shafqat, F., Khan, M.N.A., Shafqat, S., SmartHealth: IoT-enabled context-aware 5G ambient cloud platform, in: *IoT in Healthcare and Ambient Assisted Living*, pp. 43–67, Springer Singapore, Singapore, 2021.

Albahri, A.S. *et al.*, A systematic review of trustworthy and explainable artificial intelligence in healthcare: Assessment of quality, bias risk, and data fusion. *Inf. Fusion*, 2023.

Dhotre, V.A. *et al.*, Big data analytics using MapReduce for education system. *Linguist. Antverp.*, 3130–3138, 2021.

Ferrag, M.A. *et al.*, Cyber security intrusion detection for agriculture 4.0: machine learning-based solutions, datasets, and future directions. *IEEE/CAA J. Autom. Sin.*, 9, 3, 407–436, 2021.

Yadav, S.P. and Yadav, S., Fusion of medical images using a wavelet methodology: A survey. *IEIE Trans. Smart Process. Comput., Institute Electron. Engineers Korea*, 8, 4, 265–271, 2019. https://doi.org/10.5573/ieiespc.2019.8.4.265.

Dhiman, G., Rashid, J., Kim, J., Juneja, S., Viriyasitavat, W., Gulati, K., Privacy for healthcare data using the byzantine consensus method. *IETE J. Res.*, 1–12, 2022.

Griot, C., Modelling and simulation for critical infrastructure interdependency assessment: A meta-review for model characterisation. *Int. J. Crit. Infrastruct.*, 6, 4, 363–379, 2010.

Moldovanu, S. *et al.*, Towards accurate diagnosis of skin lesions using feedforward back propagation neural networks. *Diagnostics*, 11, 6, 936, 2021.

Batool, A., Hussain, M., Abidi, S.M.R., A brief review of big data used in healthcare organization-survey study. *J. NCBAE*, 1, 3, 2022.

Das, S. *et al.*, A combined neuro fuzzy-cellular automata based material model for finite element simulation of plane strain compression. *Comput. Mater. Sci.*, 40, 3, 366–375, 2007.

Kaur, J., Saxena, J., Shah, J., Fahad, Yadav, S.P., Facial emotion recognition, in: *2022 International Conference on Computational Intelligence and Sustainable Engineering Solutions (CISES)*, IEEE, 2022, https://doi.org/10.1109/cises54857.2022.9844366.

Hussain, S.M. and Begh, G.R., Hybrid heuristic algorithm for cost-efficient QoS aware task scheduling in fog–cloud environment. *J. Comput. Sci.*, 64, 101828, 2022.

Radulescu, C.Z. and Radulescu, M., A hybrid multi-criteria approach to the vendor selection problem for sensor-based medical devices. *Sensors*, 23, 2, 764, 2023.

Kabir, S. *et al.*, A similarity measure based on bidirectional subsethood for intervals. *IEEE Trans. Fuzzy Syst.*, 28, 11, 2890–2904, 2020.

Kennedy, E.P., *Control of Switched Reluctance Machines*, Diss. Dublin City University, 2005.

Heidari, A. and Jabraeil Jamali, M.A., Internet of Things intrusion detection systems: A comprehensive review and future directions. *Cluster Comput.*, 1–28, 2022.

Viera, E., Kaschel, H., Valencia, C., Heart rate variability control using a biofeedback and wearable system. *Sensors*, 22, 19, 7153, 2022.

8

An Intelligent IoT-Based Healthcare System Using Fuzzy Neural Networks

Chamandeep Kaur[1]*, Mohammed Saleh Al Ansari[2],
Vijay Kumar Dwivedi[3] and D. Suganthi[4]

[1]Department of Computer Science and IT, Jazan University, Jazan, Saudi Arabia
[2]College of Engineering, Department of Chemical Engineering,
University of Bahrain, Bahrain
[3]Department of Mathematics, Vishwavidyalaya Engineering College, Ambikapur,
District Surguja, Chhattisgarh, India
[4]Department of Computer Science, Saveetha College of Liberal Arts and Sciences,
SIMATS, Thandalam, Chennai, India

Abstract

Twenty-four percent of all sectors' energy use is in the residential sector. Intelligent sensors and smart appliances have sped up the development of energy management systems for private residences. Finding a happy medium between user convenience and energy efficiency is the goal. When calculating the efficiency of a smart house, heating, ventilation, and air conditioning (HVAC) systems may account for as much as 65% of total energy consumption. Research has shown that reducing energy usage is the major objective of combining a fuzzy logic system with other tactics. However, these strategies almost always compromise user experience. In this research, propose a fuzzy inference system (FIS) that takes humidity into account as another input to ensure that the thermostat settings are always optimal for user comfort. The temperature changes within the house as input to the proposed FIS in an effort to reduce energy use. As the number of laws increases, so does the time spent drafting new rules in FIS, which in turn increases the likelihood of human mistake. A combinatorial method is recommended for automatic rule generation. The plans are assessed using Surgeons FIS and Mamdani FIS. The sophisticated FIS system requires a small storage space and processing power, which is well-suited for usage with an Internet of Things (IoT) operating method. The suggested method reduces energy usage by 25%.

**Corresponding author*: kaur.chaman83@gmail.com

Satya Prakash Yadav, Sudesh Yadav, Pethuru Raj Chelliah and Victor Hugo C. de Albuquerque (eds.)
Advances in Fuzzy-Based Internet of Medical Things (IoMT), (121–134) © 2024 Scrivener Publishing LLC

Keywords: HVAC system, demands of management, FIS and SURGUON, RIOT

8.1 Introduction

In present decades, there has been a rise in the level of concern based on the management of energy consumption [1]. According to a reliable source, the residential sector ranks third in terms of energy consumption among all economic sectors that consume energy, such as industrial, transportation, residential, and commercial sectors [2]. The housing division is responsible for random 20% and 16% of global energy consuming, respectively. The rapid growth in the global population is also expected to result in a 24% increase in global electricity demand by 2035 [3]. Heating, ventilation, and air conditioning (HVAC) appliances make up the majority of household energy usage, making them the primary target for energy consumption reduction among all household appliances [4].

The primary electrical loads seen during peak hours are HVAC appliances [5].

A smart home's HEMS contributes to energy management by boosting use, reliable, efficient, and green. To promote energy efficiency and demand response, utilities and smart grids have implemented time-of-use rates and real-time pricing (RTP) to encourage load management among energy customers [6, 7].

However, it is frequently noted that user approval and engagement are crucial for the success of these projects [8]. The use of a thermostat or another device can improve demand response and user participation by allowing users to program and plan their equipment appropriately [9, 10]. In response to these fluctuating prices, HEMS either schedules or reduces the load [11–13].

The Internet of Things (IoT) has demonstrated values in the field of energy saving, thanks to the development of embedded devices and intelligent sensors and the accessibility of the Internet [14–16]. Sensors are utilized to track changes in the environment and assist in managing the expansion. The use of sensors to monitor changes in the environment and help in managing some equipment automatically to maintain a comfortable environment at home [17, 18]. Home appliances like lights, air conditioning, and other items now have IoT capabilities and are connected to the Internet, allowing for mobile device control from a distance [19–21]. The cost and complexity of processing are rising daily, along with the number of household gadgets and sensors [22, 23]. An interface between software and hardware is provided by the operating system. When IoT is taken into account, it poses a unique set of memory, size, power, and processing capability restrictions for the operating system [24, 25].

8.1.1   Work with HEMS

Researchers have discovered two electric load types in HEMS: thermostatically and manually controlled. Heat pumps, air conditioners, and other HVAC equipment are examples of thermostatically controlled shipments. HVAC equipment is one of the primary sources of peak traffic during peak periods. The energy consumption of these devices can be minimized through load shedding and scheduling. The literature covers a broad spectrum of work on load shedding and scheduling various home appliances.

8.1.2   Based for Algorithms in DSM

It has been noted in the literature that nature-based algorithms are frequently utilized for preparation purposes because they offer academics a stunning source for solving challenging challenges from various research and problem fields. To minimize electricity costs and provide customer satisfaction regarding appliance waiting times, a mathematical technique called wind-driven optimization has been applied. Three classes of appliances were created, and the K-WDO, a mix of the WDO and the Knapsack Problem, was applied. Simulations were run in contrast to particle swarm optimization (PSO), showing that the proposed method reduces costs more effectively. To enhance user experience in residential buildings, a neural network- and Q-learning algorithm-based approach to energy management has been described. The strategy reduced peak productivity, energy use, and carbon footprints. A new AC technology shifts load to improve demand responsiveness and smart grid power balance. Its duration reduced user comfort. The proposed method also uses just one kind of HVAC equipment to assess its efficacy. Underwater wireless sensors have had a great deal of trouble communicating because of the energy holes. A suggested routing scheme reduces energy gaps and concentrates interference. The suggested method has shown promising results in simulations, with an increase in the proportion of packets that reach their final destination. The effectiveness of demand response in HEMS is now being studied in a number of different ways, from traditional control methods to more advanced feedback controllers. The user's occupancy has been taken into consideration in HVAC building model predictive control (MPC). This approach's high computing cost and difficulty building a specific system are drawbacks.

8.1.3   Fuzzy Inference System for DSM

To react to the RTP, an HVAC control strategy was created. The study has been proposed the implementation of a dynamic demand response controller (DDRC) that is capable of modifying the thermostat setting in response to a predetermined setback and assessing the power price value at 25-minute intervals. User. The EnergyPlus software was utilized to incorporate the house model, while MATLAB is employed to conduct the dynamic demand response control (DDRC). One limitation of the proposed methodology pertains to its employment of a limited temperature maintenance range without considering user preferences. The process of defuzzification is executed through the utilization of the center of gravity (CoG) methodology, whereby parameters' membership functions are established in the form of triangles. The value obtained after defuzzification is indicative of the extent to which a set point initialization will be altered based on the output parameter that determines the degree of load change reduction required. The goal of this study is to optimize energy consumption while preserving the optimal indoor thermal conditions. Nevertheless, the comfort of the user is compromised. An algorithm based on fuzzy logic rules and the integration of wireless sensors was developed. In MATLAB, a wireless user-interface thermostat has been modeled. The proposed design unit utilized real-time user occupancy characteristics, electricity price, load demand, and external temperature, and for better heating and cooling system energy efficiency, lower the thermostat set points. Demand response participation, energy utilization, and occupant comfort are performance metrics.

Defuzzification is accomplished using the center of gravity approach, where parameter membership functions are defined as triangles. The defuzzified value indicates how much a set point's original value will change, whereas the output determines how much load reduction can be applied. However, user comfort was compromised in the process. The cost, PAR, user comfort, and energy use of Sugeno and Mamdani Fuzzy Inference Systems (FIS) were assessed. Sugeno FIS beat all other techniques when MATLAB simulations were used to calculate energy consumption. The proposed method recommended a cost-effective approach and the elimination of peak creation, albeit resulting in user discomfort.

Due to advancements in communication and technology, the use of a programmable communicating thermostat (PCT) comes highly recommended. When the value of an exchange rate changes, a PCT will automatically modify the thermostat's temperature setting. The PCT is a thermostat that does not need batteries. The never-ending chatter with clients. Three distinct AC units with varying power outputs were modeled by the authors in SIMULINK. The thermostat for load optimizer that is compatible with both RTP and ToU pricing schemes benefits from the addition of PCT to the fuzzy logic approach (FLA) in order to maximize efficiency. In order to passively cool a home, a fuzzy controller that makes use of ventilation has been developed. The cooling load was reduced by applying a multi-objective evolutionary method to improve the suggested controller. The suggested technique included thermal comfort but focused primarily on the heating and cooling system's cooling load.

8.2   Problem Formulation

The term "fuzziness" refers to the uncertainty that results from linguistic notions that lack a specific limit. In HEMS, measuring user comfort is regarded as needing to be more practical and precise. The system will function more naturally with the use of fuzzy logic. Using fuzzy logic, researchers can compute using terms that support reasoning of human and decision-making.

8.2.1   Controller for FIS Logic

Mathematical models properly reflect physical quantities in conventional controllers. A nonlinear function maps fuzzy logic controller (FLC) inputs to outputs. Thus, they are quite useful for modeling nonlinear HVAC systems. FLC requires no mathematical modeling. Figure 8.1 shows the FLC system conceptually.

FIS smears FIS operators to the antecedent, achieves insinuations from the antecedent to the consequent, aggregates the determination crossways FIS rules to create FIS output, then fuzzifiers the output to provide crisp inputs. The proposed model is tested and evaluated in this research by comparing it to the Mamdani FIS and the Sugeno FIS. In this study, the Mamdani FIS and the Sugeno FIS are used to test and assess the suggested model. The variables used to construct Mamdani FIS rules are language-specific and include things like premise and conclusion variables. Unique to each language consideration, such as premise and conclusion variables, when building Mamdani FIS rules. If the outside and inside temperatures are both normal, the occupancy rate is low, the Internet service provider (ISP) is not too expensive, and the humidity is not too high, then the energy consumption is low.

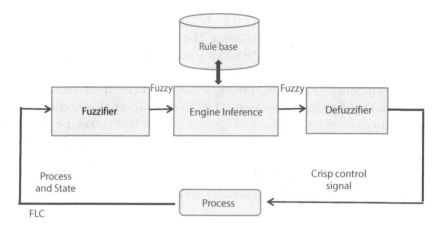

Figure 8.1 Controller for fuzzy logic.

The Mamdani FIS formula is given below:

$$Z = \frac{R\ \mu c(Z)\ zdz}{R\ \mu C(z)dz}$$

8.2.2   The Proposed Model

Numerous variables can be used as inputs to the fuzzy logic system's rule base. However, the suggested research considers factors directly affecting user comfort and minimizing energy use. This study explores the incorporation of humidity. As a proposed FIS input parameter, they provide a system feedback loop for user pleasure and low power consumption. The criteria for the FIS are the current interior and outdoor temperatures, a pricing mechanism, the presence of inhabitants, an initialized start point, and the comparative humidity in the house or region. To get accurate readings of environmental factors in real time, wireless sensors are a must. The recommended controller-unit research prospective is included into the IoT functioning method RIOT, which would be beneficial as the number of factors to watch and the efficiency of Internet-based control rise with the IoT. FIS decides how much power the controller needs to run efficiently. A relay is utilized to turn the heater ON or OFF. An actuator that regulates the heater's operation will receive a command from the proposed controller when the current temperature varies per the thermostat set point.

The RAM required by the fuzzy inference rule base is 960 bytes. And the total memory needed for our proposed system is 2 kB. It is perfect for any IoT operating system, since it requires less memory and uses fewer computing resources to traverse lookup tables. RIOT is the operating system for IoT software. A microkernel-based operating system called RIOT addresses issues with memory and power consumption constraints and varied software needs of devices. Small networked devices with low memory requirements with real-time controlling capabilities can use RIOT. The proposed controller can be implemented perfectly on the system, thanks to all of RIOT's features. A combinatorics approach is developed to construct the fuzzy rule base system using the input parameters, which is otherwise challenging to program manually and defines a total of 480 rules.

8.2.3   Model of Residential Heating System

A thermostat, a heater, their thermal characteristics, and the heater's operation inside a room to simulate changes in room temperature are included as model elements. A model of the system's heat intake and loss was used to build the thermal model. After the computations are complete, the thermostat's controller section reads the indoor room temperature value and, if the room temperature deviates from the set point temperature, sends a control signal. The elements of various home heating systems are described:

1. Heater
The quantity of temperature increase delivered to the room is used to simulate the heater component. The air is hot when the heater is on, at a flow rate of MHeater and a constant theater temperature.

$$dQgain\ dt = (THeater - TRoom) \times MHeater \times cair,$$

2. Thermostat
The thermostat controls whether the heater is on or off in the living room by calculating the delta between the basic regulator value and the room's temperature. The thermostat calculates the difference every 5 minutes.

3. Room
The technology considers heat intake from the heater and heat loss from the room to the outside when calculating the temperature variation. By this, the heat loss (dQloss dt) was computed. In the following equation,

Rthermal represents the equivalent thermal resistance of the home, and Toutside is the current external temperature.

$$dQloss\ dt = TRoom - Toutside$$

8.3   House Heating System

Tasks that are outside of the Simulink software environment must be finished before modeling can begin. Define model specifications, then generate mathematical equations. To verify the accuracy of the simulation, gather data on the model's output signal and parameter values. A heater (plant model) that heats a space (environment model) to a predetermined temperature under the control of a thermostat (controller model). Thermal energy gain to the room is by convection of heated air from the heate. Despite the fact that this is a simple model, the procedures for designing the algorithm and the model structure are the same as those used for models that are more complex. The following Figure 8.2 will explain the heat of the system.

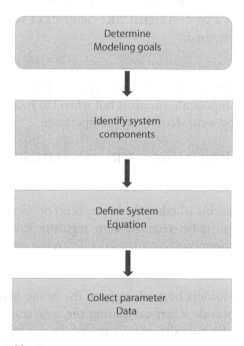

Figure 8.2 Residential heating system.

8.4   Simulation Results of FIS

Examination of the proposed schemes using simulation. A 2-kW heater is taken into consideration for the effect of a moisture factor studied utilizing a 15-kW HVAC in an urban area, and effects of a response circle in the FIS are studied in a small room. Setting the thermostat and humidistat to the current Figure 8.3 temperature and humidity level at startup has been shown to increase user satisfaction.

This section also covers the impact of incorporating a feedback loop into the FIS to reduce energy use. The day when the outside temperature dropped below 0°C was considered the coldest. Due to the extremely low temperature, it will probably require more energy to keep the interior temperature (°CT.FIS, where 610 kWh of energy is used up in a single month. In this case, Sugeno FIS's monthly energy consumption with a feedback loop is 300 kWh, while Sugeno FIS without a response loop results in a monthly energy consumption of 60 kWh as a result of the heater's response to indoor and outdoor temperatures. For this example, a feedback loop reduces Sugeno FIS's monthly energy usage to 300 kWh, but a response loop reduces it to 60 kWh due to the heater's reaction. considering both the indoor and outdoor climates as seen in Figure 8.4. In contrast to the previous method, which left the heater ON and consuming energy because it did not account for changes in the room temperature, the heater is turned to OFF state as the outside temperature rises in the afternoon to save energy. FIS with a 2.31-kWh feedback loop boosts the effectiveness of the suggested FIS to meet the goal of reducing energy use.

Performs better than the previous method. Without the additional feedback loop, energy consumption employing Mamdani FIS and Sugeno FIS, the energy usage is 501 kWh and 493 kWh, whereas employing a feedback

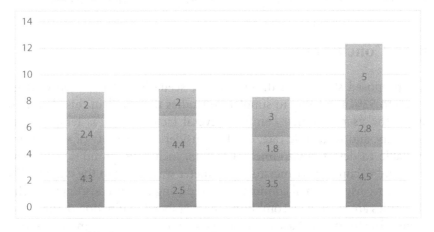

Figure 8.3 Monthly electricity cost incurred.

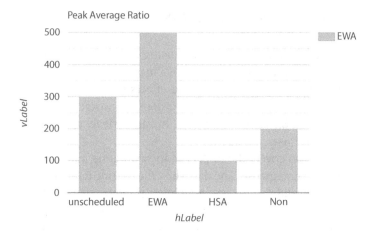

Figure 8.4 Final indoor and outdoor temperatures.

loop reduces this to 100 kWh and 90 kWh, respectively. The peak-to-average ratio (PAR) is a key parameter that is referenced and recorded when the consumed energy is decreased by means of load restriction or load shifting. Scheduling appliances tends to raise the PAR when changing the load from low peak to high peak. When added to Mamdani FIS, humidity increased efficiency by 10%, but added to Sugeno FIS, humidity decreased efficiency by 5%. The behavior of the proposed FLC is best described by its main purpose of reducing energy use. One benefit of the proposed FLC is improving the PAR for chilly cities. Maintenance of User Comfort with Proposed FIS. Set points were used by the proposed Fuzzy Logic Controller (FLC). Therefore, it can be said that having knowledge of humidity aids in maintaining user comfort as well as reducing energy use.

8.5   Conclusions

The proposed strategy in the worst-case scenario reduces energy usage by up to 55% according to simulation studies that confirm this claim. To assess the user's thermal comfort, several factors, such as temperature, humidity, and metabolic rate, can be considered. A variety of sensors are available to detect environmental factors, including humidity, temperature, and occupancy. A moisture parameter was added to the current FIS to improve user thermal comfort while reducing energy consumption. The FIS's rules are created by combining the membership function of the given inputs. The fuzzy rule base increases as the input parameter increases. It is advantageous to define more rules to deal with various scenarios. A combinatorial algorithm that assigns antecedents to the fuzzy rules' consequents based on user intuition was also limited. Simulations in MATLAB were run for a month to demonstrate the viability of the suggested method to cut energy use by up to 20%. The proposed method preserved customer comfort while yielding an up to 28% reduction in electricity costs.

One can conclude that Mamdani FIS with moisture exceeds current methods in place. In contrast, Sugeno FIS is effective in the chilling area when the moisture factor is included by comparing the outcomes of two diverse and well-known fuzzy inference systems. The FIS indicated in this paper has fewer memory requirements, minimal processor requirements, and real-time functionality. The suggested FIS method can be incorporated into RIOT, an operating system for networked IoT that primarily targets low-power devices with memory limitations. The proposed research may be improved by adding more input factors for real-world conditions when determining the necessary energy consumption. The suggested system primarily addresses HVAC, an expansion to encompass additional housing appliances is also an option to conserve energy and keep users comfortable. It would be ideal for future work to improve the suggested system so that it operates autonomously, using sensor data for temperature and humidity to choose the thermostat set points without user input automatically. Making the system adaptable to user schedules is another potential development of this technology. Renewable energy sources are integrating themselves into the energy management system due to global warming and the depletion of fossil fuels. Combining inference system programming with microcontrollers and IoT platforms allows for the transmission of control signals in the form of PWM outputs that vary dependent on the input of temperature and humidity sensors. Additional investigation may take into account potential outcomes associated with sustainable energy sources. This system may be scaled up and linked to a microgrid by using the same fuzzy controller on many individual residences.

References

1. Energy Information Administration, *Household Energy Consumption and Expenditures, Consumption by End Use*, Energy Information Administration (EIA), Washington, DC, USA, 2010.
2. Conti, J., Holtberg, P., Beamon, J., Schaal, A., Sweetnam, G., Kydes, A., *Annual Energy Outlook with Projections to 2035*, Report of U.S. Energy Information Administration (EIA), EIA, Washington, DC, USA, 2010.

3. Ahmad, M.W., Mourshed, M., Yuce, B., Rezgui, Y., Computational intelligence techniques for HVAC systems: A review. *Build. Simul.*, 9, 359–398, 2016.

4. Borenstein, S., Jaske, M., Rosenfeld, A., *Dynamic Pricing, Advanced Metering, and Demand Response in Electricity Markets, Center for the Study of Energy Markets*, University of California, Berkeley, CA, USA, 2002.

5. Keshtkar, A., Arzanpour, S., Keshtkar, F., Ahmadi, P., Smart residential load reduction via fuzzy logic, wireless sensors, and smart grid incentives. *Energy Build.*, 104, 165–180, 2015.

6. Javaid, S., Javaid, N., Iqbal, S., Aslam, S., Rahim, M.H., Optimizing energy consumption of air-conditioning systems with the fuzzy logic controllers in residential buildings, in: *Proceedings of the 2018 International Conference on Computing, Mathematics and Engineering Technologies*, Sukkur, Pakistan, March 3–4, 2018.

7. Grygierek, K. and Ferdyn-Grygierek, J., Multi-objectives optimization of ventilation controllers for passive cooling in residential buildings. *Sensors*, 18, 1144, 2018.

8. Woolley, J., Pritoni, M., Modera, M., Center, W.C.E., Why occupancy-responsive adaptive thermostats do not always save-and the limits for when they should, in: *Proceedings of the 2014 ACEEE Summer Study on Energy Efficiency in Buildings*, Asilomar, CA, USA, August 17–22, 2014.

9. Yadav, S.P., Mahato, D.P., Linh, N.T.D., S.P. Yadav, D.P. Mahato, N.T.D. Linh (Eds.) CRC Press, Boca Raton, 336, 2020, https://doi.org/10.1201/9781003038467.

10. Khan, T.A., Abbas, S., Ditta, A., Khan, M.A., Alquhayz, H., Fatima, A., Khan, M.F., IoMT-based smart monitoring hierarchical fuzzy inference system for diagnosis of covid-19. *Comput. Mater. Contin.*, 65, 3, 2591–2605, 2020.

11. Kumar, S., Kalra, G., Bhardwaj, H.K., Rajoria, Y.K., Kumar, D., Boadh, R., Internet of medical thing and FIS evaluation for selecting and delivering the best health insurance coverage. *J. Pharm. Negat. Results*, 13, Special Issue 8, 3438–3446, 2022.

12. Silva-Ramírez, E.-L. and Cabrera-Sánchez, J.-F., Co-active neuro-fuzzy inference system model as single imputation approach for non-monotone pattern of missing data. *Neural Comput. Appl.*, 33, 8981–9004, 2021.

13. Khanmohammadi, S., Chou, C.-A., Esfahlani, F.Z., Hourani, A., A fuzzy inference system for predicting human error and its application in process management, in: *IIE Annual Conference. Proceedings*, Institute of Industrial and Systems Engineers (IISE), p. 2032, 2014.

14. Bhardwaj, J., Nayak, A., Yadav, C.S., Yadav, S.P., A review in wavelet transforms based medical image fusion, in: *Evolving Role of AI and IoMT in the Healthcare Market*, F. Al-Turjman, M. Kumar, T. Stephan, A. Bhardwaj (Eds.), Springer, Cham, 2021, https://doi.org/10.1007/978-3-030-82079-4_9.

15. González, J.C., Dalforno, C., Suppi, R., Luque, E., A fuzzy logic fish school model, in: *Computational Science–ICCS 2009: 9th International Conference,*

Proceedings, Part I, Baton Rouge, LA, USA, vol. 9, Springer Berlin Heidelberg, pp. 13–22, May 25-27, 2009.

16. Janani, S.R., Subramanian, R., Karthik, S., Vimalarani, C., Healthcare monitoring using machine learning based data analytics. *Int. J. Comput. Commun. Control*, 18, 1, 1–10, 2023.

17. Chowdhury, S., Sesharao, Y., Abilmazhinov, Y., IoT based solar energy monitoring system, Maisagalla Gopal *et al., IOP Conf. Ser.: Mater. Sci. Eng.*, 981, 032037, 1–8 2021.

18. Ramadan, A., Kamel, S., Hamdan, I., Agwa, A.M., A novel intelligent ANFIS for the dynamic model of photovoltaic systems. *Mathematics*, 10, 8, 1286, 2022.

19. Kumar, S., Wajeed, M.A., Kunabeva, R., Dwivedi, N., Singhal, P., Jamal, S.S., Akwafo, R., Novel method for safeguarding personal health record in cloud connection using deep learning models. *Comput. Intell. Neurosci.*, 2022, 1–14, Mar.19, 2022.

20. Mokni, M., Yassa, S., Hajlaoui, J.E., Omri, M.N., Chelouah, R., Multi-objective fuzzy approach to scheduling and offloading workflow tasks in fog–cloud computing. *Simul. Model. Pract. Theory*, 123, 102687, 2023.

21. Abo-Sennah, M.A., El-Dabah, M.A., Mansour, A.E.B., Maximum power point tracking techniques for photovoltaic systems: A comparative study. *Int. J. Electr. Comput. Eng.*, 11, 1, 2088–8708, 2021.

22. Roy, S. *et al.*, A multi-criteria prioritization-based data transmission scheme for inter-WBAN communications. *J. Inst. Eng. (India) B*, 104, 1, 1–7, 2023.

23. Dehghandar, M. and Rezvani, S., Classification of COVID-19 individuals using adaptive neuro-fuzzy inference system. *J. Med. Signals Sens.*, 12, 4, 334, Oct. 1, 2022.

24. Quan, Y., Chaoyang, D., Qing, W., A fuzzy adaptive fusion algorithm for radar/infrared based on wavelet analysis, in: *2007 IEEE International Conference on Control and Automation*, IEEE, pp. 1344–1348, May 2007.

25. Vyas, S., Gupta, S., Bhargava, D., Boddu, R., Fuzzy logic system implementation on the performance parameters of health data management frameworks. *J. Healthc. Eng.*, 2022, 1–11, 2022.

9

An Enhanced Fuzzy Deep Learning (IFDL) Model for Pap-Smear Cell Image Classification

Rakesh S.[1]*, Smrita Barua[2], D. Anitha Kumari[3] and Naresh E.[4]†

[1]*Department of BCA, Nitte Institute of Professional Education, Nitte University, Mangalore, India*
[2]*Department of Agricultural Statistics, Assam Agricultural University, Jorhat, Assam, India*
[3]*Department of CSM, TKRCET, Meerpet, Telangana, India*
[4]*Department of Information Technology, Manipal Institute of Technology Bengaluru, Manipal Academy of Higher Education, Manipal, India*

Abstract

The conventional method of categorizing cervical cancer types relies heavily on the expertise of pathologists, which is associated with a lower degree of precision. The utilization of colposcopy is an essential element in the prevention of cervical cancer. Colposcopy has been a crucial component in the reduction of cervical cancer frequency and humanity rates over the past five decades, in conjunction with precancer screening and treatment. The rise in workload has resulted in reduced diagnostic efficiency and misdiagnosis during vision screening. The utilization of the convolutional neural network (CNN) model in medical image processing has demonstrated its superior performance in the cervical cancer type within the realm of cavernous learning. The present study puts forth two convolutional neural network architectures based on deep learning for the identification of cervical cancer through the analysis of colposcopy images. The models employed in this research are VGG19 (TL) and Colposcopy Ensemble Network (CYENET). The utilization of VGG19 as a transfer learning approach has been implemented in the CNN architecture for research purposes. The Colposcopy Ensemble Network has been developed as a novel model for the automatic classification of cervical cancers from colposcopy images.

Corresponding author: rakesh.s@nitte.edu.in
†*Corresponding author*: naresh.e@manipal.edu

Satya Prakash Yadav, Sudesh Yadav, Pethuru Raj Chelliah and Victor Hugo C. de Albuquerque (eds.)
Advances in Fuzzy-Based Internet of Medical Things (IoMT), (135–148) © 2024 Scrivener Publishing LLC

The model's precision, selectivity, and responsiveness are evaluated. The VGG19 model exhibited a classification accuracy of 70.3%. The outcomes for VGG19 (TL) are moderately satisfactory. The kappa score analysis of the VGG-19 perfect inferred that the model falls within the moderate classification category. The findings of the experiment indicate that the CYENET model demonstrated noteworthy levels of sensitivity, specificity, and kappa scores, specifically, 90.4%, 95.2%, and 88%, correspondingly. The CYENET model exhibits an enhanced classification accuracy of 90.1%, surpassing the VGG19 (TL) model by 10%.

Keywords: Precancer, CNN, VGG19, CYENET, colposcopy

9.1   Introduction

Late-stage cervical cancer is thought to be incurable, making it the second most lethal disease affecting women after breast cancer. Recent years have seen significant advancements in the ability to use images to diagnose illness. According to the World Health Organization (WHO), 7.5% of all cancer deaths in women are attributable to cervical cancer, which ranks as the fourth most common malignancy worldwide with a reported incidence of 500,000 new cases in 2018. In poor and middle-income nations, where the annual death toll from cervical cancer is over 3,100, early detection is a potential lifesaver. It is believed that 5% of all cervical cancer cases are associated with HIV, and that women living with HIV have a 6-fold increased risk of developing cervical cancer compared to women who do not have HIV. The efficiency of screening has been rethought in light of many factors, such as ready availability of equipment, uniformity of screening tests, sufficient supervision, and prompt diagnosis of cervical cancer. Several tools improved the workflow's efficiency, practicality, and cost. PAP smear image screening is mostly used to treat cervical cancer, but it requires more microscopic checks to diagnose cancer and non-cancer patients and requires trained specialists, but it may miss positive cases. PAP and Human papillomavirus (HPV) tests are expensive and insensitive. However, underdeveloped nations employ colposcopy. Colposcopy screening improves PAP smear images and HPV tests. Successful cervical cancer screening programs reduce illness and mortality. Due to a lack of skilled healthcare laborers and money, cervical cancer screening facilities in low- and middle-income countries are few and treatment of discovered abnormalities. This condition is still not totally treatable, especially if it is discovered in a poor country. Therefore, programs aimed at prevention and screening are vital. Preventative colposcopy for cervical cancer has become a common surgical treatment. Clinical outcomes for patients with this kind of cancer may benefit from earlier diagnosis and staging. Several investigations have been done using a wide variety of techniques for extracting information from digital colposcopy pictures. The primary objective of this research is to provide medical professionals, regardless of their degree of expertise, with resources useful during colposcopy examinations. Cervical colposcopy images, as well as segments of interest, may be enhanced by computer-aided diagnosis (CAD) devices, allowing for easier detection of irregularities. To provide an accurate diagnosis, professionals need to have sufficient knowledge and skill; however, these approaches may assist. Pathological areas may be an indicator of neoplasms, making their diagnosis during a colposcopy examination crucial. Acetowhite, aberrant vascularization, mosaic regions, and punctures are all examples of these abnormalities. Conventional colposcopy pictures often include a mechanism that may help detect abnormalities. Exclusion of specular reflection, cervix segmentation, act white field segmentation, detection of mosaic areas, vasculature and puncture, and categorization are only a few examples of inconsistencies in zone segmentation that have been addressed in previous publications.

9.2 Work Related

Machine learning methods were used to refine segmentation, and random forests performed best when used as a classifier for cervical cancer. Unattended learning strategies, such as the employment of support vector machine (SVM) supports, have also been utilized to handle the various picture or superpixel patches that result from the extraction of objects. For nonoverlapping cells, an innovative superpixel-based Markov random field segmentation was proposed and realized. Optimized multifilter SVM settings identify cervical cells. Artificial Neural Network (ANNs) classified cervical cell types with 70% accuracy. The cervical cancer subtype medical evidence was balanced unsupervised. Particle Swarm Optimization (PSO) using KNN membership values beat simple categorization models. Cervical cancer cells are segmented and Gabor-classified. Over 80% accurate healthy-malignant cell distinction. The recommended model's least square support vector machine (LSSVM) identified convolutional neural network (CNN) features better. Radical Basis Function (RBF)-SVM beat logistic regression and random forest. Feature-based assessments were 90%–92% accurate. New architectures tree model detect cancer cells and perform well in diverse applications. Cervical cancer diagnosis with convolutional neural networks is common. Early cervical cancer cell identification and classification using CNN-based deep learning.

ELM sorted photographs. CNN transfer and fine-tuning refers to the transfer learning approach applied to Convolutional Neural Networks. Comparing ELM (extreme learning machine), MLP (master limited partnership), and AE (Autoencoder) classifiers. The stacked soft-max autoencoder has 90.25% cervical cancer dataset accuracy. Machine learning predicted cervical cancer patient risk. Cervical screening machine learning projected risk. Since population risk factors are scarce, predictive machine learning algorithms may benefit from reduced dimensionality. Poor methods that learn each item individually assist many projects minimize dimensionality and categorization. Medical experts may swiftly evaluate whether additional diagnostic tests are needed using colposcopy image categorization. This study describes the computerized colposcopy-based cervical cancer prediction method. Article's essential contribution:

(i)   CYENET, a deep convolutional neural network, is used to identify cervical cancer in colposcopy pictures. This technique can extract discriminative features using ensemble methods without segmentation or feature engineering.

(ii) Automates cervical image screening with a notable improvement in diagnosis accuracy.

(iii) Experiments are conducted with the help of the Intel Offshore development centre (ODT) dataset. Colposcopy images are data-augmented to prevent model overfitting. This technique allows for the precise learning of target features.

Table 9.1 The related works of screening cancer.

Method	Dataset	Advantage	Disadvantage
Colpo net [12]	Colposcopy images	Accuracy is better	Accuracy by relevant information
Inception [13, 15]	Herlev dataset	Accuracy is high	Investigate of network studies cervical cells
CCN model [16, 11, 18]	Cervical smear dataset	Specificity and sensitivity	1.5% false image
CNN-SVM model [10, 12–15]	Herlev and 1 dataset	Good robuster	Need hands feature
Collective model [1–9]	PAP Slight copy	Class problem 95%	Cells are difficult to identify

9.3 Methods and Materials

Colposcopy images can detect cancer early. Transition zone (TZ) colposcopic examination determines whether irregular cytology patients require additional treatment. This research relies on the TZ title. Colposcopy perception of distinguishing characteristics has significant intra- and interobserver variation. Type 1 TZs are entirely ectocervical. Type 2 and Type 3 transition regions are endocervical. The newest Squamocolumnar junction (SCJ) was Type 2 when completely visible in the TZ. The new SCJ was Type 3 and not evident even with external instrumentation. It evaluates abnormal cytology patients but does not diagnose them. Colposcopies might vary. The clinician's experience is colposcopy's main drawback. Colposcopy detected invasive and preinvasive cervix lesions with excellent sensitivity but poor accuracy in several tests. The ensemble learning strategy uses seven machine learning algorithms to identify hepatocellular carcinoma and categorize hyperspectral images using collaborative representation classification with boosting. Figure 9.1 shows the suggested automated cervical cancer screening method's flow map. Colposcopically, the TZ is between the old and new SCJ. Colposcopies must identify the TZ.

9.3.1 Deep Neural Network Model

Many fields of image processing, such as medical image analysis, have succeeded in using CNN models. An apparent computer vision difficulty is identifying cervical cancer in colposcopy pictures. Neural networks, particularly convolutional networks, are used to categorize situations into one of three types in comparing deep learning to traditional characteristics. To improve the extraction of technical cervical cancer characteristics from colposcopy pictures, propose a CYENET architecture combining depth's key benefits and a parallel convolutional filter. The proposed model uses several convolution layers to excerpt distinct the same input in addition to the standard intricacy layers seen at the network's outset. The overfitting problem is mitigated using convolutional filters to eliminate the skewed components. CNN model training, data preprocessing, and classification outcomes comprise the proposed model's three main parts (Figure 9.2). Table 9.2 describes the CYENET model's network, which consists of a convolution layer, a max-pooling layer, and a set of filters of variable sizes in a parallel convolutional block.

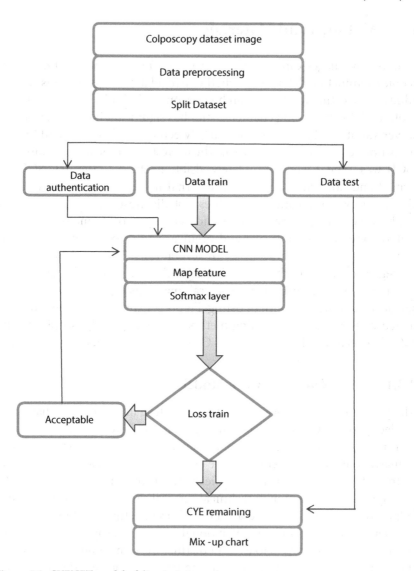

Figure 9.1 CYENET model of diagnosing cancer.

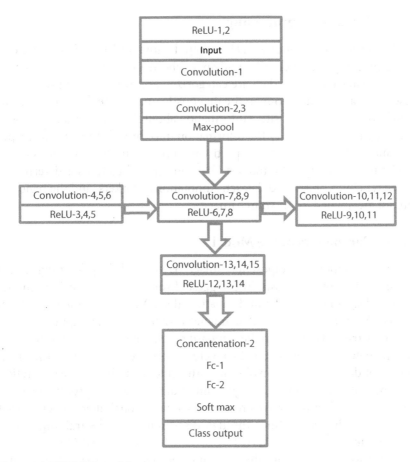

Figure 9.2 CYENET model.

Table 9.2 Architecture of CYENET.

Layer type	Filter size	Stride	Input	Output
Convolution 1 [23]	5*4	2*2	3*112*112	64*112*112
Max-pool-1 [13, 14]	3*2	2*2	74*119*111	64*59
Convolution 2 [16, 17]	1*3	1*2	64*56*56	64*56*56
Convolution 3 [1, 8]	3*2	2*2	138*28*28	128*28*28

9.3.2   Dataset Preprocessing

Intel ODT and smartphone ODT gathered a total of 5,679 images are collected by using the Intel ODT and smartphone ODT dataset for sreening the cerivical cancer. The data are categorized according to the presence or absence of a transition zone in the diagnostic image. The dataset is preprocessed to remove any sensitive information about the cases. First, diagnostic records are used to classify the information into three distinct groups: types 1, 2, and 3. Due to the lack of expertise required for using MATLAB's image labeler tools, the region of interest (ROI) in cervical pictures is determined by referencing a pretrained dataset. Annotations, markers, and the region of interest are applied to the source image.

9.3.3   Parameters of the Model

This study employs a colposcopic image-based dual deep learning model for cervical lesion diagnosis. The suggested solution comprises fine-tuning transfer learning VGG_19 and creating the CYENET architecture from scratch. A single convolutional neural network filter handles input data from 1*1 to the trained data set in the standard neural network design. CNNs can identify patterns in any section of a picture since they are spatially invariant. The input data undergo convolution with a filter resulting in the generation of an output that retains the original input data while also producing a feature map with discriminative properties. Convolutional filters are employed to extract multilayer features through discrimination. The training timing incorporates three distinct kernel sizes, namely, 1*1, 3*3, and 5*5.

Activation purposes are the scientific equipped with logic that decides whether or not it should be activated (or "fired") based on the degree to which an input is relevant to the model prediction. Piecewise linear functions, like ReLU, return a direct value if the input is positive and a zero value otherwise. Since the ReLU activation avoids simple saturation and converges quickly, it is employed. It gets around the issue of not being able to output values larger than 1 that plagues logistic regression with the tan hyperbolic function. In each of the concealed layers, use the ReLU activation function. Its definition is:

$$F(x) = Max\ (0,x), \tag{9.1}$$

ReLU's activation function is designed to break out of its infinite iteration eventually. The characteristics supplied by one kernel may be combined with those of another using the concatenation layer. Overfitting may be mitigated by using local response normalization to channel-wise normalize the activation function after each concatenation layer. Two methods exist for normalizing the local response:

(i)   on either side of the channel.
(ii) The suggested approach performs local response normalization as channel standardization for pixel-wise standardization in the specified coat.

9.4   Results

MATLAB 2020b runs the experiment on an Intel i9-powered 24 GB Quadro NVIDIA RTX 6000 workstation. Kaggle's experimental data. Colposcopy cervical cancer datasets are 85% training, 15% validation, 15% testing. Training uses 7,498 photos, validation 1,884. Multi-GPU, 64-batch, and 0.0001 beginning learning rate train the model. Section 9.3 stated that CYENET and VGG 19, with adjustment, utilize the copy dataset with limits. Assessing the deep learning model's accuracy, specificity, and sensitivity, the confusion matrix models multiclass categorization. Figure 9.3 evaluates the classification model, VGG_19's training accuracy, and the CYENET model trained on epoch 50's training dataset using the confusion matrix.

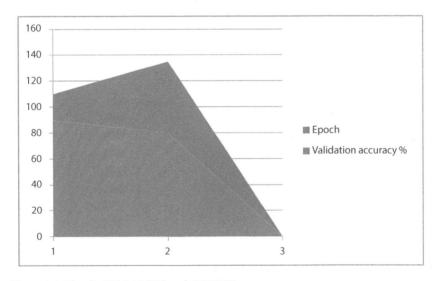

Figure 9.3 Plot the VGG 19 (TL) and CYENET.

The CYENET model has 95.1% training accuracy and the VGG_19 (TL) model 87%. Figure 9.4 shows the validation curve for the planned CYENET and just adjusted VGG-19 versus epoch. The model's accuracy increases with training epochs. The CYENET model validates at 95.3% after 23 epochs. Due to the 0.0001 learning rate, the complex VGG-19 model experienced early accuracy fluctuation. VGG 19 validated at 60.8%. The CYENET model's more durable and simple design makes cervical screening using colposcopic pictures better than the VGG19 model.

Figure 9.5 displays authentication loss curve for both the CYENET and visual geometry networks (Vgg)-19 models as proposed. The validation loss curve shift is the determining factor for the model convergence of the network proposed. In contrast to VGG 19, CYENET exhibits a notably rapid convergence, yielding a loss value of 0.292, while VGG 19 joins to a harm value of 0.9885. The VGG 19 validation model exhibits instability in contrast to the CYENET model, which demonstrates stability and a smoother loss curve.

The harmonic mean of model recall and precision yields the F1 score. While period differences may impact Cohen's Kappa measures, they are the most effective technique to measure agreement. Addressing class differences between two groups with many classes. The proposed models VGG-19 (TL) are evaluated concerning F1 and Cohen's kappa scores; these scores and the colposcopy pictures are used in the cervical cancer

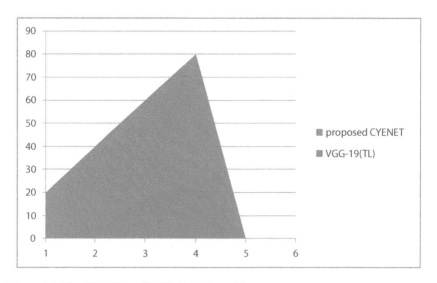

Figure 9.4 The CYENET and VGG 19 (TL) model.

diagnostic process. Cohen's Kappa proposed VGG 19 (TL) and CYENET is 88%, whereas F1 score is 91.0% and 40.80%. Compared to models from the literature and the competing model VGG 19, the suggested model

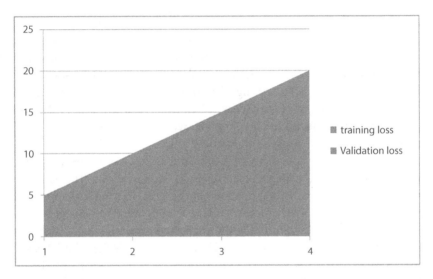

Figure 9.5 The CYENET and Vgg-19 (TL) model.

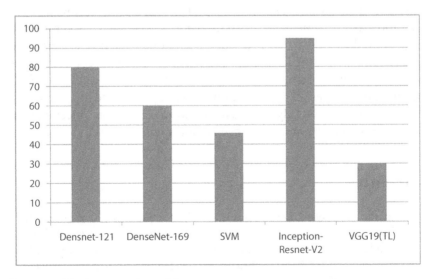

Figure 9.6 Metrics comparison of the system.

CYENET performs very well. Figure 9.6 shows the variation depiction of the model.

9.5   Conclusion

To determine the subtype of cervical cancer shown in colposcopic pictures, a novel deep learning architecture, CYENET, is presented. Oversampling creates a more evenly distributed collection of images for classification purposes. In this study, two such models are shown. One method uses VGG19 architecture for transfer learning. The other is a new model, CYENET, specifically designed to classify cervical cancer types using the ODT colposcopy picture collection. Classification accuracy, specificity, and the F1 measure are used to assess both models. The VGG19 (TL) model has a sensitivity of 33.3%, a specificity of 79.0%, and a Kappa of 50.5%, according to Cohen. VGG19 has a 70.3% accuracy in its classifications. The outcomes for VGG (TL) are satisfactory, in general. The VGG19 model's kappa value suggests that it is suitable for intermediate classification, which agrees with its overall performance. Similarly, the suggested CYENET has a high level of sensitivity (90.4%), specificity (95.2%), and kappa (80%). The CYENET model outperforms the VGG19 (TL) model by 20% in terms of classification accuracy, reaching 91.3%. When comparing CYENET's findings against those of similar efforts, it becomes clear that this instrument has great potential as a diagnostic aid for physicians. The suggested approach of classifying cervical cancer may help a certain group of people who do not need intrusive treatment. Improved categorization efficiency means that the proposed CYENET may help doctors and other medical professionals improve the diagnostic sensitivity and accuracy of colposcopy screening for cervical cancer. The theoretical deep learning model will be tested in the future on a variety of datasets. Combining sophisticated image processing methods with CNN algorithms to develop a cervical precancer diagnosis system is another way to improve upon the approach.

References

1. Kavitha, R., Jothi, D.K., Saravanan, K., Swain, M.P., Gonzáles, J.L.A., Bhardwaj, R.J., Adomako, E., Ant colony optimization-enabled CNN deep learning technique for accurate detection of cervical cancer. *BioMed. Res. Int.*, 2023, 2023. https://www.sciencedirect.com/science/article/pii/S2667305322000709

2. William, W. *et al.*, A review of image analysis and machine learning techniques for automated cervical cancer screening from pap-smear images. *Comput. Methods Programs Biomed.*, 164, 15–225, 2018.

3. Jeyshri, J. and Kowsigan, M., Fusing expert knowledge and deep learning for accurate cervical cancer diagnosis in pap smear images: A multiscale U-net with fuzzy automata. *Int. J. Intell. Syst. Eng.*, 11, 2, 763–771, 2023.

4. Malli, P.K. and Nandyal, S., Machine learning technique for detection of cervical cancer using k-NN and artificial neural network. *Int. J. Emerg. Trends Technol. Comput. Sci.*, 6, 4, 145–149, 2017.

5. Alquran, H., Mustafa, W.A., Qasmieh, I.A., Yacob, Y.M., Alsalatie, M., Al-Issa, Y., Alqudah, A.M., Cervical cancer classification using combined machine learning and deep learning approach. *Comput. Mater. Contin*, 72, 3, 5117–5134, 2022.

6. Shanthi, P.B., Hareesha, K.S., Kudva, R., Automated detection and classification of cervical cancer using pap smear microscopic images: A comprehensive review and future perspectives. *Eng. Sci.*, 19, 20–41, 2022.

7. Yaman, O. and Tuncer, T., Exemplar pyramid deep feature extraction based cervical cancer image classification model using pap-smear images. *Biomed. Signal Process. Control*, 73, 103428, 2022. https://doi.org/10.1016/j.iswa.2022.200133

8. Shao, J., Zhang, Z., Liu, H., Song, Y., Yan, Z., Wang, X., Hou, Z., DCE-MRI pharmacokinetic parameter maps for cervical carcinoma prediction. *Comput. Biol. Med.*, 118, 103634, 2020.

9. Ghoneim, A., Alrashoud, M., Song, E., Lu, J., Machine learning for assisting cervical cancer diagnosis: An ensemble approach. *Future Gener. Comput. Syst.*, 106, 199–205, 2020.

10. Bhatt, A.R., Ganatra, A., Kotecha, K., Cervical cancer detection in pap smear whole slide images using convnet with transfer learning and progressive resizing. *PeerJ Comput. Sci.*, 7, e348, 2021.

11. Attallah, O., Cervical cancer diagnosis based on multi-domain features using deep learning enhanced by handcrafted descriptors. *Appl. Sci.*, 13, 3, 1916, 2023.

12. Kalbhor, M., Shinde, S.V., Jude, H., Cervical cancer diagnosis based on cytology pap smear image classification using fractional coefficient and machine learning classifiers. *Telkomnika*, 20, 5, 1091–1102, 2022.

13. Waly, M., II, Sikkandar, M.Y., Aboamer, M.A., Kadry, S., Thinnukool, O., Optimal deep convolution neural network for cervical cancer diagnosis model. *Comput. Mater. Contin.*, 70, 2, 1–18, 2022.

14. Kuko, M. and Pourhomayoun, M., Single and clustered cervical cell classification with ensemble and deep learning methods. *Inf. Syst. Front.*, 22, 5, 1039–1051, 2020.

15. Suphalakshmi, A. *et al.*, Cervical cancer classification using efficient net and fuzzy extreme learning machine. *J. Intell. Fuzzy Syst.*, 16, 200133, 1–10, 2022.

16. Sarwar, A., Sharma, V., Gupta, R., Hybrid ensemble learning technique for screening of cervical cancer using Papanicolaou smear image analysis. *Personalized Med. Universe*, 4, 54–62, 2015.

17. Parraga, F.T., Rodriguez, C., Pomachagua, Y., Rodriguez, D., A review of image-based deep learning algorithms for cervical cancer screening, in: *2021 13th International Conference on Computational Intelligence and Communication Networks (CICN)*, IEEE, pp. 155–160, September 2021.

18. Liu, W., Li, C., Xu, N., Jiang, T., Rahaman, M.M., Sun, H., Wu, X. *et al.*, CVM-Cervix: A hybrid cervical Pap-smear image classification framework using CNN, visual transformer and multilayer perceptron. *Pattern Recognit.*, 130, 1088295, 2022.

19. Mustafa, W.A., Halim, A., Ab Rahman, K.S., A narrative review: Classification of pap smear cell image for cervical cancer diagnosis. *Oncologie*, 22, 2, 53–63, 2020.

20. Ramzan, Z., Hassan, M.A., Asif, H.M., Farooq, A., A machine learning-based self-risk assessment technique for cervical cancer. *Curr. Bioinform.*, 16, 2, 315–332, 2021.

21. Tripathi, A., Arora, A., Bhan, A., Classification of cervical cancer using deep learning algorithm, in: *2021 5th International Conference on Intelligent Computing and Control Systems (ICICCS)*, pp. 1210–1218, IEEE, May 2021.

22. Fekri-Ershad, S. and Ramakrishnan, S., Cervical cancer diagnosis based on modified uniform local ternary patterns and feed forward multilayer network optimized by genetic algorithm. *Comput. Biol. Med.*, 144, 105392, 2022.

23. Chen, H., Liu, J., Wen, Q.M., Zuo, Z.Q., Liu, J.S., Feng, J., Xiao, D., CytoBrain: Cervical cancer screening system based on deep learning technology. *J. Comput. Sci. Technol.*, 36, 347–360, 2021.

24. Yu, S. *et al.*, Automatic classification of cervical cells using deep learning method. *IEEE Access*, 9, 32559–325685, 2021.

25. Lilhore, U.K., Poongodi, M., Kaur, A., Simaiya, S., Algarni, A.D., Elmannai, H., Hamdi, M., Hybrid model for detection of cervical cancer using causal analysis and machine learning techniques. *Comput. Math. Methods Med.*, 2022, 2022.

10

Classification and Diagnosis of Heart Diseases Using Fuzzy Logic Based on IoT

Srinivas Kolli[1]*, Pramoda Patro[2], Rupak Sharma[3] and Amit Sharma[4]

[1]*Department of Information Technology, Vallurupalli Nageswara Rao Vignana Jyothi Institute of Engineering & Technology, Vignana Jyothi Nagar, Pragathi Nagar, Nizampet (S.O.), Hyderabad, Telangana, India*
[2]*Department of Engineering Mathematics, Koneru Lakshmaiah Education Foundation, Hyderabad, Telangana, India*
[3]*Department of Computer Application, SRM Institute of Science and Technology, NCR Campus, Sikri Kalan, Modinagar, Ghaziabad, India*
[4]*Department of Computer Science and Engineering, College of Computing Sciences & IT, Teerthanker Mahaveer University, Moradabad, India*

Abstract

The Internet of Medical Things (IoMT) technology improves healthcare system sensor data collection for heart disease diagnosis and prognosis. This research aims to predict cardiovascular disease using medical data and imaging. Two-stage healthcare data classification and prediction are offered. The second stage is unnecessary if the first predicts cardiovascular disease. Echocardiography pictures were categorized to predict heart disease after the initial data classification utilizing patient sensors. The hybrid Faster R-CNN with SE-ResNet-101 model for sensor input and hybrid linear discriminant analysis with modified ant lion optimization (HLDA-MALO) classified echocardiogram pictures. Combining and validating the two categorization techniques yielded cardiovascular disease predictions. HLDA-MALO detects 90.85% of normal sensor data and 90.31% of unusual data. Faster R-CNN with SE-ResNeXt-101 transfer learning produced the best image classification results. The model has 98.01% accuracy, 98.9% recall, 91.33% specificity, 98.05% F-score, and 99.10% maximum accuracy.

Keywords: IoMT, cloud, heart illness, hybrid analysis, R-CNN, echocardiography

---

**Corresponding author*: kollisreenivas@gmail.com

Satya Prakash Yadav, Sudesh Yadav, Pethuru Raj Chelliah and Victor Hugo C. de Albuquerque (eds.)
Advances in Fuzzy-Based Internet of Medical Things (IoMT), (149–162) © 2024 Scrivener Publishing LLC

10.1   Introduction

Wearable gadgets, the Internet of Things (IoT), and mobile networks are examples of cutting-edge healthcare innovations that facilitate the connection of resources, persons, and institutions and the uploading of health information. Physicians, nurses, hospitals, clinics, and universities all play important roles in a well-rounded healthcare system. The framework is dynamic and covers an extensive range of topics, including detecting and preventing illness and evaluating the healthcare system. Management, intelligent healthcare, and cutting-edge biotechnology make use of automated networks including the IoT, the Internet, artificial intelligence (AI), big data, storage networking, and 5G. By incorporating emerging technologies into behavioral frameworks and safeguarding protocols, it will help to detect potential health concerns in a timely manner and formulate proactive interventions, such as treatment surveillance and the creation of novel assessments, to prevent problems from worsening. In 2019, the worldwide intelligent medical market was worth an estimated USD 143 billion, and it is projected to increase at a Compounded Annual Growth (CAGR) of 16% from 2021 to 2027, as reported by a study of the market.

In contrast, telemedicine systems exhibit a high degree of variability. They are often made with a specific therapeutic objective in mind like the distant monitoring of cardiac function or the facilitation of stroke rehabilitation. Telemedicine systems possess the attribute of cost reduction and alleviation of healthcare system overload. However, their efficacy is compromised as patient volume and disease prevalence increase. These technological advancements facilitate continuous patient health monitoring in real time, without necessitating hospitalization, while improving their physical agility and movement. The Internet of Medical Things (IoMT) pertains to specific applications of IoT technology in the healthcare industry. The diagram presented in Figure 10.1 illustrates the standard multi-tier architecture of an Internet of Things application, which consists of the perception, network, and application layers. IoMT places significant emphasis on the perception layer, which comprises two discrete sublayers, namely, information access and information acquisition.

To identify and perceive bulges and collect information regarding persons and entities, IoMT's info-gathering sublayer makes use of a wide variety of signal processing and therapeutic perception devices. The information access sublayer bridges all gaps between the information collection sublayer and the network using short-range transmission including Wi-Fi, ZigBee, and Bluetooth. The service sublayer and the network transmission

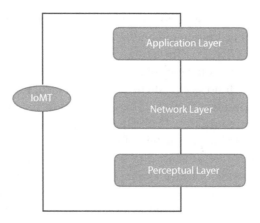

Figure 10.1 Architecture of the IoT.

sublayer are two more layers that make up the network layer. If IoMT is a living organism, the network transmission sublayer would be its brain. Perception layer data are delivered in a synchronous, accurate, reliable, and barrier-free manner through a variety of networks such as the Internet, mobile communications networks, and specialized networks. The service layer is in charge of bringing together various databases, metadata, and other data from many sources across various networks [1–4]. The application layer comprises two sublevels, namely, medical information sets and decision-making applications [5]. The data applications encompass a range of functions, such as medical device management, patient data management, and material data management. The utilization of decision-making applications encompasses the examination of patient data, illnesses, pharmaceuticals, diagnoses, treatments, and related areas [6]. Two classification techniques are employed, and their results are verified to predict the occurrence of cardiovascular disease. The hybrid linear discriminant analysis with modified ant lion optimization (HLDA-MALO) method, which combines modified ant lion optimization and linear discriminant analysis, is employed for the purpose of classifying sensor data. The study utilizes the hybrid Faster R-CNN with SE-ResNet-101 model for the purpose of arranging echocardiography images.

10.2   Related Works of IoMT

The development of a system for diagnosing heart illnesses using IoMT was documented in reference [7]. The system was created through the utilization of a modified superior labrum anterior to posterior swarm optimization (MSSO) technique in conjunction with an adaptive neuro-fuzzy inference system (ANFIS). The utilization of the Levy flight strategy has enhanced the search proficiency of the MSSO-ANFIS. The ANFIS learning process commonly follows a gradient-based approach, which is susceptible to being trapped in local minima. The utilization of the maintenance and support service organization (MSSO) technique has been implemented to improve the learning parameters of the adaptive neuro-fuzzy inference system for the purpose of achieving superior outcomes. An approach to monitoring patients with heart conditions utilizing the Internet of Things and an adjusted neural network known as deep learning modified neural network (DLMNN) was proposed in a scholarly article. This method aims to help in the identification and management of heart disease. The study involved the authentication of a cardiac patient from a specified medical facility through the utilization of SHA-512 and the substitution cypher. Subsequently, the IoT sensor device is affixed to the patient's physique, and the sensor information is transmitted to the cloud in a synchronous manner. The technique was employed to securely encode and transmit the sensor data to the cloud [8]. The categorization process was ultimately completed subsequent to the decryption of the encoded data [10]. In medical diagnosis for conventional neural network (MDCNN) was applied to predict cardiac disease. The diagnosis infrastructure for the acute esophageal necrosis (AEN) was built using the sound heart datasets for Physio bank Physio Net A training and PASCAL B training. To improve prognostics of heart illnesses, employed a learning-aided mode [9]. The outcome was that the reduction in features affected the accuracy and processing speed of classifiers. employed an enhanced deep learning classifier to categorize cancer, Alzheimer's disorders, and brain imaging. The optical circuit switching (OCS) approach enhanced the performance of the classifier. The best features from the preprocessed photos were selected for analysis using the OCS technique in this case, and they included the multi-texture and gray-level characteristics. Methods for slicing and reducing features have been considered for improved performance [10]. A patient's cardiovascular illness was detected using the convolutional neural network (CNN). The proposed method first used CNN to model temporal data to predict cardiac disease. Performance could be enhanced by using element extraction and selection methods [11]. A fuzzy-based decision tree algorithm was proposed for the early diagnosis of heart illness using a continuous and remote patient monitoring system [12]. The chosen structure would help classify reduced data by improving model presentation if redundant and irrelevant networks were removed from the data. A model for predicting heart illness using a maximum-relevance-minimum-redundancy feature extraction method and back propagation neural network has been developed [13, 14]. The effectiveness of classification and prediction was assessed using a numerical medical dataset [15, 16]. Heart disease was predicted using a semi-supervised generative adversarial network [17, 18]. Images from echocardiography were used in that investigation to assess the presence of cardiac disease [19, 20].

10.3 Hybrid Model for Hortonworks Data Platform (HDP)

The model has been employed in AI and machine learning (ML) methodologies to classify and forecast medical data. Databases and wearable sensors are integral components in conducting advanced research. The model under consideration operates through a bifurcated process consisting of two distinct phases. In the initial phase, medical sensors affixed to a patient's physique produce sensor data, which is subsequently succeeded by categorizing echocardiography images in the subsequent stage. The heart disease prediction process involves completing various classification techniques, followed by the validation and combination of their results. The classification model yields outcomes in binary values, indicating the existence or nonexistence of the ailment under consideration. The investigation involved the recording and sampling of sensor data, with the electrocardiogram (ECG) sensor being recorded at 100 Hz. Information is transmitted via Bluetooth and saved in comma-separated value (.csv) and binary file formats. The experiment on image classification utilized personalized echocardiography image data collected under a medical doctor's supervision in a private setting. The study utilized SE-ResNet-101 with the hybrid Faster R-CNN to categorize echocardiography images. Wearable sensors in the form of pulse oximeters, ECG, and blood pressure and temperature sensors were utilized to gather medical information. By being applied to the human body, these sensors capture information from the ECG, heart rate, blood pressure, and body temperature. IoT technology was used to collect the data and store them in the cloud. Two stages of this research were carried out, each with its unique difficulties. Heart disease was predicted using the results of the two stages. Based on the results of stage 1, users might assess the effects of a condition by BP, ECG monitoring, and heartbeat [21, 22].

The model under consideration is depicted in Figure 10.2 and operates in the following manner: Initially, medical data are gathered by placing

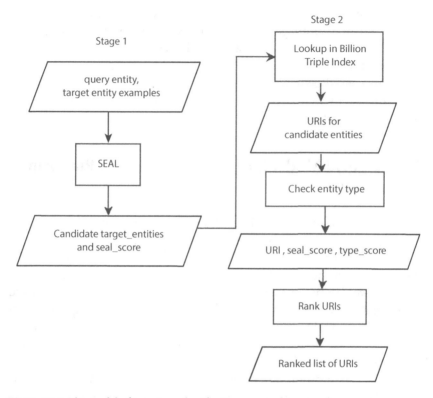

Figure 10.2 The model of two-stage classification.

sensors for electrocardiography, blood pressure, and pulse oximetry onto the human body. The sensor data provided by the patient are relevant to the field of cardiac illness. The electrocardiogram finds the orientation of impulses during their propagation through the myocardium [22, 23].

Here, is analyzed the depth of the two-stage retrieval method for the ELC task. The service, excellence, advocacy and leadership (SEAL) method is employed at the initial stage for set enlargement. SEAL has the ability to manage relational instances. Therefore, first one gives SEAL query entity and target entity pairs. SEAL creates a candidate list of further relation instances, or entity pairs, by learning wrappers over these relation instances. Eliminate entity pairs that include a query entity by filtering them out. The other partner in the dyad becomes a potential solution to the ELC task. Only utilize target entity examples as seeds if SEAL is unable to locate related instances. Then, SEAL returns the things that can fit the provided list, which also serve as potential answers for the ELC assignment. Along with each candidate it outputs, SEAL also outputs a score. Type-checking and ranking are dealt with in the second stage. The Billion

Triple Index was employed. Conduct a lookup in the Billion Triple Index for each entity in the candidate list generated by the first stage. The index returns multiple URIs for each query. Type fields from the websites that matched the top URIs. Target type DBpedia and target entity are two fields that the ELC task specifies as taken. Target type matches receive a typing score of 2, target entity matches receive a score of 1, and no type matches but valid URIs welcome a score of 0. The list excludes candidate entities for which no URI was discovered. At this point, have entity name, URI, type score, and SEAL score candidate tuples order the entities based on type scores, and then handle collisions based on SEAL scores.

10.4   Ant Lion Optimization and Hybrid Linear Discriminant

10.4.1   ALO

The ant lion optimizer (ALO) is a heuristic find algorithm that emulates the searching strategy of the ant lion in nature and is characterized by the absence of parameters. The utilization of a roulette wheel and casual walk by the ALO presents a noteworthy circumventing stagnation in local optima. The selection of ant lions by ALO is used to erratic movement of ants surrendered them facilitate the investigation of the search area. Additionally, the adaptive reduction of boundaries in ant lion traps ensures exploitation. The arithmetical system of the ALO was elucidated by employing subsequent methods. Equation 10.1 is a proper characterization of the ant's random walk, as ants exhibit stochastic movement patterns in their natural habitat while foraging for food.

$$Zk = [0, \text{cum sum}(2s(k1)-1), \text{cum sum}(2s(k2)-1),...\text{cum sum}(2s(kn)-1] \tag{10.1}$$

The variables in question are denoted as follows:

- N represents the upper limit of iterations, and consume refers to the sum of values accumulated over time.
- K represents the step taken in the random walk process.
- S k is the function in Equation 10.2, where Zk denotes the random walk of the ant.

$$s(k) = \begin{cases} 1 \, if \; rdm > 0.5 \\ 0 \, if \; rdm \le 0.5 \end{cases} \tag{10.2}$$

where rkj is the variable j's minimum at iteration k, the is the variable j's maximum at iteration k, pj is the variable j's lowest random walk, and qj is its highest. In contrast to ants, which move randomly, ant lion can use these processes to build a trap that is appropriate for its fitness.

$$rk = \frac{rk}{J} \tag{10.3}$$

$$t^k = \frac{tk}{J} \tag{10.4}$$

where J=10kK, K is the current iteration (=2 for k > 0.1K, =3 for k > 0.5K, =4 for k > 0.75K, =5 for k > 0.9K, and =6 for k > 0.95K). In essence, the exploitation accuracy may be controlled by the constant.

Each ant's update mechanism was taken into consideration to be comparable to the continuous algorithm in order to build in ALO. The primary distinction between binary and conventional ALO was how the binary technique updated ants by flipping among 0 and 1; the assumption is shown in equation 10.5.

$$S^k = \begin{cases} 2\,if\ dm <|| tanh(GZkj)| \\ 0 \qquad\qquad otherwise \end{cases} \tag{10.5}$$

The expression "tanh" refers to the hyperbolic tangent function, while "S^k" represents the binary coding format of the location of an ant. Incorporating elitism into the swarm intelligence algorithm is a noteworthy characteristic, as it enables the attainment of the optimal solution at each stage of the optimization process. Nevertheless, this attribute proved to be unsuitable for binary coding.

10.4.2   Linear Discriminant Analysis

LDA has the two distinct types of categories, even though it can potentially uncover different patterns if extended. A function for multiple linear discrimination is created to distinguish between classes, which is represented by multiple hyperplanes in the feature space. The linear discriminant analysis model operates under the assumption that all categories can be linearly separated. Linear discriminant analysis (LDA) is a widely recognized technique utilized for identifying underlying patterns. LDA classifiers have been employed in various medical applications, such as the classification of breast and lung cancer, as well as the analysis of electrocardiogram signals. This is achieved by enhancing Fisher criterion I(Y), which is instrumental in minimizing the overlay between the sections in the low-dimensional feature space. The corresponding projection Y exhibits a higher degree of class separation.

10.5 Result

A region proposal network (RPN) has been developed to facilitate object identification by utilizing region proposal techniques to ascertain object positions. A solitary network executes the region proposal network operation, which produces regional proposals. The SE-ResNeXt-101 model, which has a significant depth, can be evaluated comprehensively across all stages on the graphics processing unit (GPU) while achieving advanced accuracy in object detection. This can be accomplished by utilizing the recommended echocardiogram in conjunction with a faster RCNN.

The proposed task has been executed utilizing the cloud. The planned model has been evaluated utilizing the MATLAB Simulink tool version 2019a. The testing was conducted on a 64-bit version of Windows 11, 16 GB of RAM, and an Intel Core i7-10700 CPU running at 4.7 to 4.9 GHz. This study's main goal was categorizing and prognosticating cardiovascular diseases. The recommended classifiers divided the data into two categories: heart illness or not.

10.5.1 Dataset Description

Every dataset has its own instances and attributes; the Cleveland dataset, for instance, contains 303 records and 76 characteristics. However, traits, as indicated in Table 10.1, in 15.

10.5.2 Performance Metrics

The output metrics in the Equation are the F-score, recall, accuracy, and precision. Based on these metrics, Table 10.2 shows the difference between actual result to the anticipated one.

Table 10.1 Descriptions of the Cleveland dataset.

Data	Class	Accuracy	Precision	Recall	Specificity	F-Score
Sensor (collected)	Normal	96	9.0	7.04	4.6	9.3
Cleveland dataset		98.	96	8.92	5.5	8.5
Sensor	Abnormal	8.1	9.8	8.83	7.2	97.0
Cleveland dataset		90.8	905.9	998.02	916.0	97.1

Table 10.2 Difference between actual result to the anticipated one [24].

Algorithm	Accuracy	Precision	Recall	Specificity	F-Score
VGG-19	99.3	90.6	4.0	83.9	89.8
ResNeXt-101	86.5	9.0	9.2	82.8	95.9
Inception-ResNet-v2	86.8	9.7	9.4	98.1	99.4
SE-ResNet-101	90.4	9.8	9.1	99.3	90.5
Proposed model	90.5	9.06	9.5	86.2	90.2

$$Accurateness = \frac{Trn + Trn}{trp + flp + Trn + FLN}\% \qquad (10.6)$$

$$Exactness = \frac{Trp + Trn}{flp} \qquad (10.7)$$

$$Memory = \frac{TRPTRN}{FLP} \qquad (10.8)$$

1. The true positive rate (TPR) refers to the accurate and comprehensive identification of positive instances within the regular class classification.
2. FLP refers to the number of fake positives, which represents the total count of incorrect instances classified as positive in a given set of standard types.
3. The TRN denotes the precise negative value that accurately categorizes incremental classification within abnormal classes.
4. FLN refers to the false negative rate, which represents the proportion of irregular courses that are incorrectly classified as regular.

The suggested HLDA-MALO technique achieved 90.31% accuracy, 96.48% precision, 90.83% recall, 90.52% specificity, and 97.98% F-score in sensor-collected medical signal abnormal class categorization. HLDA-MALO had 90.48% accuracy, 90.59% precision, 90.02% recall, 90.80% specificity, and 90.01% F-score on Cleveland dataset anomalies. Figure 10.3 shows accuracy normal data.

The Faster R-CNN-SE- model had been found to exhibit superior classification accuracy in the categorization of echocardiogram images for cardiac disease prediction, as mentioned in Figure 10.4.

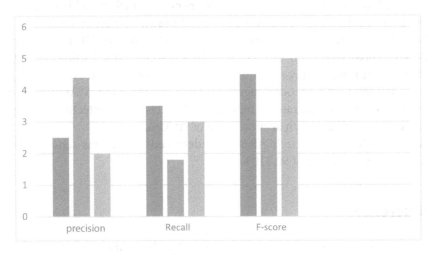

Figure 10.3 The accuracy normal data.

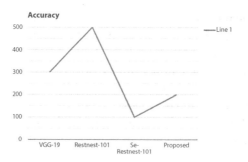

Figure 10.4 Comparison of image classification accuracy.

10.6   Conclusions

The present investigation employed machine learning techniques to establish an Internet of Medical Things-centered predictive model for cardiac disease. The proposed model was subjected to two experimental trials. The outcomes of the preceding stage are dependable and proficient in anticipating heart illness. The initial phase involved categorizing medical data from a wearable detector fixed to the patient's physique. In contrast, the subsequent stage entailed the organization of data by utilizing echocardiography imagery. The employed categorization techniques are validated to forecast the occurrence of heart illness. The sensor data categorization was achieved using a hybrid linear discriminant analysis with modified ant lion optimization (HLDA-MALO) technique. The study employed a hybrid model that combined Fast R-CNN with SE-ResNet-101 for the purpose of classifying echo images. The models were trained using datasets about heart illness sourced from the UCI repository, which encompassed the Cleveland and echocardiography datasets. The LDA-MALO hybrid methodology demonstrated a high level of precision in detecting average sensor data, achieving an accuracy rate of 90.85%.

Additionally, the approach effectively identified anomalous sensor data, with an accuracy rate of 90.310%.

References

1. Raj, R.J.S., Shobana, S.J., Pustokhina, I.V., Pustokhin, D.A., Gupta, D., Shankar, K., Optimal features selections-based medical images classifications using deep learning models in internet of medical things. *IEEE Access*, 8, 58006–58017, 2020, doi: 10.1109/ACCESS.2020.2981337.

2. Wang, M., Wu, C., Wang, L., Xiang, D., Huang, X., A feature selections approach for hyperspectral images based on modified ant lion optimizer. *Knowl. Based Syst.*, 168, 39–48, 2019, doi: 10.1016/j.knosys.2018.12.031.

3. Paul, S.M.V., Balasubramaniam, S., Panchatcharam, P., Malarvizhi Kumar, P., Mubarakali, A., Intelligent framework for prediction of heart disease using deep learning. *Arab. J. Sci. Eng.*, 1–11, 2021, doi: 10.1007/s13369-021-06058-9. https://www.mdpi.com/2076-3417/13

4. Yadav, S.P., Mahato, D.P., Linh, N.T.D., *Distributed Artificial Intelligence*, S.P. Yadav, D.P. Mahato, N.T.D. Linh (Eds.) CRC Press, 2020, https://doi.org/10.1201/9781003038467.

5. de Carvalho Junior, H.H. *et al.*, A heart disease recognition embedded system with fuzzy cluster algorithm. *Comput. Methods Programs Biomed.*, 110, 3, 447–454, 2013.

6. Uyar, K. and İlhan, A., Diagnosis of heart disease using genetic algorithm based trained recurrent fuzzy neural networks. *Proc. Comput. Sci.*, 120, 588–593, 2017.

7. Sanz, J.A. *et al.*, Medical diagnosis of cardiovascular diseases using an interval-valued fuzzy rule-based classification system. *Appl. Soft Comput.*, 20, 103–111, 2014.

8. Kumar, S.U. and Inbarani, H.H., Neighborhood rough set based ECG signal classification for diagnosis of cardiac diseases. *Soft Comput.*, 21, 4721–4733, 2017.

9. Adeli, A. and Neshat, M., A fuzzy expert system for heart disease diagnosis, in: *Proceedings of International Multi Conference of Engineers and Computer Scientists*, Hong Kong, vol. 1, March 2010.

10. Yadav, H., Singh, S., Mishra, K.K., Srivastava, S., Naruka, M.S., Yadav, S.P., Brain tumor detection with MRI images, in: *2022 International Conference on Computational Intelligence and Sustainable Engineering Solutions (CISES)*, IEEE, 2022, https://doi.org/10.1109/cises54857.2022.9844387.

11. Kasbe, T. and Pippal, R.S., Design of heart disease diagnosis system using fuzzy logic, in: *2017 International Conference on Energy, Communication, Data Analytics and Soft Computing (ICECDS)*, IEEE, pp. 3183–3187, August 2017.

12. Chandna, D., Diagnosis of heart disease using data mining algorithm. *Int. J. Comput. Sci. Inf. Technol.*, 5, 2, 1678–1680, 2014.

13. Reddy, G.T. and Khare, N., Heart disease classification system using optimised fuzzy rule based algorithm. *Int. J. Biomed. Eng. Technol.*, 27, 3, 183–202, 2018.

14. Dhotre, V.A. *et al.*, Big data analytics using MapReduce for education system. *Linguist. Antverp.*, 3130–3138, 2021.

15. Ephzibah, E.P. and Sundarapandian, V., A neuro fuzzy expert system for heart disease diagnosis. *Comput. Sci. Eng.*, 2, 1, 17, 2012.

16. Gadekallu, T.R. and Khare, N., Cuckoo search optimized reduction and fuzzy logic classifier for heart disease and diabetes prediction. *Int. J. Fuzzy Syst. Appl.*, 6, 2, 25–42, 2017.

17. Sarangi, L., Mohanty, M.N., Patnaik, S., Detection of abnormal cardiac condition using fuzzy inference system. *Int. J. Autom. Control*, 11, 4, 372–383, 2017.

18. Anooj, P.K., Clinical decision support system: Risk level prediction of heart disease using weighted fuzzy rules. *J. King Saud Univ.-Comput. Inf. Sci.*, 24, 1, 27–40, 2012.

19. Bouali, H. and Akaichi, J., Comparative study of different classification techniques: Heart disease use case, in: *2014 13th International Conference on Machine Learning and Applications*, IEEE, pp. 482–486, 2014.

20. Latha, C.B.C. and Carolin Jeeva, S., Improving the accuracy of prediction of heart disease risk based on ensemble classification techniques. *Inform. Med. Unlocked*, 16, 100203, 2019.

21. Bhatla, N. and Jyoti, K., An analysis of heart disease prediction using different data mining techniques. *Int. J. Eng.*, 1, 8, 1–4, 2012.

22. Pandey, P.S. *et al.*, A smart parking system based on IoT technologies. *Linguist. Antverp.*, 59–64, 2021.

23. Sagir, A.M. and Sathasivam, S., A novel adaptive neuro fuzzy inference system based classification model for heart disease prediction. *Pertanika J. Sci. Technol.*, 25, 1, 1–18, 2017.

24. Rahman, M.Z., Akbar, M.A., Leiva, V., Tahir, A., Riaz, M.T., Martin-Barreiro, C., An intelligent health monitoring and diagnosis system based on the internet of things and fuzzy logic for cardiac arrhythmia COVID-19 patients. *Comput Biol Med.*, 154, 106583, 2023.

11

Implementation of a Neuro-Fuzzy-Based Classifier for the Detection of Types 1 and 2 Diabetes

Chamandeep Kaur[1], Mohammed Saleh Al Ansari[2],
Vijay Kumar Dwivedi[3] and D. Suganthi[4]*

[1]Department of Computer Science and IT, Jazan University, Jazan, Saudi Arabia
[2]College of Engineering, Department of Chemical Engineering, University of Bahrain, Sakhir Bahrain
[3]Department of Mathematics, Vishwavidyalaya Engineering College, Ambikapur, Surguja, India
[4]Department of Computer Science, Saveetha College of Liberal Arts and Sciences, SIMATS, Thandalam, Chennai, India

Abstract

In 2019, the death rate increased above 1.5 million throughout the globe due to diabetes, according to data published by the Globe Health Organization, and it affected about 450 million people worldwide. It has been noted that many people with diabetes failed to recognize their condition in its earliest stages, leading to a rise in the commonness of type 2 diabetes. To prevent this from happening, a novel neural classifier based on fuzzy logic for diagnosing diabetes at an early stage. We add some unknown neuro-fuzzy rules with temporal bounds for preliminary sorting. Fuzzy cognitive maps (FCMs) with time intervals improve these levels before making a final categorization judgment. The suggested model's primary focus is on time-based detection of diabetes severity. In addition, the decision-making procedure in diabetes forecasting uses a set of neuro-fuzzy criteria for picking the most relevant variables. Trials done both from the repository and with the typical diabetes detection models available on the market demonstrated the suggested model's efficiency in performance.

*Corresponding author: suganthiphd@gmail.com

Satya Prakash Yadav, Sudesh Yadav, Pethuru Raj Chelliah and Victor Hugo C. de Albuquerque (eds.)
Advances in Fuzzy-Based Internet of Medical Things (IoMT), (163–178) © 2024 Scrivener Publishing LLC

Keywords: Diabetes, type 1 and type 2, fuzzy logic, neural classifier, fuzzy cognitive maps

11.1   Introduction

Diabetes is a set of metabolic illnesses considered by high blood glucose levels above the usual range. Diabetes is caused due to the lack of ability to release enough insulin or use the insulin generated by the liver. As a result, blood sugar levels rise, and diabetes develops. Chronic hyperglycemia due to abnormalities in insulin production constitutes the diabetes mellitus (DM) category of metabolic diseases. Glucokinase deficiency is an inherited disorder of the glucose-insulin signaling system that results in persistent neonatal diabetes. Worldwide, the number of persons living with diabetes is assumed to almost double from 177 million in 20 centuries to 370 million by 2030, according to the World Health Organization (2003) projections. By 2025, experts predict that the number of people with diabetes will have increased by 64%, reaching 53.1 million. There were an expected 285 million individuals (6.4% of the total population) with diabetes in the year 2010, and this value is expected to climb to roughly 439 million, which is 7.7% by 2030. Both type 1 and type 2 diabetes mellitus are the most general forms. The first type of diabetes, known as insulin-dependent diabetes mellitus (IDDM), is characterized by impaired insulin production from pancreatic beta cells. Reduced sensitivity of target tissues to insulin is the root cause of type 2, also known as non-insulin-dependent diabetic mellitus (NIDDM). Insulin resistance is a decrease in the body's sensitivity to insulin, and its causes are well-known. Metabolic changes occur in both forms of diabetes mellitus, affecting the primary nutrients. Lack of insulin or insulin resistance hinders glucose metabolism by making it difficult for cells elsewhere in the body, excluding the brain, to take in and use glucose effectively. This leads to elevated blood sugar levels, a decline in glucose consumption by cells, and an increase in the utilization of fats and proteins.

Feature selection is crucial to any decision-making system, since it is the means through which feature discount is achieved. In addition to improving overall performance and prediction accuracy rate with less training period, feature selection algorithms also aid in expediting the training process. Finding the relevant qualities in the record set and eliminating the irrelevant ones are part of the feature selection process. Feature selection aims in acquiring a subset of abilities that adequately defines the challenge at hand while incurring as little performance loss as possible. There are several advantages, one of which is improved gadget performance which helpful for keeping track of data, learning the ropes of the process, and seeing how everything fits together.

Preprocessing helps save time and money by decreasing the amount of data that must be stored. Regarding feature selection, there are two main trends: clear-out tactics and wrapper method. Filter models use the generic characteristics of the training records to choose features independently of any predictor. In contrast, wrapper models must improve a predictor as part of the choosing procedure. This method is more specific than the other version, and wrapper models generally perform better. Electronic health records and other forms of biological data storage rely heavily on temporal information. Conditions and patient states develop and change throughout time, and knowing what came before is essential to comprehend what is happening now and what could happen in the future. Time may be expressed computationally and systematically, and formal techniques explain the logic and knowledge needed for this. Events and their temporal usage are formalized via the development of structures or representations. Because time markers are vague, imprecise, and intermittent across and within temporal occurrences, it may be difficult to reason about the past, present, and future in terms of their semantic, causal, and granular subtleties and linkages. This dissertation represented medical processes and modeled healthcare delivery throughout time using formal temporal representations, analytical methodologies, and reasoning.

In this study, neuro-fuzzy based classifier diabetes offer a novel weighted genetic-based feature selection technique that can distinguish between the two types of diabetes and pick the appropriate characteristics to predict type 1 and type 2 cases. To determine the proper features, carry out the reduction of tuple, and tides up the input data, the suggested feature selection algorithm's main benefits stand out. In addition, a novel neuro fuzzy-based rule and algorithm classified based on time with time restrictions is developed for calculating the illness level in the body and uses fuzzy-based rules to carry out the first categorization stage. Fuzzy time-bound cognitive maps are developed to categorize data into groups further. Eighty percent of the data are used for training in this fuzzy cognitive map (FCM), and the remaining 20% is used for testing. The suggested system's employing fuzzy rules with time-based constraints is a substantial advantage. For feature selection, classification, and time-based constraint analysis, the outcomes of these choices are sent into a filter, where they work in tandem to provide valuable suggestions.

11.2 Methodology

The suggested model for predicting diseases is represented in Figure 11.1. It has 11 main parts such as the repository dataset, data acquisition system, and user domain. The repository dataset includes diabetes datasets along with the other standard datasets. Data redundancy is avoided, thanks to the data acquisition system, which extracts just the specific information it needs from the dataset. Using a data-collecting agent, the user domain removes the most helpful feature from the repository under the specified rules and regulations. The decision-maker controls the whole system and can manipulate any part. The geographical agent provides diabetes-related geographical information. The fuzzy inference system is in charge of the fuzziness and smoothness adjustments. For the decision-maker to make timely and accurate judgments on medical datasets, it relies on temporal information provided by the temporal agent. Genetic algorithms and temporal rules are two halves of the data preprocessing puzzle. Here, fuzzy temporal rules are used with the weighted genetic algorithm to preprocess data and choose the most contributing characteristics.

The classification phase includes two subcomponents: the neuro-fuzzy temporal-based classifier system and the fuzzy-based reasoning map to categorize the data correctly. The rule maker's role is to ensure that the

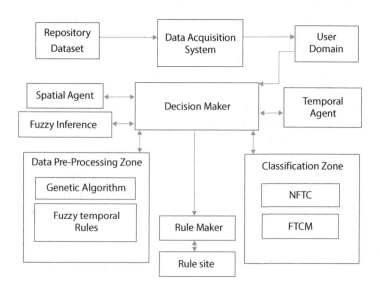

Figure 11.1 Disease-predicting model of the proposed idea.

decision-maker can access the appropriate rules at the right moment. The diabetes classification rules may be found in the rule base.

11.3   Proposed Approach

This paper introduces the fuzzy-based temporal rule and a moderated weighted genetic algorithm-created variable selection, as well as the neuro-fuzzy temporal rule-based arrangement algorithm and the already-existing fuzzy reasoning map (FCM) for efficient organization, to create the first kind of medical skilled system for expecting the onset and severity of diabetes. What follows is a comprehensive explanation of the planned medical professional system.

11.3.1   Feature Selection

Using data from the UCI Diabetic Repository, feature selection is performed for this thesis. Later, after consultation with domain experts, fresh and additional features are introduced to better fit Indian circumstances. This paper offers a novel approach to feature selection that considers genetics. The primary advantage of this approach is that it may be used to determine which variables are most helpful in expecting type 1 and type 2 diabetes. Additionally, questions from the customer and a completed survey to fulfill their desire will be considered. The essential characteristics of type 1 and type 2 are classified by the feature selection approach based on the user's data. Type 1 is characterized by a lack of ability to create insulin, but type 2 results from resistance of insulin. Cells of type 1 diabetics cannot take in sugar (glucose) because of insulin manufacturing issues. However, sugar is a required ingredient for all humans to generate energy. Type 2 diabetes is more common in adults, although it may occur at any age. The level of damage is high here and requires immediate attention. Tiredness, hunger, dry mouth, impaired eyesight, and itchy skin are frequent diabetic symptoms. Type 1 diabetes symptoms include frequent urination, weight loss, and blurred eyesight. It has been discovered that yeast infections are an extra severe symptom for those with type 2 diabetes. Both men and women experience this often. The following procedures (shown in Figure 11.2) are used in the newly created feature selection approach.

Convenient and most contributing landscapes that are beneficial for making real choices throughout the testing procedure may be identified with the help of the suggested feature selection-based algorithm. Fuzzy-based temporal rule and average weighted genetic algorithm-based feature

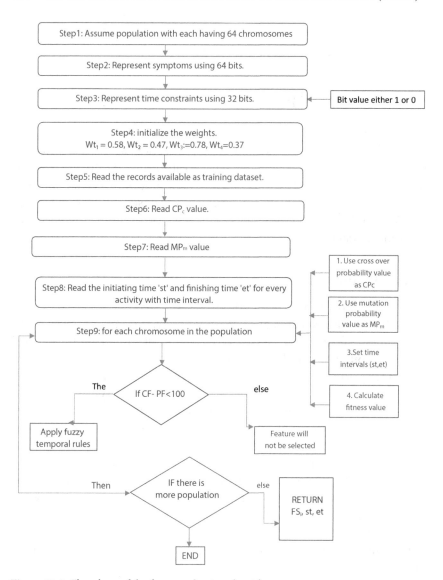

Figure 11.2 Flowchart of the feature selection algorithm.

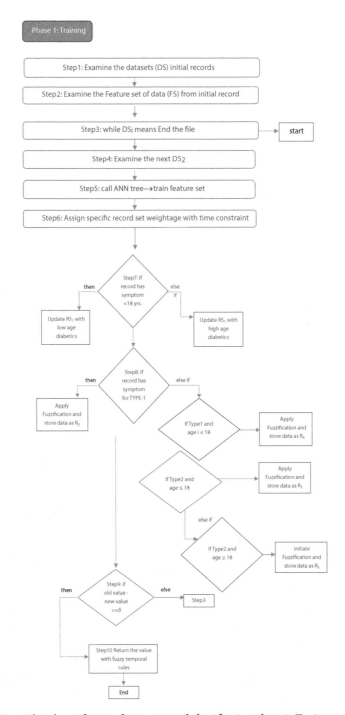

Figure 11.3 Flowchart of neuro-fuzzy temporal classification phase 1: Testing.

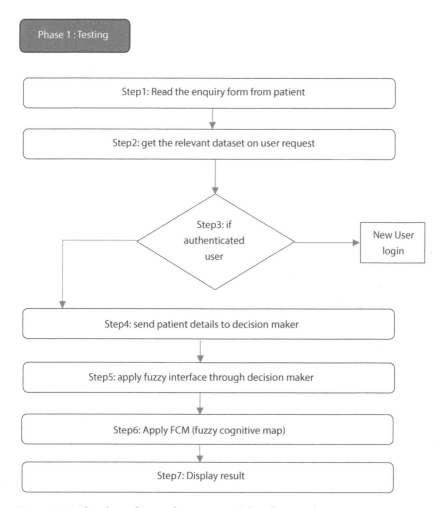

Figure 11.4 Flowchart of neuro-fuzzy temporal classification phase 2: Testing.

selection algorithm fuzzy temporal rules, fitness methods, and attribute sections have been presented and used to identify and pick the most contributing traits. In this context, characteristics serve as chromosomes, generating populations, mutating, and crossing between people. To execute the mutation process and the crossover procedures with the erratically set weights, the values of the feature are translated to 64 bits, and then the time is converted to 32 bits. Here, the consequences play a crucial part in determining medical files. After that, it uses the feature weights to determine the fitness value. Here, the fitness number and fuzzy temporal criteria are used to make the final judgment on features. Ultimately, the features with the most contributions will be chosen as an outcome.

11.3.2 Neuro-Fuzzy Temporal Classification

This part will examine a recently suggested classifier that combines neural network-based fuzzy logic and temporal restraints: The neutral network-based classifier with the fuzzy logic and temporal constraint system. This study's main contribution is incorporating time constraints into feature selection, categorization, and finally a temporal reasoning-based execution as shown in Figures 11.3 and 11.4. The stages that make up the suggested classifier are as follows.

This method uses the inference engine and human judgment to conclude based on fuzzy rules.

A deductive inference may be made using the following fuzzy rules:

Here is an example of a set of rules that may be applied to the diabetes dataset as shown in Figure 11.5:

Expert opinion and clinical characteristics are used in the creation of fuzzy rules. The inference engine uses forward chaining inference with the rules defined in this thesis to get optimal conclusions. And it does rule matching and control firing by constructing a discriminative network. The regulations required for conclusive decision-making on medical datasets are derived using both the conventional benchmark dataset and the streaming dataset, with the advice of medical professionals and fuzzy intervals and temporal limitations taken into account. The suggested neural temporal fuzzy classification uses all of these vague secular principles to make sound judgments about datasets.

```
Case 1

DECLARE Blood_glucose, t1, t2, Parents_and_Ancestors, Type1_Diabetic

IF (Blood_glucose > 7.8 mmol/1) AND ([t2 - t1] >= 5 Years) AND (Parents_and_Ancestors with diabetic > 1) THEN
    Type1_Diabetic = True
    // predicted, based on history of family members.
END IF

case 2

DECLARE insulin_value, HbA1c, t1, t2, Diabetics

IF (insulin_value >= 200) AND (insulin_value < 250) AND (HbA1c >= 8.0%) AND (HbA1c < 9.0%) AND ([t2 - t1] >= 360 days) THEN
    Diabetics = "High Medium"
    // It requires 5 units of regular insulin dosage, pre-breakfast and pre-dinner.
END IF

Case 3
DECLARE Starting_stage_of_Diabetes, Skin_disorder, Sudden_weight_loss, Loss_of_muscle_mass, Giddiness, t1, t2, Type2_diabetic

IF (starting_stage_of_Diabetes = True) AND (Skin_disorder) AND (Sudden_weight_loss OR Loss_of_muscle_mass) AND (Giddiness) AND ([t2 - t1] >= 365 days) THEN
    Type2_diabetic = "Low"
    // Predicted based on symptoms
END IF
```

Figure 11.5 Represents program code for some sample rules.

11.4   Result with Discussion

Trials were conducted in this study utilizing both publicly available "benchmark" datasets and accurate data gathered from hospitals. In addition, rules were created with input from domain experts. The work's benchmark dataset came from the UCI Repository at the University of California, Irvine. Type 1 kind and type 2 kind diabetes are represented by separate categories for 788 entries. Records such as pregnancy count, BP, thickening of the skin, serum secretion for more than 1 hour, BMI value, and age were acquired from the UCI Repository dataset for all patients over 21. The suggested feature selection approach considers and selects five characteristics: glucose, BP, skin thickness issue, BMI value, and insulin values. Table 11.1 offers real-world data used to assess the suggested model in this study, which was implemented as a first-level classifier. Fuzzy-based cognitive maps (FCM) with frequent time intervals are used to make a final determination in the classification process, refining these levels further. The suggested model's primary focus is on time-based detection of diabetes severity. The most critical parameters for the decision-making process in diabetes prediction are selected using a set of neuro-fuzzy algorithms. Trials done both from the repository and with the typical diabetes detection models available on the market demonstrated the suggested model's efficiency in performance.

In addition, a follow-up procedure is required, the details of which will differ from patient to patient based on his or her medical background. The patient's medical records, which were kept from 2008 to 2014, are also considered in this investigation. Patients from Bengaluru, Chennai, Hyderabad, Kochi, and Pune were considered. In Figure 11.2, we have an example of the examination of computational time by city.

Table 11.1 Patients' particulars.

Variables	Particulars
Number of patients examined	260
Men and women	115 and 145
Age category	10–65
Observation period	90 days to 5 years
Time gap for the follow-up	7 days

Figure 11.2 demonstrates that the training and testing durations differ considerably across cities as a function of the quantity of data used in the analysis. Compared to other Indian cities like Chennai, Bengaluru, and Kochi, Pune and Hyderabad have shorter training and testing times. It uses a genetic algorithm that considers time yield appropriate training and testing durations.

The effectiveness of the proposed classifier is shown in Figure 11.6 for both the complete dataset and the characteristics of interest. Here, five trials with varying numbers of data are used to evaluate the performance of the suggested neural network classifier, which takes fuzzy logic and time limitations into account. The input dataset's classification accuracy measures the efficiency.

Considering that the suggested neural classifier performs better on the chosen featured dataset than it does with full features, Figure 11.7 demonstrates the usefulness of the suggested neural classifiers. This is because temporally constrained contributing characteristics converge more quickly to optimal choice values. However, as more factors are included, the decision-making process becomes more complicated, resulting in longer decision times and lower accuracy.

The comparison of the fuzzy classifier's performance under time restrictions and without is shown in Figure 11.6. Here, we provide the results of five studies conducted on patient data gathered from several hospitals in many major Indian cities.

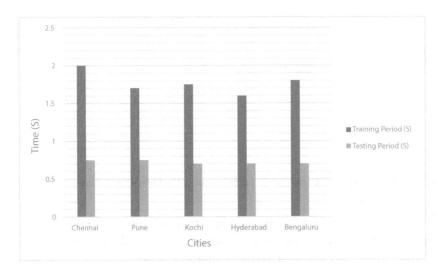

Figure 11.6 Time study.

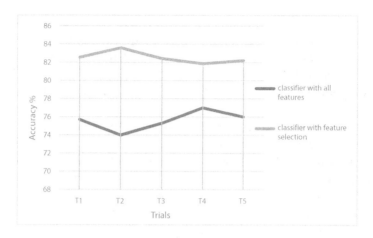

Figure 11.7 Performance study.

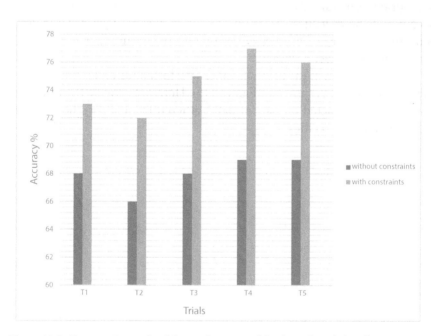

Figure 11.8 Comparative study of the performance of the fuzzy-based classifier.

As shown in Figure 11.8, the suggested fuzzy classifier with time restrictions significantly outperforms the baseline version without temporal constraints. This is because material limitations provide:

- Efficient analysis of the past.
- Leading to the formation of rules for performing temporal reasoning.
- Enabling learning and prediction capabilities.

In addition, the qualitative temporal logic enabled by the time constraint imposed with the fuzzy classification algorithm improves the decisions' accuracy.

Fuzzy classifiers with feature selection and the fuzzy-based classifier negotiating feature selection and time limitations are contrasted and compared in Figure 11.7. Five separate tests were performed using subsets of the gold standard benchmark patient records.

As seen in Figure 11.9, the suggested classifier that uses feature selection performs better than the one that does not. This is since deductive inferences on learned rules are operated via the use of time-constrained choices of features, resulting in a higher detection accuracy. Furthermore, the suggested classifier's findings have been evaluated using a real-world dataset and confirmed with the help of domain experts. The studies performed here reveal no qualitative difference between the system's judgments and those of human experts. The suggested approach is much more reliable and valuable for treatment planning. The submitted model does better than the modern methods in all five studies over a wide range of

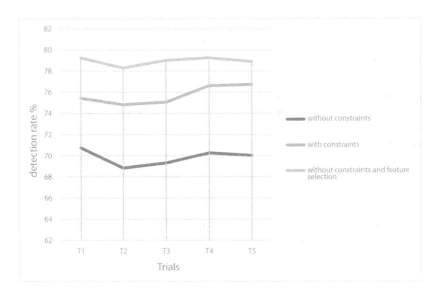

Figure 11.9 Study of detection accuracy.

patient data. Experiments were run on a random sample of data, and the suggested model was evaluated using the same method. Fuzzy logic, neural networks, temporal restrictions, and optimization methods were used in all previous efforts to make predictions. However, they fell short of the current standards. The suggested model correctly predicted illnesses and severity levels using fuzzy-based temporal rules. The enhancement promoted the evolution of a genetic algorithm, the use of a temporal logic system, fuzzy logic system, a neural network system, and feature selection methods. Compared to current illness prediction systems, the suggested approach fares rather well.

11.5   Conclusion and Future Scope

Applying a neural network with fuzzy logic and temporal limitations, as well as a genetic algorithm-based feature selection technique, a novel illness prediction system has been created and applied for accurate diabetes diagnosis. The newly suggested classifier uses fuzzy logic and temporal restrictions to make better decisions based on medical information. A novel genetic algorithm-based feature selection technique has been created to improve prediction accuracy. The accuracy of illness predictions made by the suggested system was higher than that of previously published methods. Adding a multi-neural network and considering fuzzy logic and time limitations would improve this work.

Bibliography

Ganapathy, S. *et al.*, An intelligent temporal pattern classification system using fuzzy temporal rules and particle swarm optimization. *Sadhana*, 39, 283–302, 2014.

Bhuvaneswari, G. and Manikandan, G., A novel machine learning framework for diagnosing the type 2 diabetics using temporal fuzzy ant miner decision tree classifier with temporal weighted genetic algorithm. *Computing*, 100, 759–772, 2018.

Elizabeth Jesi, V. and Aslam, S.M., An intelligent disease prediction and monitoring system using feature selection, multi-neural network and fuzzy rules. *Neural Comput. Appl.*, 34, 22, 19877–19893, 2022.

Kumar, P.M. *et al.*, Cloud and IoT based disease prediction and diagnosis system for healthcare using Fuzzy neural classifier. *Future Gener. Comput. Syst.*, 86, 527–534, 2018.

Soltani, A. *et al.*, A new expert system based on fuzzy logic and image processing algorithms for early glaucoma diagnosis. *Biomed. Signal Process. Control*, 40, 366–377, 2018.

Polat, K. and Güneş, S., An expert system approach based on principal component analysis and adaptive neuro-fuzzy inference system to diagnosis of diabetes disease. *Digit. Signal Process.*, 17, 4, 702–710, 2007.

Talari, P., Suresh, A., Kavitha, M.G., An intelligent medical expert system using temporal fuzzy rules and neural classifier. *Intell. Autom. Soft Comput.*, 35, 1, 2023. https://www.ncbi.nlm.nih.gov/pmc/articles/PMC8659829/

Medina-Quero, J. *et al.*, Ensemble classifier of long short-term memory with fuzzy temporal windows on binary sensors for activity recognition. *Expert Syst. Appl.*, 114, 441–453, 2018.

Ordóñez, F.J. *et al.*, Online activity recognition using evolving classifiers. *Expert Syst. Appl.*, 40, 4, 1248–1255, 2013.

Aruna, P., Puviarasan, N., Palaniappan, B., An investigation of neuro-fuzzy systems in psychosomatic disorders. *Expert Syst. Appl.*, 28, 4, 673–679, 2005.

Aamir, K.M. *et al.*, A fuzzy rule-based system for classification of diabetes. *Sensors*, 21, 23, 8095, 2021.

Kumar, T.R., Pavan, K.V.S., Kukati, R., Quantitatively examines the feasibility of different configurations of the aftermarket supply chain enabling additive manufacturing. *Solid State Technol.*, 63, 5, 492–507, 2020.

Beriha, G.S. *et al.*, Assessment of safety performance in Indian industries using fuzzy approach. *Expert Syst. Appl.*, 39, 3, 3311–3323, 2012.

Muhammad, L.J. *et al.*, Fuzzy rule-driven data mining framework for knowledge acquisition for expert system, in: *Translational Bioinformatics in Healthcare and Medicine*, pp. 201–214, Academic Press, 2021. https://www.ncbi.nlm.nih.gov/pmc/articles/PMC8659829/

Subasi, A., Automatic detection of epileptic seizure using dynamic fuzzy neural networks. *Expert Syst. Appl.*, 31, 2, 320–328, 2006.

Torres-García, A.A. *et al.*, Implementing a fuzzy inference system in a multi-objective EEG channel selection model for imagined speech classification. *Expert Syst. Appl.*, 59, 1–12, 2016.

Liao, S.-H., Chu, P.-H., Hsiao, P.-Y., Data mining techniques and applications–A decade review from 2000 to 2011. *Expert Syst. Appl.*, 39, 12, 11303–11311, 2012.

Nancy, J.Y., Khanna, N.H., Kannan, A., A bio-statistical mining approach for classifying multivariate clinical time series data observed at irregular intervals. *Expert Syst. Appl.*, 78, 283–300, 2017.

Yadav, H., Singh, S., Mishra, K.K., Srivastava, S., Naruka, M.S., Yadav, S.P., Brain tumor detection with MRI images, in: *2022 International Conference on Computational Intelligence and Sustainable Engineering Solutions (CISES)*, IEEE, 2022, https://doi.org/10.1109/cises54857.2022.9844387.

Sengur, A., Wavelet transform and adaptive neuro-fuzzy inference system for color texture classification. *Expert Syst. Appl.*, 34, 3, 2120–2128, 2008.

Pourpanah, F., Lim, C.P., Saleh, J.M., A hybrid model of fuzzy ARTMAP and genetic algorithm for data classification and rule extraction. *Expert Syst. Appl.*, 49, 74–85, 2016.

Jain, A. *et al.*, Optimized levy flight model for heart disease prediction using CNN framework in big data application. *Expert Syst. Appl.*, 223, 119859, 2023.

Thakkar, H. *et al.*, Comparative anatomization of data mining and fuzzy logic techniques used in diabetes prognosis. *Clin. eHealth*, 4, 12–23, 2021.

Khezri, M. and Jahed, M., A neuro–fuzzy inference system for sEMG-based identification of hand motion commands. *IEEE Trans. Ind. Electron.*, 58, 5, 1952–1960, 2010.

Hameed, K. *et al.*, An intelligent IoT based healthcare system using fuzzy neural networks. *Sci. Prog.*, 2020, 1–15, 2020.

Pujahari, R.M., Yadav, S.P., Khan, R., Intelligent farming system through weather forecast support and crop production, in: *Application of Machine Learning in Agriculture*, pp. 113–130, Elsevier, 2022, https://doi.org/10.1016/b978-0-323-90550-3.00009-6.

Houssein, E.H. *et al.*, Deep and machine learning techniques for medical imaging-based breast cancer: A comprehensive review. *Expert Syst. Appl.*, 167, 114161, 2021.

12

IoMT Type-2 Fuzzy Logic Implementation

Sasanko Sekhar Gantayat[1]*, K. M. Pimple[2] and Pokkuluri Kiran Sree[3]

*[1]Department of CSE (Honors), Koneru Lakshmaiah Education Foundation
(Deemed to be University), Vaddeswaram, Guntur, Andhra Pradesh, India
[2]Department of Electronics and Telecommunication Engineering, Dr. Rajendra
Gode Institute of Technology and Research, Amravati, India
[3]Department of Computer Science and Engineering, Shri Vishnu Engineering
College for Women (A), Bhimavaram, Andhra Pradesh, India*

Abstract

Monitoring data streams lays the groundwork for creating clever context-aware apps. Multiple wireless sensors might be dispersed across a localized region and keep an eye on environmental variables to spot disasters like fire and flood. Measurements are sent to a back-end system, which then makes determinations about the presence or absence of irregularities that might have unfavorable consequences. A system present using data streams from several sensors can accurately identify events as they happen in real time. Time series prediction is used in the proposed framework to derive upcoming insights from total values and contextual information over consensus theory to efficiently aggregate data. A second type of fuzzy inference method is used to precisely identify events from the unanimously merged and forecasted components of context. Reasoning skills under uncertainty of phenomenon identification are provided by the type-2 inference process. The effectiveness of a method can vary based on the specific problem domain and characteristics of the data. Benefits are the advantage of the proposed method include accuracy fast computation and low source. Drawbacks are situations that may arise when the method may not perform well. Further compare our approach to type-1 fuzzy inference and other processes to see how effective it is in reducing false positives.

Keywords: Back-end system, type 1 and type 2, aggregate data, fuzzy inference, false positives

*Corresponding author: sasankosekhar@kluniversity.in

Satya Prakash Yadav, Sudesh Yadav, Pethuru Raj Chelliah and Victor Hugo C. de Albuquerque (eds.)
Advances in Fuzzy-Based Internet of Medical Things (IoMT), (179–194) © 2024 Scrivener Publishing LLC

12.1 Introduction

12.1.1 Motivational

A wireless sensor network (WSN) is composed of a collection of sensors that are interconnected wirelessly and have the ability to detect and observe specific phenomena. Each individual sensor possesses distinct sensing capabilities. Here sensors have distinct sensing capabilities to conduct measurements. The basic benefit of wireless sensor networks is the self-governing characteristic of the sensors. Once situated in a designated area of focus, such as a forest, these devices have the capability to conduct measurements autonomously and transmit the data to adjacent devices within their spatial proximity. The data are then relayed to a centralized processing method, which is referred to as the monitoring system (MS) henceforth. The MS acquires contextual information and subsequently analyzes it to first detect particular phenomena and subsequently respond to distinct occurrences. These occurrences are associated with crucial elements such as breaches of predetermined limitations. Therefore, the implementation of a monitoring infrastructure is crucial in security applications. This can be achieved by utilizing a monitoring system that employs a rapid and effective mechanism for generating alerts upon meeting predetermined criteria [1, 2]. These criteria are associated with sensor malfunctions, depletion of resources, or other anomalies. The prompt detection of malfunctions is crucial, particularly in time-sensitive applications where prompt reactions are necessary. An example scenario involves the utilization of an MS within a power plant setting. In this context, a multitude of contextual information streams is received by a collection of sensors, which are subsequently processed and aggregated to generate security awareness.

Environmental monitoring has been identified as a noteworthy domain of application, as evidenced by scholarly literature [3]. The field of environmental monitoring has garnered considerable attention due to the adverse impacts that environmental degradation can have on human well-being. The prompt emphasizes the importance of promptly recognizing alterations in the environment and making informed decisions to ensure the preservation of a satisfactory standard of living for human beings.

12.1.2 Contribution and Organization

The present study's contribution can be summarized as follows: 1) System offers the ability to monitor contextual information flows and identify the occurrence of false alarms. The method employed considers sensors as a collective unit. The approach does not depend solely on the observations of individual sensors. The mechanism employed here integrated a set of techniques that included the proposed methodology, which involves several expert opinion aggregation and decision-making techniques. Firstly, data fusion is utilized to combine the opinions of multiple experts while excluding any outliers. Secondly, a consensus operator is employed to determine the level of agreement among the experts regarding a particular phenomenon. Thirdly, time series forecasting is utilized to forecast the forthcoming behavior of the team on their recent opinions. Finally, fuzzy logic-based inference is employed to handle the uncertainty associated with determining the timing of an event. A thorough sensitivity analysis was conducted on the planned mechanism using the fundamental model parameters. Additionally, a comparison has been made to evaluate the performance against various baseline solutions.

12.2 Related Work

12.2.1 Sensor Monitoring System

Intelligent apps are built on contextual data stream monitoring techniques. Opportunities are newly developed to integrate intelligence into new systems and engage people [4]. Sensors observe a sub-area and provide information to an MS. Sensor network networks temporal and geographical environmental data [5]. The MS uses contextual information to make environmental judgments and alarms [6] to describe the MS architecture. A tree-building approach allows energy-efficient computations, and a series of trials shows its benefits [7]. Proposes a network to observe the quality of indoor air. A base station gathers all information from independent nodes with sensors for humidity, temperature, light, and air quality, and a specialized O program supervises the readings. Many researchers focus on danger detection.

12.2.2 Environmental Monitoring System

Due to environmental impacts on people, environmental monitoring is also popular [4]. It describes a framework for integrating open-source and environmental monitoring networks. Sensors are permanent infrastructure, individuals are mobile monitoring networks, and a back-end system makes environmental protection judgments. WSNs monitor soil moisture, humidity, and temperature.

12.2.3   FIS Monitoring System

FL has the potential to be an effective method for producing high-quality systems in the context of monitoring operations. Decision-making, whether it is for basic alarms or more involved reasoning, is aided by the suggested FL systems, which also deal with the uncertainty associated with the distribution of sensor information. The model was developed to estimate the velocity of the particles of ground vibrations. The system uses blast face distance and vibration monitoring point location as independent factors in an FL scheme. Prediction models using the FL are explored, where one such model is used to attempt to estimate ambient gamma radiation levels. The method of defect detection via FL data fusion is discussed. The FL is used to lessen the chances of mistakes and false positives. For settings with ambient intelligence, it is suggested to use a type-2 FL system. The system profiles users based on what it learns about their habits.

12.2.4   Data Fusion and Detection of Outliers

Fusion, prediction, consensus, and decision-making methods exist. WSNs have researched outlier detection extensively. Contains a comprehensive survey. Outlier detection methods include statistical decomposition. Statistics frequently need sensor data distribution expertise. Parametric techniques may not work in real life. Nearest neighbor algorithms are efficient for unilabiate but do not assume stream distribution. Multivariate closest-neighbor techniques are computationally costly. Multivariate data demand suitable input parameters and higher processing costs, rendering neighbor-based techniques unsalable. Clustering and neighbor-based algorithms have comparable limitations, whereas classification methods are computationally costly, Use the cumulative sum (Cum Sum) technique, which is computationally efficient and does not need streaming data distribution expertise.

12.2.5   Prediction Techniques

Time series forecasting is commonly used to predict future random variable values. Polynomial or linear predictors estimate future random variable values. Both linear and polynomial approaches need coefficient. Prediction can use neural networks. Brain networks process information like biological brain networks. Fast linear prediction is needed. The linear predictor allows the suggested MS to make rapid judgments. The methods are chosen because of their simplicity and quickness. When forecasting the sensor team's future value, the linear analyst is employed across a defined window of observations. Then, the prediction process begins, the predictor is performed.

12.2.6   Consensus Methods and Metrics

Authors compare consensus metrics. They compare entropy-based consensus with distance-based pairwise consensus. Favor similarity-based consensus and standard deviation-based consensus. Technology uses the metric. It compares group members' viewpoints. Unlike previous methods, it evaluates the consensus by evaluating each pair. Probabilistic or FL reasoning may aid decision-making. Probabilistic methods manage event occurrence. Fuzzy logic is a precise method of reasoning, computation, and deduction that associates discourse objects with imprecise, incomplete, unreliable, uncertain, partly true, or partially possible information.

12.3   Rationale

12.3.1   Description Scenario

A collection of n sensors S = {s1, s2, ..., sn} monitors specified regions of the same occurrence that reports their actual valued data X = {x1, x2, ..., xn} to MS. It infers events from incoming readings and informs registered end users/applications. The MS should indicate a fire incident if sensors assess ambient temperature or local fire risk increases. The team reports helping the MS to reduce false warnings and identify events. The MS bases alert on majority opinion.

The MS also addresses the problem that sensors might provide incorrect results (missing values, outliers) for numerous causes.

Random and linguistic uncertainty exists. Statistical mistakes in sensor readings cause random uncertainty, whereas linguistic ambiguity is caused by addressing each expert's phenomenon characterization. FL and type-2 fuzzy sets handle random and linguistic ambiguity. The uncertainty-controlling mechanism is on top of the fusion process, since sharp alert levels might cause false alarms. As the fusion process's final result, FL determines whether the measured or aggregated value is incorrect (because of random uncertainty), excessive (due to linguistic ambiguity), or inadequate. Decision-making methods based on thresholds would fail in this case. Second, a type-2 fuzzy logic system (FLS) incorporates both membership function uncertainty and sensor measurement uncertainty into its final output calculation. In a dynamic setting, such as a multisensory one, it is impossible for specialists in a membership function to have a complete view.

12.3.2   Fuzzy Set of Type 2

Type 2 is suggested for the MS's response to measurements. Type-1 FLS is avoided because it has limitations in its application environments. Type 2 manages more uncertainty than Type 1. Type 2 and Type 1 s vary in two ways:

    (i)   Adaptiveness: type-1 sets vary according to the change in input

    (ii) Innovation, the lower and upper membership functions of the same type-2 fuzzy set may be utilized concurrently to compute each limit of the type-reduced interval.

    (iii) Type-1 FLSs have restrictions. Type-1 FLSs have discrete memberships.

Experts should be able to define fuzzy variable membership degrees in type-1 FLSs. Experts cannot always determine the grade of membership. In that instance, unreliability is noticed in both the cases (e.g., whether a measurement is low or high) and the membership grades for each variable.

12.3.3   Driven Uncertainly Mechanism

The MS manages contextual data and makes decisions at each interval. Figure 12.1 depicts architecture. V This mechanism includes these processes:

(1) The fusion process: That shows sensor agreement and the prediction process analyzes the data to anticipate future aggregated measurements. (2) Type-2 fuzzy inference method: This method, which employs type-2 fuzzy sets to deal with membership function definition ambiguity, is implemented using a type-2 fuzzy logic system and incorporates fusion, consensus, and prediction. The degree of consensus, which is a real value in the range [0, 1], reflects the degree to which different sensors infer the

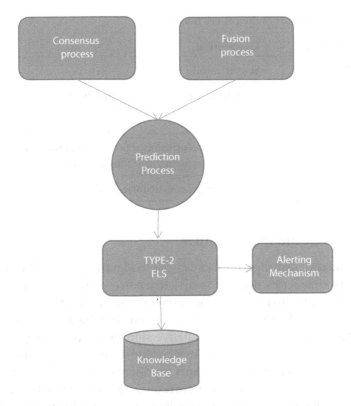

Figure 12.1 MS architecture processes fed to a type 2.

same phenomena. To evaluate the present risk, a degree of danger is calculated using a FIS method. If the DoD is more than a certain value, the MS will issue an alarm.

12.3.4   Fusion Data of Multi-Sensor

Multi-sensor data fusion produces accurate measurements using contextual data from n sensors. To comprehensively assess incoming data, we need observation that reflects the team's perspective on the phenomenon. Table 12.1 represents the different eliminating sensors that differ from the mean (measurement distribution) yields the fused measurement. These sensors enable "compact" measurements, remove outliers from measurements that disagree with the team. Using the remaining sensors, make the final measurement, use the cumulative sum idea drift method for outlier identification and the linear opinion pool approach for final total measurement.

Table 12.1 List of the paper's notations.

Notation	Description
S	Sensor count
W	Examined window (Integer number)
n	Sensor count
y	Fusion Process (instance program running in a computer) aggregated measurement
M	Prediction process historical values

12.3.5   Detection of an Outlier

The cumulative sum algorithm endeavors to identify any alterations in the contextual time series, denoted as $x_i[t]$, that corresponds to a sensor labeled as SI. This applies to n sensors and discrete time instances, represented by $t = 1, 2, \ldots$. The algorithm utilized in this study is a change point detection technique that relies on the cumulative sum of the disparities between the present value at time t and the mean value up to time t. The mean of the distribution of sensor measurements represents the overall average. The depiction of slopes in a series may correspond to potential outliers.

The likelihood densities of the analyzed variable, which is responsible for generating the signal, are denoted as h. Alternative methodologies entail utilizing the mean run length. One possible methodology involves the selection of either the mean detection delay or false alerts. The selection of h is crucial, as it has a significant impact on the identification of outliers. A smaller bandwidth (h) value is likely to result in a greater number of outliers, whereas a larger bandwidth value is expected to produce a smaller number of outliers. It is recommended to utilize training data and subsequently establish the appropriate value for h. The scheme we employ involves utilizing training data to determine the value of h. This approach was selected due to its computational efficiency in comparison to alternative methods, which may present challenges in developing an analytical model.

The cumulative sum algorithm generates a pair of signals as its output.

12.3.6   Sensor Confidence

A heuristic is used to assess c_i. A system is needed that reacts to events in real time instead of resource-intensive methods. The periodic window

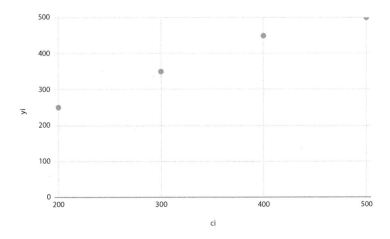

Figure 12.2 Plot ci is very low and MS decreases the level of the sensor.

technique tracks outlier occurrences for each sensor. The window size is W. The system records sensor behavior for W. The MS ignores outlier sensors with low ci that impact measurements aggregated with other data. ci for sensor SI is calculated t from t-W to The technique detects sensor outliers for each W. After W expires, outlier counts are reset to zero and a new era begins in the period [tW+1, t2W]. Thus, the technique removes prior behavior and does not penalize sensors for "abnormal" outlier occurrence rates in the previous frame. Figure 12.2 shows ci versus form and threshold.

12.3.7   FIS Process of Type 2

The anticipated value is determined using fused measurement history. Scalability depends mainly on fusion and consensus methods. The application domain's lowest and maximum values determine input normalization in [0,1]. If the MS detects a fire, limit the sensor temperature. DoD is also [0,1]. A DoD near unity indicates great risk, i.e., a strong opinion that a dangerous occurrence happens. DoD < 0. Three linguistic values—Low, Medium, and High—are considered for inputs and outputs. The values of the fuzzy variable are either low or high, correspondingly. In the context of fuzzy logic, the term "medium" refers to a fuzzy variable that exhibits a value in proximity to 0.5. An instance of a diminished y value suggests that the amalgamated calculation is in proximity to a lower threshold of sensors (such as zero for a temperature). The residual linguistic values are rationalized in a comparable manner. Type-2 fuzzy set-top and lower boundaries

Table 12.2 The sensor data reach the upper limit.

Rule	DoC input	DoD output
1	Any 2	Less
2	Less or Medium	Less
3	High	Medium
4	Less	Less
5	Medium or High	Medium
6	High	High
7	Any	High

are established by experts for each respective fuzzy set. Triangle membership functions are utilized for the sake of simplicity. Table 12.2 presents the rules pertaining to FL. In the event that the Department of Defense surpasses a predetermined threshold value within the range of zero to one, the monitoring system will issue an alert. Otherwise, it will proceed with generating sensor reports.

12.4   Performance Evolution

The suggested mechanism aims to improve accuracy, early detection and false alarms in test experiments by incorporating environmental parameters such as water and heat. Table 12.3 shows experimental system parameters. The test is conducted using a cross-validation approach with a model-trained. The Intel Berkeley Research Lab3 dataset comprises millions of measurements from 54 lab-deployed sensors. Fifteen sensors measured 1,000 temperatures, yielding 15,000 readings. Insert bogus numbers to test the proposed mechanism's false warnings. As these measurements do not identify any dangerous events, assume high temperature. Use genuine flood event data from water level sensors4. The riverbank had sensors. Use all available sensors to measure n = 10 sensors. Since the flood occurred in the past, the alarm probability is unity in this dataset. Here, 250 measurements before and during the flood are normalized in [0,1]. Use these data to determine whether the MS can detect the occurrence in time. Finally, obtain = 2 and = 5 for the confidence calculation because if one wants to discount the observations from any sensor that detects outliers for more

Table 12.3 The parameter readings.

Limits	Ranges
n Sensor	6,12,15
A fault of p-value	0.01,0.05,0.1,0.2,0.3,0.4,0.6
distance M	15,500,1000
window Down of w	20,500,1000
Missing value w	0.4, 0.6

than 5. With the Cum Sum technique, small values for h +, h -, k +, and k - in order to "easily" generate outliers and, therefore, to construct the total measurement on the top of data extremely near to the mean.

It contains five interrelated components i.e., fuzzifier, and rules base, Inference engine type reducer and DE fuzzifier. The Social Security Administration's system relies on. While it is true that a single sensor may readily deduce an alert, this is not the best technique since erroneous reporting could be the cause of a single reading. Instead of relying on individual readings, the suggested T2FLS determines the occurrence of an event only when team readings, together with comparable future projections of the aggregated reading, point to its presence. Similarly do a t-test analysis to see whether or not the boost approach provides statistically significant compared to the SSA. Table 12.4 displays the t-test cutoff points.

12.4.1 Comparison with a Type 1 in FIS

T2FLS and T1FLS are compared on Intel Berkeley Research Lab dataset with implanted incorrect values. T1FLS input: the measurement y and y^*.

Table 12.4 TIFLS base rule.

Rule	Y	DoD
1	Less	Less
3	Less	Medium
5	Less or Medium	Medium
6	High	High
8	Any	High

Table 12.5 Alert differentiation for Rof-SSA and RoFA-T2FLS.

P	Rof- SSA	RoFA-T2FLS
2%	1.057	10.010
4%	1.234	0.001
10%	1.234	0.002
16%	1.986	0.017

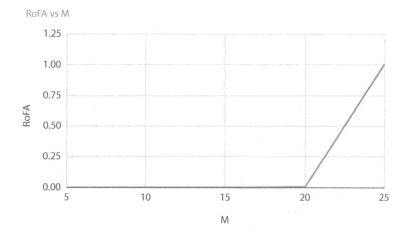

Figure 12.3 t values of m in difference in RoFA.

T1FLS does not use on DoC like T2FLS. The T1FLS also randomly selects ci for every sensor si in [0, 1]. Table 12.5 shows the T1FLS FL rule base. Figure 12.3 shows the RoFA different values of M.

12.4.2   Comparison with Other Models

Flood forecast and installation descriptions. Medium density fiberboard (MDF) tested on the upper Charles River. Three nodes—rainfall, temperature, and pressure—are from the suggested system. In this implementation, the model averages 10 false warnings (RoFA = 0.01). Evaluate the T2FLS with a simple prediction model (SPM) over sensor measurements using the Intel Berkeley Research Lab dataset with inserted incorrect values. When a sensor's historical value exceeds the threshold, the SPM alerts. The SPM averages the linear predictor from Section IV-D with a

Table 12.6 Alerts of fault difference of pie and p.

Percentage	RoFASSA	RoFAT2FLS	RoFAT2FLS
1%	0.123	0.0132	Zeros
4%	0.124	0.0133	Zeros
6%	0.125	0.0135	Zeros
18%	0.126	0.0137	Zeros
10%	0.129	0.0139	Zeros

polynomial predictor. SPM false alarms average 181% more than T2FLS. $n \to 15$ sensors provide similar results. The similarity of SPM is to the SSA mechanism, but it uses future sensor readings to "convey" the SSA's shortcomings. Table 12.6 represents of p and pie, which are false alerts.

12.4.3   Discussion on Sensor Coverage Impact

The sufficiency of sensors for the monitoring process is contingent upon the specific application, the area being observed, and the hardware utilized. Phenomena are interrelated and have a significant impact on each other.

The placement of sensors can be impacted by various issues that affect the coverage of the surrounding area. Numerous research endeavors are focused on the determination of the most effective placement of sensors and the resolution of the coverage issue. Sensor coverage models are representative of the sensing capacity and quality of sensors. Abstraction models are utilized to quantify the efficacy of sensors in detecting physical phenomena at specific locations.

The mathematical formulation of a sensor coverage model involves the use of a coverage function that takes into account the distance between a given point and the sensor's location. Various studies have indicated and hypothesized that varying applications may necessitate distinct levels of coverage. An exemplar scenario that necessitates extensive coverage is a military surveillance application. This is due to the requirement of monitoring a region through the simultaneous operation of multiple nodes. The rationale behind this is to ensure that the security of the area is not compromised even if some nodes fail to function. In certain cases, environmental monitoring applications may necessitate a minimal level of coverage.

12.5 Conclusions

A system is offered that integrates a suite of methods for integrating data from disparate sensors (contextual data streams) monitoring the same phenomena.

A fusion method to combine data from several sensors and filter irrelevant readings. Here, methods are discussed for deducing the degree to which a group of sensors agrees on an observation. For forecasting the team's future measurements, we can use time series prediction.

The reported measurements are subjected to a combination of the abovementioned methods, and the findings are input into a fuzzy logic system, which is then tasked with deducing the level of hazard associated with a given occurrence. Decisions in uncertain situations, such as those seen in dynamic settings or while defining membership functions, may be made with the help of the type-2 fuzzy logic system that has been presented. Simulations conducted using real-world context data demonstrate the effectiveness of the suggested method. A technique is demonstrated that can detect occurrences of phenomena early while reducing the number of false positives.

The forthcoming research endeavors entail the formulation of an adaptation method that is congruent with environmental attributes. This mechanism of adaptation will be discussed.

The task involves the provision of membership functions and the adaptation of a fuzzy rule base in accordance with predetermined performance metrics. The metrics under discussion are subject to the influence of environmental factors, as reported by a team of sensors. Consequently, the system exhibits complete alignment with alterations in the surroundings and possesses the capability to facilitate more universal applications.

References

1. Ullah, I., Youn, H.Y., Han, Y.H., Integration of type-2 fuzzy logic and dempster–shafer theory for accurate inference of Iot-based health-care system. *Future Gener. Comput. Syst.*, 124, 369–380, 2021.
2. Dhiman, N. and Sharma, M.K., IoMT tsukamoto type-2 fuzzy expert system in medical diagnostic. http://dx.doi.org/10.2139/ssrn.4117243
3. Kolomvatsos, K., Anagnostopoulos, C., Hadjiefthymiades, S., Data fusion and type-2 fuzzy inference in contextual data stream monitoring. *IEEE Trans. Syst. Man, Cybern. Syst.*, 47, 8, 1839–1853, 2016.

4. Yuan, X. *et al.*, A stable AI-based binary and multiple class heart disease prediction model for IoMT. *IEEE Trans. Industr. Inform.*, 18, 3, 2032–2040, 2021.

5. De Miguel, L. *et al.*, Extension of restricted equivalence functions and similarity measures for type-2 fuzzy sets. *IEEE Trans. Fuzzy Syst.*, 30, 9, 4005–4016, 2021.

6. Chakraborty, A. *et al.*, A framework of intelligent mental health monitoring in smart cities and societies. *IETE J. Res.*, 1–14, 2023, https://doi.org/10.1080/03772063.2023.2171918.

7. Yang, L. *et al.*, Generative adversarial learning for trusted and secure clustering in industrial wireless sensor networks. *IEEE Trans. Ind. Electron.*, 70, 8, 2023.

8. Rodríguez-Rodríguez, I., Rodríguez, J.V., Campo-Valera, M., Applications of the internet of medical things to type 1 diabetes mellitus. *Electronics,* 12, 3, 756, 2023.

9. Yeom, C.-U. and Kwak, K.-C., Adaptive neuro-fuzzy inference system predictor with an incremental tree structure based on a context-based fuzzy clustering approach. *Appl. Sci.*, 10, 23, 8495, 2020.

10. Sachdeva, P., Shukla, R., Sahani, A., A review on artificial pancreas and regenerative medicine used in the management of type 1 diabetes mellitus. *J. Med. Eng. Technol.*, 46, 8, 693–702, 2022.

11. Rocca, J., *GA Optimized Fuzzy Logic Controller for the Dissolved Oxygen Concentration in a Wastewater Bioreactor,* Thesis, University of Guelph, Ontario, Canada, 2012.

12. Shafqat, F., Khan, M.N.A., Shafqat, S., SmartHealth: IoT-enabled context-aware 5G ambient cloud platform, in: *IoT in Healthcare and Ambient Assisted Living*, pp. 43–67, Springer Singapore, Singapore, 2021.

13. Albahri, A.S. *et al.*, A systematic review of trustworthy and explainable artificial intelligence in healthcare: Assessment of quality, bias risk, and data fusion. *Inf. Fusion*, 96, 156–191, 2023.

14. Ferrag, M.A. *et al.*, Cyber security intrusion detection for agriculture 4.0: Machine learning-based solutions, datasets, and future directions. *IEEE/CAA J. Autom. Sin.*, 9, 3, 407–436, 2021.

15. Dhiman, G., Rashid, J., Kim, J., Juneja, S., Viriyasitavat, W., Gulati, K., Privacy for healthcare data using the byzantine consensus method. *IETE J. Res.*, 1–12, 2022, https://doi.org/10.1080/03772063.2022.2038288.

16. Griot, C., Modelling and simulation for critical infrastructure interdependency assessment: A meta-review for model characterisation. *Int. J. Crit. Infrastruct.*, 6, 4, 363–379, 2010.

17. Yadav, S.P., Blockchain security, in: *Blockchain Security in Cloud Computing. EAI/Springer Innovations in Communication and Computing*, K. Baalamurugan, S.R. Kumar, A. Kumar, V. Kumar, S. Padmanaban (Eds.), Springer, Cham, 2022, https://doi.org/10.1007/978-3-030-70501-5_1.

18. Batool, A., Hussain, M., Abidi, S.M.R., A brief review of big data used in healthcare organization-survey study. *J. NCBAE*, 1, 3, 2022.

19. Das, S. *et al.*, A combined neuro fuzzy-cellular automata based material model for finite element simulation of plane strain compression. *Comput. Mater. Sci.*, 40, 3, 366–375, 2007.

20. Hussain, S.M. and Begh, G.R., Hybrid heuristic algorithm for cost-efficient QoS aware task scheduling in fog–cloud environment. *J. Comput. Sci.*, 64, 101828, 2022.

21. Radulescu, C.Z. and Radulescu, M., A hybrid multi-criteria approach to the vendor selection problem for sensor-based medical devices. *Sensors*, 23, 2, 764, 2023.

22. Yadav, S.P. and Yadav, S., Fusion of medical images using a wavelet methodology: A survey, in: *IEIE Trans. Smart Process. Comput.*, Institute Electron. Engineers Korea, 8, 4, 265–271, 2019. https://doi.org/10.5573/ieiespc.2019.8.4.265.

23. Kennedy, E.P., *Control of Switched Reluctance Machines*, Thesis, Dublin City University, Ireland, 2005.

24. Heidari, A. and Jabraeil Jamali, M.A., Internet of Things intrusion detection systems: A comprehensive review and future directions. *Cluster Comput.*, 26, 6, 3753–3780, 2022.

25. Gurugubelli, S., Chekuri, R.B.R., Kumar, T.R., The method combining laser welding and induction heating at high temperatures was performed. *Des. Eng.*, 592–602, 2021.

26. Viera, E., Kaschel, H., Valencia, C., Heart rate variability control using a biofeedback and wearable system. *Sensors*, 22, 19, 7153, 2022.

13

Feature Extraction and Diagnosis of Heart Diseases Using Fuzzy-Based IoMT

Tribhangin Dichpally*, Yatish Wutla, Vallabhaneni Uday and Rohith Sai Midigudla

Department of Computer Science Engineering with Specialization in Artificial Intelligence and Machine Learning, Vellore Institute of Technology, Amaravati, India

Abstract

Asthma, cancer, heart disease, and diabetes are prevalent global health challenges. Distinguishing between various types of heart diseases can be challenging. The utilization of smart wearables necessitates the implementation of fog computing and Internet of Things (IoT) solutions in medical diagnosis. The utilization of edge, fog, and cloud computing is recommended for achieving efficient and precise results. The hardware is responsible for the collection of patient data. Cardiac properties are assessed by extracting signals. The compilation of feature extraction from other properties is also undertaken. The optimized cascaded convolution neural network (CCNN) is utilized by the diagnostic system to obtain these properties. The hyperparameters of the CCNN are optimized through the utilization of galactic swarm optimization (GSO). The GSO-CCNN model exhibits an accuracy of 3.70% when compared to other models such as LSTM, CNN, and CCNN. The results indicate that the proposed approach can be considered a dependable improvement over the current approach.

Keywords: IoMT, database, CNN, galactic of utilization, GSO

*Corresponding author: tribhangin@gmail.com

Satya Prakash Yadav, Sudesh Yadav, Pethuru Raj Chelliah and Victor Hugo C. de Albuquerque (eds.) Advances in Fuzzy-Based Internet of Medical Things (IoMT), (195–210) © 2024 Scrivener Publishing LLC

13.1   Introduction

The current economy relies on cloud and fog computing concepts to supply on-demand service resources to consumers. Industry and academics depend on these disciplines [1, 2]. Cloud computing's high reaction time disqualifies it from real-time applications. Because they may provide varying response levels depending on the intended uses, big data analytics, cloud computing, Internet of Things (IoT), and edge computing have all been developed [3–5]. Since edge devices may leverage processing, storage, and communication to enhance networks such as security system, privacy, and flexibility, cloud computing is preferable for real-time or latency-sensitive applications [6]. New applications may now use the robust infrastructure and services made available by cloud computing frameworks [7]. Energy consumption and network latency have all been reduced with gateways, nodes, and routers in fog computing [8–10]. Recent studies of fog computing's use in healthcare have shown that minimizing response and processing times is among the most challenging and vital Quality of Service (QoS) constraints [11–13].

Healthcare is the most critical application sector requiring accurate and real-time "fog computing" outcomes for beneficial advances [14]. Fog computing may improve healthcare security by bringing resources closer to consumers to reduce latency [15]. Early findings allow critical cardiac patients to be treated faster. It delivers results quickly, but complex data and high accuracy make it problematic. Thus, new research employing deep learning and its many variants on a large dataset may reach great accuracy [16–18]. Current methods collect healthcare data via file input data and IoT sensors, notably for heart patients. Healthcare patient data are downloaded at 250 MB per minute or more [19]. Cloud and edge resources are needed to capture and provide data and video for high-volume applications. The data collected from IoT networks' intelligent devices are stored and analyzed by either cloud servers or edge nodes [20–22]. "Edge-Fog-Cloud-derived computation model" to provide cardiac patients with expert computer services other people that require actual results to convey healthcare and other results with low response time, energy use, and high accuracy [23–25].

13.2   Literature Survey

Satyanarayana's health fog system uses edge computer devices and integrated deep learning to diagnose heart problems autonomously. This healthcare service architecture manages cardiac patient data and collects

IoT data as a fog service. Fog bus was used to install and evaluate the recommended model's execution time and power consumption. This health fog approach offers enhanced QoS and forecast accuracy for numerous fog computing scenarios.

Using modified slap swarm optimization (MSSO) and adaptive neuro-fuzzy inference system (ANFIS), Khan and Algarni devised an internet of medical things (IoMT) system for cardiac illness diagnosis that improved search ability using the Levy fly approach. Historically, input data were collected from medical records to determine cardiovascular disease risk factors. These factors included glucose levels, cholesterol levels, chest discomfort, sex, age, BP, and more. It is possible that ANFIS's diagnostic, which relied on gradient-based learning using a standard learning procedure, was stuck in a cycle of local minima. An optimal result for ANFIS, the learning parameters were optimized using the MSSO method. When compared to other approaches, the findings from the developed MSSO-ANFIS model are encouraging.

S. K. Sood and I. Mahajan created an "adaptive neuro-fuzzy inference system" to identify high-risk coronary heart disease sooner using a cloud-based cyber-physical localization system. This approach tracked high- or middle-risk cardiac disease using ECG measurements. If ECG readings are abnormal, messages are sent to users' phones and healthcare professionals to take quick action to monitor patients' health. The simulations showed that the model classified danger levels quickly and accurately.

"IoT-enabled ECG captures dynamic features" retrieved statistical data and analyzed them using the "Pan Tompkins QRS detection" approach to generate dynamic features. The classification step used "dynamic and statistical features" to predict cardiac arrhythmia. This model analyzes ECG

Table 13.1 Advantages and traditional methods of an IoT health of heart disease.

Methodology	Features	Challenges facing
Ensembled learning process	The prediction offered in time	The performing is enhanced with various selection techniques
DLMNN	High security is returned in less minutes	Feature selection for enhancing the predictive ones.
MDCNN	It is often high level/ saves	Tested using wear devices

data for cardiac risk. General practitioners might readily assess cardiac disease using this model.

Many medical systems use the Internet of Things to gather sensor information to diagnose and predict cardiac problems. Despite many studies on the diagnosis of heart disease, results are inaccurate. Table 13.1 describes heart disease IoT healthcare approaches. Based on this research, IoT healthcare needs new strategies to accurately identify cardiac disease early on.

13.3   Prediction of Heart Disease by IoMT

The provision of Internet services has grown more reliant on IoT and cloud computing in recent years. Since medical datasets tend to be large, edge and fog computing frameworks are used to provide consumers with low-latency, energy-efficient services while addressing issues with latency, security, privacy, mobility, and network capacity. Applications that need real-time or low-latency processing make use of fog computing in tandem with cloud services. Due to the better processing capabilities of edge devices or fog nodes, cardiac patient data may be handled successfully in a fog computing environment. When compared to traditional cloud data centers, this method may dramatically reduce delay, response time, and latency. Despite the requirement to handle a greater number of patients with cardiac problems, current systems display increased reaction times, workloads, resource utilization, and energy usage. The system's design and architecture are shown in Figure 13.1.

The system referred to as the "prediction of intelligent heart disease framework" collects patient data related to heart conditions through the utilization of Internet of Things devices. The computer hardware mechanisms encompassing ecological, medical, and activity sensors on patients are of significant importance. The collection of bodily measurements encompasses a range of parameters, activity level, BP, ECG report, oxygen saturation level, breathing rate, and ECG. Servers analyze heart disease prediction data and provide them to worker or broker nodes. From the above given data, the worker will extract the independent parameters. The lowest and maximum mean, standard deviation, and autocorrelation values provide additional structures. Fog bus powers the intelligent heart disease prediction system that uses broker, worker, and cloud data centers. Based on retrieved characteristics, optimized cascaded convolutional neural networks (CCNNs) forecast heart illness. Galactic swarm optimization (GSO) optimizes cascaded network layers, hidden neurons, and CCNN

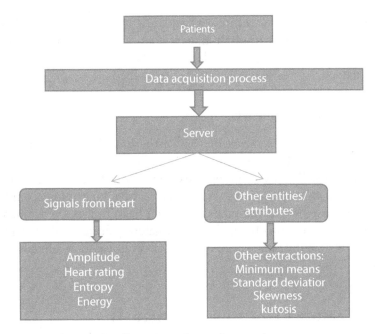

Figure 13.1 Prediction of intelligent heart disease framework.

activation functions. The heart disease detection model reduces mean square error (MSE) prediction loss. Normal and abnormal output categories provide system monitoring and safety.

13.3.1   Configuration of the System

This "lightweight fog service" enables intelligent heart illness prediction system analyses IoT and smart device data from heart patients. This fog bus model predicts cardiac problems. Fog bus is a platform-free cloud-fog deployment and development framework. This structure sends tasks and data to fog worker nodes from numerous "healthcare sensors with gateway devices" IoT sensors. Fog broker nodes also handle tasks and resources. Using encryption, authentication, and blockchain, a security manager makes this environment resilient and reliable. Fog bus also uses HTTP RESTful APIs for cloud integration.

13.3.2   IoT

Smart healthcare merges hardware and software for "end-to-end integration of Edge-Fog-Cloud" for accurate and fast results. Hardware, software.

Three sensors—environment, activity, and medical—provide data. Medical sensors include glucose, respiration, temperature, oxygen, EMG, EEG, and ECG. Gateway devices—tablets, laptops, and phones—transfer cardiac patient data.

13.3.3   Deep Framework

The third step involves the utilization of the deep learning unit, which employs the data to train convolutional neural network (CCNN) to classify the "data points." These data points are essentially feature vectors obtained. As a result of this, the forecast is formulated by taking into account the assignment assigned to the manager, which has produced a diminished quantity of information obtained from the gateway devices. Ultimately, the findings indicate the presence or absence of cardiovascular ailment in the patient.

13.4   Feature Extraction from Signals

Peak amplitude, total harmonic distortion, heart rate, zero-crossing rate, entropy, "standard deviation," and energy are calculated from the gathered signals Y to perform feature extraction. It helps in cleaning up datasets by eliminating unnecessary information. It boosts learning velocity by decreasing computing complexity and expanding the number of generalization stages in the prediction. The new features are a condensed version of the old ones.

13.4.1   Overall Current Distortion of Signal

According to the definition given in, the proportion of the total power of all harmonic components to the power of the fundamental frequency is the proper definition of HD, which is formulated in

$$thd = \sum_{v=0}^{n/h} H \qquad (13.1)$$

the maximum harmonic order is termed as the harmonic order vth amplitude is derived as hv, and the amount of samples per period is denoted as N and the harmonic order is denoted as h.

13.4.2   The Entropy Function

It "measures the signal deviation from the mean." This fluctuation's power is assessed in variance.

$$dt = \sum = |X|2 \tag{13.2}$$

Finally, dt and X2 are the total number of features identified from signals.

13.4.3   Mean of Minimum and Maximum

Dataset mean calculated by addition to values and the data division.

$$\mu = \frac{\sum_y d}{d} \tag{13.3}$$

The dataset's total values are d, and all values are yd. The lowest and biggest values in the dataset are minimum of the mean and the maximum values.

13.5   Optimized Cascaded CNN

The model predicts cardiac disorders using CCNN. It processes signal and data characteristics. GSO algorithm optimizes CCNN layers, hidden neurons, and activation functions. This improves cardiac disease detection to maximize prediction rate and reduce error. CNN layers form CCNN. CNNs are convolutional, pooling, and fully linked feedforward neural networks. To optimize the prediction rate and minimize error, this enhances heart disease diagnosis. CNNs are a kind of feedforward neural network that combines convolutional, pooling, and fully connected layers. CNN architecture. Local perception using a convolution kernel in a rectangular input data area yields a feature map. Weight sharing distributes convolution kernel biases and weights for each feature map. Pooling summarizes and reduces the feature map. Maximum and average pooling also maximize or intermediate smaller feature map areas. Without affecting the retrieved characteristics, these data are minimized the threshold in the cascaded network. The CNN convolution layer receives data and signals characteristics, which are then sent to the pooling layer. The fully connected layer computes the entropy loss, which is 00.4 if the CCNN has just one network or less than the threshold if the combining layer output passed to the initial layer of the following net. The utilization of fully linked layers yields outcomes that are systematically classified. The threshold is a concept that denotes a specific point or level at which a particular phenomenon or event is triggered or becomes significant. The cascaded convolutional neural network (CCNN) is optimized through the implementation of a poured net, unseen nerve cell, and activation function layers. The GSO algorithm exhibits a superior recognition rate. The optimized CCNN design, which has been optimized using GSO, is depicted in Figure 13.2.

In convolutional neural network activation functions, there are 5–25 hidden neurons. The completely linked layer calculates the entropy loss. The limit of is often employed in the last convolutional layer to boost output nonlinearity. Fewer neurons are engaged in the processing of ReLU.

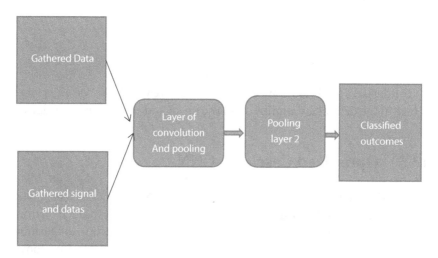

Figure 13.2 The GSO optimized CCNN design.

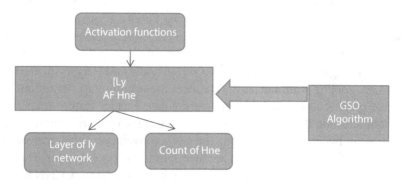

Figure 13.3 CCN with GSO parameter.

It takes six times as long for the sigmoid and tanh activation functions to converge. When there are no gradients, leaky ReLU is employed. Any real integer may be converted to a value between 0 and 1 using the sigmoid activation function. The encoded solution of the CCNN model is seen in Figure 13.3.

13.5.1   GSO

The GSO method is used in an intelligent healthcare model that employs IoT-assisted fog (Figure 13.4) computing to improve the accuracy with which cardiac illnesses may be predicted. The activation function, hidden neurons, and hidden layers of a cascaded network may all be optimized using this method. The mistake rate is reduced while the accuracy rate is increased, thanks to this optimization. Because of its many advantages, including the ability to get local optimal solutions, a quicker convergence rate, the ability to obtain local solutions in order to obtain the global optimum, and the ability to strike a good balance between the exploitation and exploration phases, the GSO algorithm has been chosen for this problem. Furthermore, new research claims decreased computing time and greater

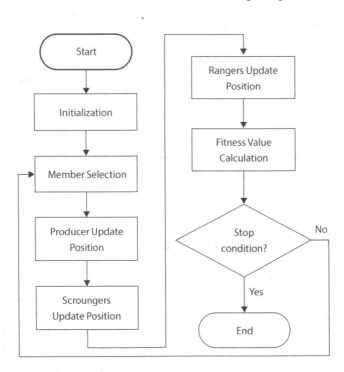

Figure 13.4 GSO algorithm flowchart.

accuracy using this technique. It is one of the metaheuristic optimization algorithms that take cues from nature. The motion of "blissful forms" like clusters and stars in response to the pull of gravity inspired this method. Here, the whole galaxy is believed to be a "point mass," which, by reducing the potential energy of neighboring galaxies, makes it intriguing. People are sorted into groups according to their numbers, and those in each group gravitate toward the most effective solutions. This approach allows for several iterations to get the best possible local optimum. In addition, the problem of convergence to a local minimum is solved during the exploration stage, resulting in a quicker convergence rate than is possible with other current methods. These mini-galaxies, often called subswarms, are home to several stars. Subswarm comprises a group of G of K tuples with figures as and B partitions of size. The entire swarm structure initializes G components randomly from incoming data.

$$Y \ CG; \ a[1,B],$$

$$G \ CY; \ a[1,K],$$ (13.4)

$$Y = G$$

Best subswarms help build superswarms or superclusters construction of superwarms or superclusters is performed, while best subwarms assist in the next phase of clustering. Hence, the superswarm includes every subswarm. Equations update superswarm location and velocity below.

$$p_{i,j} = (v_{i,j} + p_{i,j})$$ (13.5)

The global best galaxy, p, is updated only if a better galaxy is found. The superswarm idea includes the finest galaxies worldwide, improving exploitation.

13.6   Results and Discussion

MATLAB 2020a ran the cardiac diagnostic model provided. The system's effectiveness was compared to standard models using performance criteria. Design model was analyzed with different optimization algorithms like particle swarm optimization (PSO) [16], gray wolf optimization (GWO) [17], whale optimization algorithm (WOA) [18], and deer hunting optimization algorithm (DHOA) [19] with the GSO-based CCNN and some classifiers like deep neural networks (DNN) [20], Recurrent Neural Networks (RNN) [21], Long Short-Term Memory (LSTM) [22], CNN [23], and CCNN [14]. e system configuration has been added in here. Experimentation was performed on Intel core i3 processor, RAM size 4 GB, and system type 64-bit OS, x64-based processor, and windows 10 edition, and 21H1 version.

13.6.1   Analysis Based on Heuristic Techniques

Existing metaheuristic-based algorithms are used to evaluate the built smart heart disease prediction system (Figure 13.5). In order to demonstrate the efficacy of a newly constructed GSO-CCNN in the detection of heart disease, the learning percentages are varied from 76% to 85% and the network is tested using several conventional performance metrics. The proposed c4.5 has much better accuracy than competing methods. Accuracy, however, is maintained at the same levels as other methods at the beginning of the learning process. The intended Bayes net has a greater error rate at early percentages of the Fumarate and nitrate reductase (FNR) measure, but this drops down after approximately 84%. NB and BAYNET also achieve superior performance when compared with other performance metrics, that the prediction rate is higher when fog is used in conjunction with IoT technology.

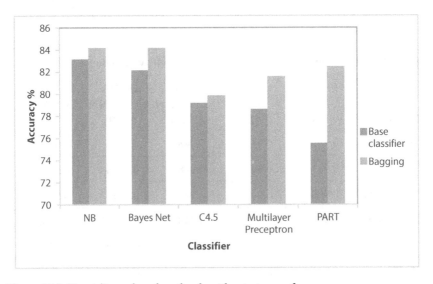

Figure 13.5 Heart disease based on the algorithm in terms of accuracy.

13.6.2   Comparative Analysis

Table 13.2 shows the effectiveness of the intelligent health care system with IoT-assisted fog computing for various metaheuristic-based algorithms and classifiers. GSO-CCNN is 40% and 3.7% more accurate. The intelligent healthcare approach also outperformed traditional procedures. The below table represents this.

Table 13.2 Analysis of the smart healthcare model.

Measures	PSO-CCNN [16]	GWO-CCNN [17]	WOA-CCNN [18]	DHOA-CCNN [19]	GSO-CCNN
"Accuracy"	0.9408	0.9366	0.9344	0.9481	0.9499
"Sensitivity"	0.9362	0.9264	0.9208	0.9926	0.93483
"Specificity"	0.9454	0.9468	0.948	0.9036	0.9725
"Precision"	0.94489	0.94569	0.94655	0.91148	0.98077
"FPR"	0.0546	0.0532	0.052	0.964	0.0275
"FNR"	0.0638	0.0736	0.0792	0.0074	0.065167
"NPV"	0.9454	0.9468	0.948	0.9036	0.9725

Table 13.3 The comparative of smart healthcare mdel with based algorithm.

Measures	PSO-CCNN [16]	GWO-CCNN [17]	WOA-CCNN [18]	DHOA-CCNN [19]	GSO-CCNN
"Accuracy"	0.9508	0.9433	0.9483	0.9405	0.9721
"Sensitivity"	0.951	0.94	0.9482	0.9314	0.97667
"Specificity"	0.9506	0.9466	0.9484	0.9496	0.96525
"Precision"	0.95062	0.94625	0.94839	0.94867	0.97683
"FPR"	0.0494	0.0534	0.0516	0.0504	0.03475
"FNR"	0.049	0.06	0.0518	0.0686	0.023333
"NPV"	0.9506	0.9466	0.9484	0.9496	0.96525

13.6.3 K-Fold Validation

Table 13.3 shows the relative investigation of the recommended intelligent healthcare system with IoT-assisted fog computing using k-fold validation for varied metaheuristic-based algorithms and classifiers, with k=5. Cross-validation resamples machine learning models on a small dataset.

The proposed GSO-CCNN algorithm is more accurate and effective than existing algorithms. At early learning percentages, the maintains precision like others. But while raising the performance improves with higher learning percentages.

13.7 Conclusion

The goal of this research is to use edge, fog, and cloud computing to usher in a new intelligent healthcare paradigm. The suggested model takes into account data from various pieces of hardware. Signals have been analyzed to determine their cardiac properties by computing parameters such as their entropy, standard deviation, and energy. By computing statistical metrics, minimum and maximum values, qualitative characteristics have been achieved. Convolutional neural networks and the gradient search optimization technique for optimizing CNN parameters enabled the diagnostic system's features. In this research, the CCNN's hyperparameters, including its hidden neurons, activation function, and outer layers, were optimized using the grid search optimization method. Based on the evaluation findings, the GSO-CCNN outperforms the DNN, RNN, LSTM, CNN, and CCNN, as well as the PSO-CCNN and DHOA-CCNN. The intelligent healthcare paradigm has seen encouraging results from the combination of the Internet of Things and fog computing. Incorporating state-of-the-art feature selection methods, optimization techniques, and classification algorithms into the proposed model has been suggested as a means of enhancing the performance of the system for predicting the occurrence of cardiac sickness. It has been determined that this variant may be used effectively in emergency circumstances when speedy action is required.

References

1. Wagan, S.A., Koo, J., Siddiqui, I.F., Qureshi, N.M.F., Attique, M., Shin, D.R., A fuzzy-based duo-secure multi-modal framework for IoMT anomaly detection. *J. King Saud Univ.-Comput. Inf. Sci.*, 35, 1, 131–144, 2023.

2. Alamelu, V. and Thilagamani, S., Lion based butterfly optimization with improved YOLO-v4 for heart disease prediction using IoMT. *Inf. Technol. Control*, *51*, 4, 692–703, 2022.

3. Bhagat, R.K., Yadav, A., Rajoria, Y.K., Raj, S., Boadh, R., Study of fuzzy and artificial neural network (ANN) based techniques to diagnose heart disease. *J. Pharm. Negat. Results*, 13, 5, 1023–1029, 2022.

4. Mazhar, T., Nasir, Q., Haq, I., Kamal, M.M., Ullah, I., Kim, T., Alwadai, N., A novel expert system for the diagnosis and treatment of heart disease. *Electronics*, *11*, 23, 3989, 2022.

5. Parveen, K., Daud, M., Siddiqu, S.Y., Smart detection of cardiovascular disease using gradient descent optimization. *Lahore Garrison Univ. Res. J. Comput. Sci. Inf. Technol.*, *6*, 03, 35–42, 2022.

6. Guo, C. *et al.*, Recursion enhanced random forest with an improved linear model (RERF-ILM) for heart disease detection on the internet of medical things platform. *IEEE Access*, 8, 59247–59256, 2020.

7. Meenal, M.R. and Vennila, S.M., Bidirectional recurrent network and neuro-fuzzy frequent pattern mining for heart disease prediction. *SN Comput. Sci.*, 4, 4, 379, 2023.

8. Rajkumar, G., Devi, T.G., Srinivasan, A., Heart disease prediction using IoT based framework and improved deep learning approach: Medical application. *Med. Eng. Phys.*, *111*, 103937, 2023.

9. Panja, S. *et al.*, Fuzzy-logic-based IoMT framework for COVID19 patient monitoring. *Comput. Ind. Eng.*, 176, 108941, 2023.

10. Safa, M., Pandian, A., Gururaj, H.L., Ravi, V., Krichen, M., Real time health care big data analytics model for improved QoS in cardiac disease prediction with IoT devices. *Health Technol.*, 4, 1–1, 2023 Apr.

11. Tarish, H.A., SS-FD: Internet of medical things based patient health monitoring system. *Period. Eng. Nat. Sci.*, 9, 3, 641–651, 2021.

12. Kavitha, D., Vidhya, A., Prema, V., Priyadharshini, M., Kumaresan, G., Sangeetha, G., An efficient IoMT based health monitoring using complex valued deep CNN and political optimizer. *Trans. Emerg. Telecommun. Technol.*, 1, e4610, 2022 Dec.

13. Rezaee, K., Yang, X., Khosravi, M.R., Zhang, R., Lin, W., Jeon, G., Fusion-based learning for stress recognition in smart home: An IoMT framework. *Build. Environ.*, *216*, 108988, 2022.

14. Yadav, S.P. and Yadav, S., Fusion of medical images in wavelet domain: A discrete mathematical model. *Ing. Solidaria*, 14, 25, 1–11, 2018. Universidad Cooperativa de Colombia- UCC. https://doi.org/10.16925/.v14i0.2236.

15. Awotunde, J.B. *et al.*, An enhanced cloud-IoMT-based and machine learning for effective COVID-19 diagnosis system, in: *Intelligence of Things: AI-IoT Based Critical-Applications and Innovations*, pp. 55–76, 2021.

16. Pirbhulal, S., Wu, W., Li, G., A biometric security model for wearable health-care, in: *2018 IEEE International Conference on Data Mining Workshops (ICDMW)*, 2018, November, IEEE, pp. 136–143.

17. Chen, L. *et al.*, ECG signal-enabled automatic diagnosis technology of heart failure. *J. Healthc. Eng.*, 2021, 1–28, 2021.
18. Neog, H., Dutta, P.E., Medhi, N., Health condition prediction and covid risk detection using healthcare 4.0 techniques. *Smart Health*, 26, 100322, 2022.
19. Kumar, S. *et al.*, Internet of Medical Thing and FIS evaluation for selecting and delivering the best health insurance coverage. *J. Pharm. Negat. Results*, 13, 8, 3438–3446, 2022.
20. Pap, I.A. and Oniga, S., A review of converging technologies in eHealth pertaining to artificial intelligence. *Int. J. Environ. Res. Public Health*, 19, 18, 11413, 2022.
21. Awotunde, J.B. *et al.*, Internet of medical things for enhanced smart healthcare systems, in: *Implementation of Smart Healthcare Systems using AI, IoT, and Blockchain*, pp. 1–28, Academic Press, 2023. file:///C:/Users/hp/Downloads/Artificial_Intelligence_Blockchain_and_IoT_for_Sma.pdf
22. Naresh, V.S., Pericherla, S.S., Murty, P.S.R., Sivaranjani, R., Internet of Things in Healthcare: Architecture, applications, challenges, and solutions. *Comput. Syst. Sci. Eng.*, 35, 6, 411–421, 2020.
23. Kaur, J., Saxena, J., Shah, J., Fahad, Yadav, S.P., Facial emotion recognition, in: *2022 International Conference on Computational Intelligence and Sustainable Engineering Solutions (CISES). 2022 International Conference on Computational Intelligence and Sustainable Engineering Solutions (CISES)*, IEEE, 2022, https://doi.org/10.1109/cises54857.2022.9844366.
24. Singh, C., Rao, M.S.S., Mahaboobjohn, Y.M., Kotaiah, B., Kumar, T.R., Applied machine tool data condition to predictive smart maintenance by using artificial intelligence, in: *Emerging Technologies in Computer Engineering: Cognitive Computing and Intelligent IoT*, ICETCE 2022. Communications in Computer and Information Science, vol. 1591, V.E. Balas, G.R. Sinha, B. Agarwal, T.K. Sharma, P. Dadheech, M. Mahrishi, (Eds.), Springer, Cham, 2022, https://doi.org/10.1007/978-3-031-07012-9_49.
25. Hayyolalam, V. *et al.*, Edge-assisted solutions for IoT-based connected healthcare systems: A literature review. *IEEE Internet Things J.*, 9, 12, 9419–9443, 2021.

14

An Intelligent Heartbeat Management System Utilizing Fuzzy Logic

K. Suresh Kumar[1]*, R. Sudha[2], T. Suguna[3] and M. K. Dharani[4]

[1]MBA Department, Panimalar Engineering College, Varadarajapuram,
Poonamallee, Chennai, India
[2]Department of CSE, Vasavi College of Engineering, Hyderabad, India
[3]Department of ECE, Panimalar Engineering College, Chennai, India
[4]Department of Artificial Intelligence, Kongu Engineering College, Erode,
Tamil Nadu, India

Abstract

Currently, there is a growing interest in the area of health monitoring management. Since all family members are likely to be busy and occupied, monitoring the health status of elderly individuals has been an increasingly critical matter. The present study aims to investigate a system has that been devised to enable caretakers to access the temperature and pulse rate data of individuals under their care who are being monitored at home. It is possible to obtain data regarding the air quality within a household, which can subsequently prompt the system to produce an alert if any hazardous gases are identified. A fuzzy logic methodology has been employed to perform and analyze the data obtained from temperature, heart rate, and gas sensors. Outliers will be detected by utilizing both trained data and sensor data. The data that have been gathered and transmitted to the cloud have the capability of being retrieved through the utilization of the ThingSpeak platform. The forthcoming research endeavors involve automating message transmission to carer and physicians through deep learning techniques after identifying outliers.

Keywords: IoT, fuzzy logic, data analysis, automate message transmission

*Corresponding author: pecmba19@gmail.com

Satya Prakash Yadav, Sudesh Yadav, Pethuru Raj Chelliah and Victor Hugo C. de Albuquerque (eds.)
Advances in Fuzzy-Based Internet of Medical Things (IoMT), (211–224) © 2024 Scrivener Publishing LLC

14.1 Introduction

The processing power of the future will go much beyond with current technology. The Internet of Things (IoT) is a cutting-edge technology that will soon be embedded in almost every physical item that encounter. The use of radio frequency identification and sensors to set up its autonomous environment, controlled and connected over the Internet. These gadgets will generate their ecosystems. With cloud computing, individuals and organizations can access programmers on demand and from anywhere. The healthcare industry is one of the most significant potential users of the Internet of Things. In this project, a health monitoring gadget that uses inexpensive sensors already on the market was developed to track vital signs, including heart rate, body temperature, and humidity.

Fuzzy logic (FL) has been implemented. Lotfi Zadeh first proposed the idea of fuzzy logic in the year 1966. In fuzzy logic, truth values may be any nonnegative integer that ranges from 0 to 5. Partial truths, in which the truth value may be anywhere from fully false to completely true, are handled by fuzzy logic. Fuzzification, inference, and defuzzification are the three main components of a fuzzy logic method.

- **Fuzzification**
  The sensors collect the raw data as input, and then the membership functions transform the data into a fuzzy collection of words and variables based on human language.
- **Defuzzification**
  The crisp output is obtained by mapping the fuzzy output using membership functions.

The algorithm employed in the implementation of fuzzy logic is outlined below:

1. The process of defining and establishing terminology and variables.
2. Initialize the rule.
3. In order to convert crisp input to fuzzy input, it is necessary to utilize membership functions.
4. Utilize the guidelines for imprecise input.
5. The process of transforming imprecise or uncertain output into a precise and definite output is known as converting fuzzy output to crisp output.

- **Inference**
  Inference is reached by using the guidelines. The system will function according to a predefined set of rules, much like an IF-THEN statement.

14.2 Literature Survey

The provision of healthcare services for elderly individuals who desire to maintain their independence is illustrated in the scholarly article denoted as [1].

To effectively monitor and maintain one's health condition, it is recommended that an individual utilizes a wearable device. This device tracks the individual's health status and facilitates communication with their concerned person and medical professionals. Data collection is enabled through sensors and wireless networks, storing the collected data in a case for communication purposes. In case of emergency, a notification has to be transmitted to the designated carer and medical professionals registered in the system. A physician can provide medical advice to patients residing in remote areas and issue prescriptions for necessary medications. This system has the potential to serve as a medication reminder.

The use of fuzzy logic in manufacturing processes is discussed [2]. Fuzzy logic is being utilized as a language control protocol for expert operations to bridge the gap between theoretical and mathematical operations. The current use of this strategy is for real-world applications in factories and pilot plants. This article highlights some of the benefits of using FIS. The potential of fuzzy logic is also discussed. An alternative for Mamdani inference is presented in article [3]. This is beneficial over the original method in that it shortens reaction times and simplifies complicated calculations, making it ideal for measuring the time spent participating in sporting events. This revised approach has a broad use in sports and strenuous physical training [4].

Maintain optimal performance by consistently monitoring the temperature and assessing the monitor's status for any potential problems. Any time their temperature or pulse rate changes, or if one goes over or below a certain threshold, their loved ones or carers will be alerted promptly. A wearer's current position is also obtained. Daily reports and data will be produced and stored in the cloud. This facilitates the regular reporting of patient data that clinicians may use as necessary retrieved from the cloud using ThingSpeak [5], an open-source IoT platform. In addition, MATLAB is supported, allowing for data analysis and visualization. Sending data from an Arduino, Beagle Bone Black, or Raspberry Pi is possible. ThingSpeak will enable us to not only log on to our sensor app but also monitor its precise position in real time. The information will be gathered and analyzed using the ThingSpeak IoT platform. ThingSpeak will function as a go-between for various sensors and software, as well as a data collector that pulls information from multiple devices into a centralized database.

A fundamental component of ThingSpeak, the Channel will include not just a location field but also data and status fields. The data are recorded in channels, analyzed and visualized using MATLAB, and responded to by alerts and tweets.

The theory, consequences, and uses of fuzzy logic are explained in article [6].

There is a linear relationship between input and output, and all implications describe the fuzzy inputs that cause that relationship to exist. The system's input and output identifiers that also need to be specified are mentioned as well. Fuzzy logic is described in the context of its use in industrial operations, particularly in water purification and the production of steel.

How body sensor networks might be most effectively used within the healthcare system is discussed in article [7]. The Internet of Things and the rising popularity of wearable technology have sparked a flurry of daily innovation [8].

In particular, wearable devices and smart objects in the healthcare domain. In this research, we propose a "body sensor network" (BSN) to connect various wearable sensors to one another [9–11]. They also focused on the safety concerns of an Internet of Things-based health monitoring system [12]. The BSN network will be used to power this system. This system is based on the Raspberry Pi platform, which allows for a high degree of security and efficiency, thanks to the use of cryptographic primitives in the construction of the communication system and authentication of smart devices and BSN [13–15].

14.3   Implementation of the System Design

14.3.1   Architecture System

The diagram depicted in Figure 14.1 illustrates the system architecture of our health monitoring system based on IoT technology, which utilizes fuzzy logic [16, 17]. The system has been engineered to function within an Internet of Things ecosystem. The patient will be equipped with an air quality sensor, temperature sensor, and pulse sensor nearby [18].

The implementation of sensors positioned on and in proximity to the patient enables the acquisition of the patient's health status and air quality,

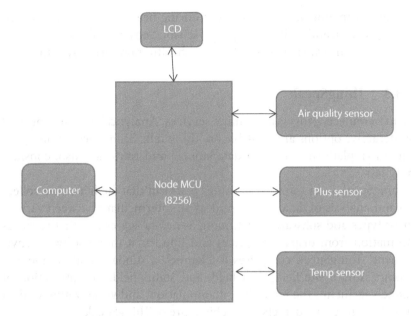

Figure 14.1 Architecture of the system.

which is subsequently transmitted to the target device via the NodeMCU ESP8266 microcontroller [19–21]. The data obtained from the microcontroller are sent to the cloud via Wi-Fi in order to facilitate the visualization and analysis of the data. It is possible to retrieve previously collected sensor data based on date and time. The data that have been gathered are retrievable via the ThingSpeak Internet of Things platform [22–24].

The most popular of the fuzzy techniques, the Mamdani inference method, has been used here. The Mamdani approach, which is based on min-max operations, is the simplest of all methods. In addition, to the Mamdani fuzzy inference does well at modelling human-like decision-making using language variables and rules. It allows humans to contribute to the fuzzy logic system, making it attractive in applications that need human input. Language also makes the system transparent and understandable [25].

14.3.2 Design System

This gadget has a built-in cloud storage service called ThingSpeak, which can be used to upload and retrieve data to and from the cloud. With this setup, we can get up-to-the-minute information. This project makes use of a NodeMCU ESP8266 microcontroller, a MAX30100 motor driver, and a few more components, sensor for monitoring heart rate, a DS18B20 temperature sensor, and a MQ-2 air quality sensor. Sensors and a microprocessor make up the experimental setup for a health monitoring system.

14.3.3 ThingSpeak

The IoT connects gadgets and online services. Analytical, monitoring, and counteractive options are available on Thing talk. ThingSpeak is an open-source IoT platform for cloud data storage and retrieval. Also, consider Thing talk.

ThingSpeak is an Internet of Things platform that facilitates the collection and analysis of data. ThingSpeak is an intermediary between various sensor types and software, functioning as a data aggregator that retrieves information from disparate devices and imports it into a software environment. ThingSpeak comprises a Channel, a fundamental component encompassing a site field, data field, and status field. The utilization of channels facilitates the recording, manipulation, and visualization of data through. Figure 14.2 depicts the architecture of ThingSpeak.

A) Key of ThingSpeak

1. The data transmission can be achieved through device configuration using either MQTT or REST API.
2. The process of collecting data from both devices and third-party sources is known as data aggregation.

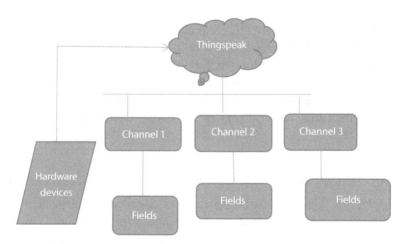

Figure 14.2 Overview of ThingSpeak.

3. The utilization of data visualization techniques is imperative for both real-time and past data representation.
4. The utilization of MATLAB data. The collected data can undergo preprocessing and subsequent analysis. Automate your IoT analytics in accordance with predetermined schedules or events.
5. This statement implies that the subject takes action based on the information provided.
6. The individual utilizes Twitter or Twilio as a means of communication.

B) Workflow of ThingSpeak

1. Data collection and channel
2. Visualizing and data analyzing
3. Data on act and using in apps

14.4 Analysis and Result

14.4.1 Measurements of Heartbeat Rate

The MAX500 is a pulse sensor that is widely used. It can detect heart rate and pulse oximetry with its two LEDs, optimized optics, photodetector, and low-noise analog signal processing. This pulse sensor can handle inputs between 1 V and 3.3 V.

MAX500 may function as both a fitness tracker and a health monitor. Figure 14.3 depicts the patient's heart rate data from the pulse sensor and stored in ThingSpeak over time.

Pulse pressure is generated and conveyed throughout the cardiovascular system when blood is discharged from the ventricles. When the pulse pressure travels through the vessels, it displaces the vessel walls, which may be monitored at different locations.

The photoelectric approach uses photoconductors to detect a pulsating blood volume change. Amplification is achieved with the use of photoresistors and phototransistors. The light is emitted using an LED, and its intensity is monitored using a photoresistor placed in an artery. Every time blood is pumped, the amount of blood in the finger grows, the optical density changes, and less light is transmitted through the finger. The resistance of the photoresistor will rise as a consequence. A voltage divider circuit

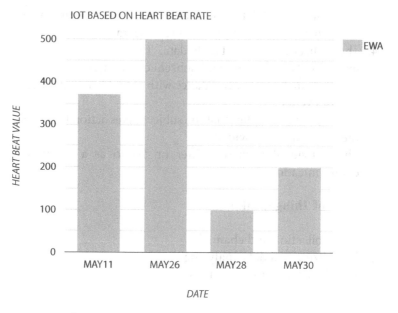

Figure 14.3 Heartbeat measurement.

made up of photoresistors allows for the generation of a voltage that varies with finger blood volume.

14.4.2   Temperature Measurements

Utilize a DS18B20 temperature sensor, which provides accurate temperature readings from 9 bits to 12 bits in Celsius and has an alert. The integrated-circuit sensor generates a voltage directly proportional to the temperature in Celsius, and this analogue signal is converted into digital representation using an analogue-to-digital converter (ADC). This sensor is equipped with a single-wire interface. Therefore, the CPU just requires a single data connection and a ground. Parasitic electricity, which is delivered over the data connection, eliminates the need for a dedicated power cord. Patient temperature readings throughout time are shown in Figure 14.4.

14.4.3   Air Measurements

Tin dioxide (SnO2), an electrode, a heater, a tiny Al_2O_3 ceramic tube, and the tube's crust comprise the MQ-2 gas sensor. Plastic and a stainless steel mesh form the crust. The heater is the most crucial part, since it supplies essential conditions for the proper operation of delicate parts. The MQ-2

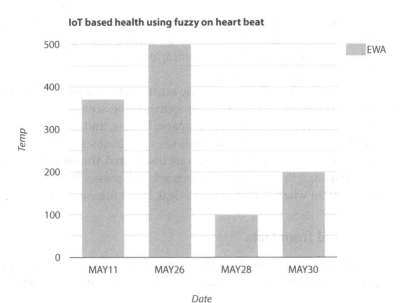

Figure 14.4 Temperature of heartbeat measures.

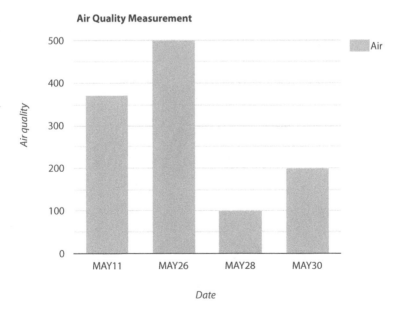

Figure 14.5 Measurement of quality of air.

sensor has six pins; four are utilized for the signal collection, while the other two provide the current necessary to warm the sensor. Figure 14.5 depicts the air quality in the patient monitoring room. The MQ-2 sensor is a tool for gauging ambient air quality.

An immediate alert will be sent if the sensor detects a potentially dangerous gas. Dangerous gases like hydrogen may be seen by this sensor. Cigarette smoke, ethanol, methane, propane, butane, and liquefied petroleum gas. These sensors are installed in homes and businesses to detect the presence of gas leaks. If dangerous gases are discovered, the measured value will be incremented to 1 and put on the graph; otherwise, it will remain at 0: a binary system where 0 means no gas leak and 1 means harmful gases.

14.4.4   Cloud from Data

The ThingSpeak channel will be used to upload information to the cloud, such as a user's heart rate, temperature, and air quality. The data from all of

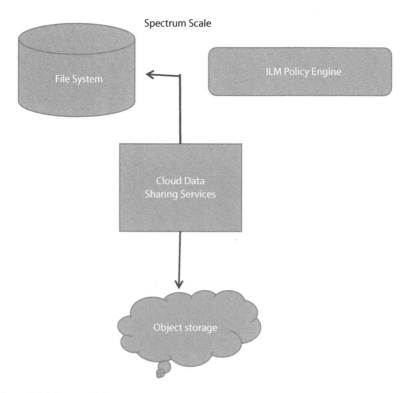

Figure 14.6 Imported data.

the sensors are tallied by ThingSpeak. Here, at the office, fuzzy logic is used in Internet of Things-based health monitoring system to analyze information like temperature, heart rate, and air quality. Channel allows for the visualization of the results.

The values that are calculated and recorded may be visualized with the help of MATLAB visualization programmers. Ensure the safety of the collected information, and it will be kept on the cloud. All of the sensors' readings that have been uploaded to ThingSpeak are shown in Figure 14.6.

14.5 Conclusion

Nowadays, individuals have a lot on their plates, so tools like IoT health observing using fuzzy logic may help them keep tabs on the health of their loved ones and those in their care. As shown in this study, building a health monitoring system using IoT is the best bet. The values measured by the sensors have been analyzed using fuzzy logic. NodeMCU ESP8266 microcontroller with built-in Wi-Fi is the heart of the gadget, and ThingSpeak is used to analyze the collected data through graphs, automate the setup fully. In the current structure, cloud-stored data such as temperature, heart rate, and air quality are downloaded, and a fuzzy logic-based determination is made. All of this can be done mechanically and quickly notify nurses and physicians of any abnormalities. Future efforts like this will help the elderly and sick at home, where they can be continually monitored, freeing up stress for carers and loved ones. Older adults will also benefit, since they can maintain independence and enjoy a higher quality of life. The system has been constructed utilizing cost-effective health monitoring devices.

References

1. Basanta, H., Huang, Y.-P., Lee, T.-T., Intuitive IoT-based H2U healthcare system for elderly people. *IEEE Conference on Networking, Sensing, and Control Mexico City*, Mexico, April 28-30, 2016.
2. Mamdani, E.H., Application of fuzzy logic to approximate reasoning using linguistic synthesis. *IEEE Trans. Comput.*, 26, 12, 11821191, 1977.
3. Tth-Laufer, E., Takcs, M., Rudas, I.J., Real-time fuzzy logic-based sport activity risk calculation model optimization Computational Intelligence and Informatics (CINTI). *2013 IEEE 14th International Symposium on, Budapest*, pp. 291–295, 2013, doi: 10.1109/CINTI.2013.6705209.

4. Kulkarni, C., Karhade, H., Gupta, S., Bhende, P., Bhandare, S., Health companion device using IoT and wearable computing. *International Conference on Internet of Things and Applications (IoTA) Maharashtra Institute of Technology*, Pune, India, 22 Jan - 24 Jan, 2016.

5. Banerjee, P.S., Karmakar, A., Dhara, M., Ganguly, K., Sarkar, S., A novel method for predicting bradycardia and atrial fibrillation using fuzzy logic and arduino supported IoT sensors. *Med. Nov. Technol. Devices*, 10, 100058, 2021.

6. Quasim, M.T., Shaikh, A., Shuaib, M., Sulaiman, A., Alam, S., Asiri, Y., Smart healthcare management evaluation using fuzzy decision making method, 2021.

7. Arunachalam, S.P., Kapa, S., Mulpuru, S.K., Friedman, P.A., Tolkacheva, E.G., Intelligent fractional-order PID (FOPID) heart rate controller for cardiac pacemaker, in: *2016 IEEE Healthcare Innovation Point-of-Care Technologies Conference (HI-POCT)*, IEEE, pp. 105–108, 2016.

8. Dahalan, A.J., Razak, T.R., Ismail, M.H., Fauzi, S.S.M., Adderley, R., Gining, J.M., Heart rate events classification via explainable fuzzy logic systems. *IAES Int. J. Artif. Intell.*, 10, 4, 1036, 2021.

9. Mahfouf, M., Abbod, M.F., Linkens, D.A., A survey of fuzzy logic monitoring and control utilisation in medicine. *Artif. Intell. Med.*, 21, 1–3, 27–42, 2001.

10. Madhuri, V.J., Mohan, M.R., Kaavya, R., Stress management using artificial intelligence. *2013 Third International Conference on Advances in Computing and Communications*, IEEE, 2013.

11. Skinner, J.F., Garibaldi, J.M., Curnow, J., Ifeachor, E.C., Intelligent fetal heart rate analysis, in: *2000 First International Conference Advances in Medical Signal and Information Processing (IEE Conf. Publ. No. 476)*, IET, pp. 14–21, 2000, September.

12. Becker, K., Thull, B., Käsmacher-Leidinger, H., Stemmer, J., Rau, G., Kalff, G., Zimmermann, H.-J., Design and validation of an intelligent patient monitoring and alarm system based on a fuzzy logic process model. *Artif. Intell. Med.*, 11, 1, 33–53, 1997.

13. Gurugubelli, S., Chekuri, R.B.R., Rajasanthosh Kumar, T., The method combining laser welding and induction heating at high temperatures was performed. *Des. Eng.*, A 578, 2013, 125–133, 2021.

14. Islam, T., Jasim Uddin Qureshi, Md., Farhan Nasir, Md., Chowdhury, R., Palit, H., Mitra, P., Fuzzy logic controlled an autonomous patient's health monitoring system through the Internet of Things, in: *2022 25th International Conference on Computer and Information Technology (ICCIT)*, IEEE, pp. 965–970, 2022.

15. El-Samahy, E., Mahdi Mahfouf, L., Torres-Salomao, A., Anzurez-Marin, J., A new computer control system for mental stress management using fuzzy logic, in: *2015 IEEE International Conference on Evolving and Adaptive Intelligent Systems (EAIS)*, IEEE, pp. 1–7, 2015.

16. Selvarajan, S., Manoharan, H., Hasanin, T., Alsini, R., Uddin, M., Shorfuzzaman, M., Alsufyani, A., Biomedical signals for healthcare using Hadoop infrastructure with artificial intelligence and fuzzy logic interpretation. *Appl. Sci.*, 12, 10, 5097, 2022.

17. Baig, M.M., Gholamhosseini, H., Harrison, M.J., Fuzzy logic based smart anaesthesia monitoring system in the operation theatre. *WSEAS Trans. Circuits Syst.*, 11, 1, 21–32, 2012.

18. Bhunia, S.S., Dhar, S.K., Mukherjee, N., iHealth: A fuzzy approach for provisioning intelligent health-care system in smart city, in: *2014 IEEE 10th International Conference on Wireless and Mobile Computing, Networking and Communications (WiMob)*, IEEE, pp. 187–193, 2014.

19. S.P., Mahato, D.P., Linh, N.T.D., *Distributed artificial intelligence*, S.P. Yadav, D.P. Mahato, N.T.D. Linh (Eds.), CRC Press, 2020, https://doi.org/10.1201/9781003038467. https://doi.org/10.1007/978-3-030-86749-2_5

20. Becker, K., Rau, G., Kaesmacher, H., Petermeyer, M., Kalff, G., Zimmermann, H.-J., Fuzzy logic approaches to intelligent alarms. *IEEE Eng. Med. Biol. Mag.*, 13, 5, 710–716, 1994. https://cours.etsmtl.ca/sys843/REFS/Books/ZimmermannFuzzySetTheory2001.pdf

21. Abdullah, A.A., Zakaria, Z., Mohamad, N.F., Design and development of fuzzy expert system for diagnosis of hypertension. *2011 Second International Conference on Intelligent Systems, Modelling and Simulation*, IEEE, 2011. file:///C:/Users/hp/Downloads/4336a113_ISMS_azian.pdf

22. Majma, N., Babamir, S.M., Monadjemi, A., Runtime verification of pacemaker using fuzzy logic and colored petri-nets. *2015 4th Iranian Joint Congress on Fuzzy and Intelligent Systems (CFIS)*, IEEE, 2015. https://www.researchgate.net/publication/311855147_Runtime_Verification_of_Pacemaker_Functionality_Using_Hierarchical_Fuzzy_Colored_Petri-nets

23. Al-Turjman, F., Yadav, S.P., Kumar, M., Yadav, V., Stephan, T. (Eds.), *Transforming Management with AI, Big-Data, and IoT*, Springer International Publishing, 2022, https://doi.org/10.1007/978-3-030-86749-2. https://digital-library.theiet.org/content/books/he/pbhe034e;jsessionid=1ioxg01yd27f9.x-iet-live-01

24. Hadjadj, A. and Halimi, K., Improving health disabled people through smart wheelchair based on fuzzy ontology, in: *2021 8th International Conference on Internet of Things: Systems, Management and Security (IoTSMS)*, IEEE, pp. 1–6, 2021.

25. Tang, V., Choy, K.L., Ho, G.T.S., Lam, H.Y., Tsang, Y.P., An IoMT-based geriatric care management system for achieving smart health in nursing homes. *Ind. Manage. Data Syst.*, 119, 8, 1819–1840, 2019.

15

Functional Fuzzy Logic and Algorithm for Medical Data Management Mechanism Monitoring

U. Moulali[1]*, Bhargavi Peddi Reddy[2], Srikanth Bhyrapuneni[3], Shruthi S.K.[4], Shaik Khaleel Ahamed[4] and Harikrishna Bommala[5]

[1]*Department of CSE, Methodist College of Engineering and Technology, Hyderabad, India*
[2]*Department of CSE, Vasavi College of Engineering, Hyderabad, India*
[3]*Department of CSE, Koneru Lakshmaiah Education Foundation, Hyderabad, India*
[4]*Methodist College of Engineering and Technology, Hyderabad, India*
[5]*Department of CSE, KG Reddy College of Engineering & Technology, Hyderabad, India*

Abstract

With the advent of wireless sensors and wearable gadgets, medical care has risen to the forefront of technological advancement. A mountain of unstructured and diverse health data is produced by the widespread use of sensors and devices in fitness. There have been several helpful approaches and frameworks established for secure and private data-sharing frameworks. However, the use of fuzzy logic systems to organize and analyze health data has received very little attention. The reliability, accuracy, and stability of wireless sensors and devices are all negatively impacted by low battery or energy levels. Accurate diagnosis and decision-making need proper categorization, elimination of noise, and interoperability of health data. Using a fuzzy logic system or algorithm to handle raw medical data uncertainties and data management may save energy and be successful. Artificial intelligence (AI), neural networks, and optimization underpin fuzzy logic. This study covers a large amount of literature on fuzzy logic systems and algorithms to improve healthcare apps and frameworks. Exploring different machine learning

---

*Corresponding author: moulaliu@methodist.edu.in

Satya Prakash Yadav, Sudesh Yadav, Pethuru Raj Chelliah and Victor Hugo C. de Albuquerque (eds.)
Advances in Fuzzy-Based Internet of Medical Things (IoMT), (225–238) © 2024 Scrivener Publishing LLC

methods and integrating cloud infrastructure elements may improve the reasoning component's versatility.

Keywords: Wireless sensors, data frameworks, FLS, neural networks, healthcare apps

15.1   Introduction

There are significant opportunities to enhance clinical outcomes and patient satisfaction, decrease healthcare costs, and impact population health as a whole, thanks to the maturation of artificial intelligence (AI) as a tool for enhancing healthcare. Large companies often have trouble keeping their servers online around the clock, but with the help of an A1 health check monitoring job, this problem can be mitigated by enforcing some initial methods that can be used to clean the storage. Increases in population and the prevalence of new diseases may strain the capacity of a community's medical infrastructure, especially in less developed regions. The truth value of a logical statement, in the context of fuzzy logic, may be thought of as a real integer between 0 and 1. It is also a kind of AI, whereas in the realm of artificial neural networks (ANNs), neuro-fuzzy is a hybrid approach that combines AI with fuzzy logic. The following Mamdani rule-based systems provide the basis of the fuzzification process.

1. Transform each of the input values into a fuzzy membership function.
2. To calculate the fuzzy output functions, step 2 is to run all relevant rules in the rule-based system.
3. Defuzz the values that were previously fuzzified.

Fuzzification converts numerical input systems to fuzzy sets. Fuzzy sets are worded. The range is 0–2. It belongs to the fuzzy set of values that are 2, but not if they are 0. Triangle and trapezoid curves describe fuzzy sets graphically. The slope indicates value change. The slope becomes sigmoid as the value declines from 2. Figure 15.1 compares Boolean and fuzzy logic.

Decision-making, security, and health data management are only a few of the applications of FL models and algorithms. WBAN sensors and strategies are the result of the rapid development of 5G and industry 5.0 wireless communication and sensor technologies. When collecting and transmitting data, low-power WBAN sensors often make mistakes. It is necessary to test fuzzy logic models and implementations. Multiple types of cancer, including those of the breast, lung, and blood, may be detected by using an

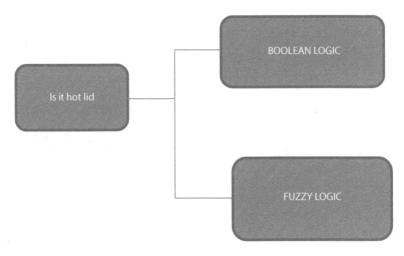

Figure 15.1 Fuzzy logic system and Boolean.

adaptive neuro-fuzzy model. Computer-aided design (CAD) aids physicians in the early diagnosis and treatment of several disorders. Patients in critical condition may be diagnosed and treated using CAD. Features are sorted by CAD. There is a resemblance between the classifiers used by CAD, decision trees, random forests, support vector machines, and adaptive neuro-fuzzy inference systems (ANFISs). In this case, modifies glow worm swarm optimization (M-GSO) is useful. DE helps improve. The findings from DE were compared to those from the classic ANFIS model, genetic algorithm (GA), DE, DE, and lion optimization approaches, among others. The implementation of this system results in a reduction of the workload for the staff members. Machine learning improves fuzzy neural networks. Medicine uses the fuzzy neural system to identify chronic illnesses. The frequency notification system (FNS) improves data management. Artificial ne brightens physics. Scientist Fojnica's ANN, an example of artificial intelligence, may improve high-stakes decision-making due to its accurate illness detection. Hierarchical ANNs work. Artificial neural networks function as computational models inspired by the human brain and are additionally employed in the development of artificial animal brains for the purpose of pattern recognition. The utilization of neurotrophic factors (NFs) holds significant importance within the medical domain, as they have proven to be effective in enhancing diagnostic capabilities. Approximately 36 different NF models are currently employed for this purpose. Figure 15.2 illustrates the diverse range of fields in which fuzzy logic systems have been employed. The utilization of neurotrophic factors holds significant prominence in the management of individuals with diabetes, particularly

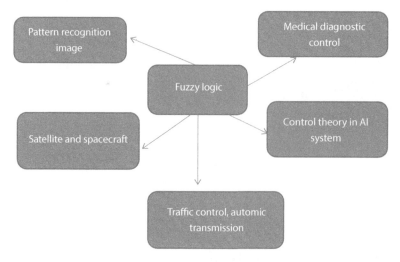

Figure 15.2 Fuzzy logic system in various fields.

in the context of treating diabetic foot ulcers and facilitating the detection of early signs indicative of diabetes. NFs exhibit therapeutic attributes that contribute to the healing process of diabetic foot ulcers while offering the capability to identify initial manifestations associated with diabetes.

FL models and algorithms work in managing health conditions, security requirements, and in making decisions. Devices have made real-time health monitoring and management easier, but uncertainties and flaws in data sensing and transmission make wireless body area network (WBAN) sensors, particularly low-power ones, difficult to use. To solve these concerns, fuzzy logic-based health management, security, and decision-making models and systems must be carefully tested.

The proliferation of wearable devices and WBAN sensors has been shown to increase at an exponential rate, which we attribute to the development of cordless communiqué systems in the industry 4.0 revolution. Vast amounts of data created are often unorganized and of varying types. There have been many suggested theories and methods for data interpretation, categorization, and analysis, but they are inconsistent and unreliable. Health data management, healthcare applications, and hospital management systems that use fuzzy logic have a track record of success.

15.2   Fuzzy Logic System Integration

Because of the difficulty in diagnosing this illness, a lot of people are focusing on developing more intelligent systems for use in medicine. They looked for tools that would make it simpler to check for diabetes complications; the corneal confocal microscopy (CCM) technology stands out as particularly useful for identifying digital signal processing network (DSPN). The high cost of this treatment, however, makes it uncommon in mainstream medical facilities that are used to screen DSPN in its earliest stages. These tests take into account the patient's current conditions like pain, vibration, harm of sensitivity, and temperature and use AI techniques for diagnosis. The fuzzy logic inference system is the utmost frequent, simple, widely used approach in making decisions because of its ability to predict future outcomes based on the current state of affairs. Figure 15.3 displays the severity level calculated by the ANFIS categorization of managed network System Inc (MNSI) data from 100 people using the presentation limitations of the system that captures EMG and muscle activity.

When it comes to healthcare, the Internet of Things (IoT) is crucial. It improves healthcare by decreasing patient wait times, unused hospital resources, and extraneous costs. The condition of patients can be determined from their normal day-to-day activities to the implementation of a number of sensors in wearable devices. This enables the Medical Internet of Things (MIoTs) to detect the patients' conditions in real time. All of the data gathered by these strategies are sent to the medical personnel through a cloud-based network so that they can make an accurate diagnosis and start treatment immediately. The backbone of the MIoTs consists of the perception, network, and application layers. As may be seen in Figure 15.4, fuzzy logic systems are very effective. This diagram depicts the five dataset classifiers (SVM, DT, RF, NB, and KNN) being used to categorize the initial patient's health data. The categorized information is similarly binary,

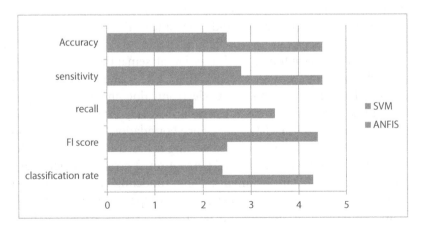

Figure 15.3 SVM models and ANFIS.

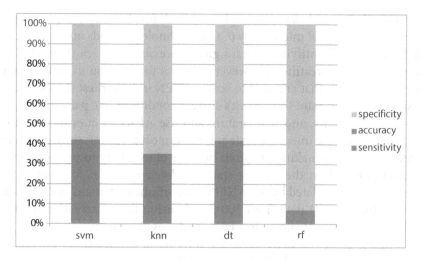

Figure 15.4 Various model parameters in recording daily life.

with a value of 0 indicating positivity and a value of 2 indicating negativity. Figure 15.4 shows that NB has the greatest accuracy (0.974%) and lowest false-positive rate (0.032%), while KNN has the highest sensitivity (0.730) and lowest false-negative rate (0.332). SVM is the most effective classifier available. However, security issues are resolved in ANFIS environments.

15.3   FLSA

Using IoT, hospitals and other medical facilities may be saved. Key health data may be difficult to find, since they are stored in text format across documentation, medical records, and electronic health records. An autonomous storage system can be beneficia determine the most effective and painless methods of automation. Fuzzy latent semantic analysis (FLSA) works well for robotic storage systems. This tactic is often used because of its success. Digital storage, browsing, electronic documentation, categorization, and searching and indexing are all necessary for secure data preservation, according to the National Science Foundation (NSF). The second most common kind of computerized sorting is based on bags words. It is a crucial part of computerized visual perception. It assembles dictionaries and grammars of digital documents. Topic modeling is beneficial; however, the fuzzy latent semantic analysis model outperforms it in redundant and nonredundant circumstances. Seven-step process based on Fuzzy logic spectrum. Figure 15.5 compares LDA-T data to alternative modeling

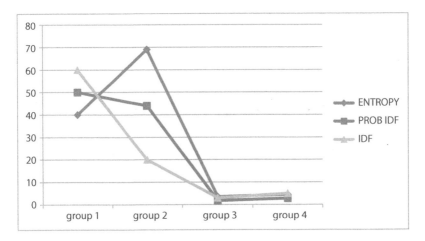

Figure 15.5 Analysis of Prob IDF with other models.

approaches including fuzzy latent semantic analysis. Warped Gibbs sampling works best. The graph shows that the FLSA (Prob IDF) approach outperforms the LDA because it remains stable as the number of topics increases, avoids potentially harmful topics, and works with discontinuous and continuous datasets.

IoT health monitoring offers remote patient monitoring. Industry 5.0 and 4G/5G allow this. WBAN sensors and wearables changed health monitoring. Data management concealment advantages. Sensors and devices generate huge heterogeneous data. Type 1 fuzzy logic makes sensory input inconsistent and ambiguous in most healthcare systems. The use of Dempster-Shafer's theory enables the extraction of accurate information and the provision of exact outcomes. Please verify the accuracy of the phrase. Erroneous indications result from heterogeneous data from sensors on the patient and related information from devices surrounding the patient. Fusing data from several nodes/sensors improves service and accuracy. Type 1 fuzzy logic decisions are wrong with massive data. Type 2 fuzzy logic makes decisions for uncertain data. Two-phase fusion is hypothesized. Phase 1 T2FL calculates an accurate membership value from patient sensor data. Phase 2 synthesizes DST node/sensor inferences. Doctors and patients evaluated inferred data. The recommended model's precision, accuracy, and recall were compared to similar models. The method merged two datasets. F1 score comparisons favor the model. Precision, repeatability, and cross-validation need 10 model runs. T2FLD outperforms COS and T1FL-COS 12%–19%. Figure 15.6 illustrates 2-fold datasets.

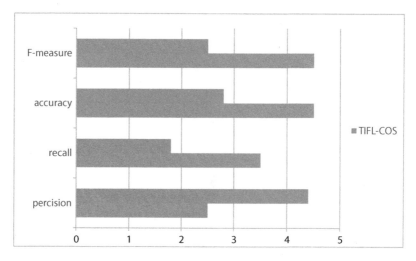

Figure 15.6 Performance of recall, accuracy, precision, and F1 measure of the T2FLD.

Using fuzzy logic and machine learning, Sengan *et al.* developed an electronic health data medical information retrieval system. An aging population, limited medical services, and rising costs have placed a strain on the healthcare system, which is simplified by this approach. Massive amounts of e-healthcare data are analyzed through machine learning. By integrating e-HCRs, evidence-based pharmaceutical services may be provided to patients based on a thorough understanding of their diseases.

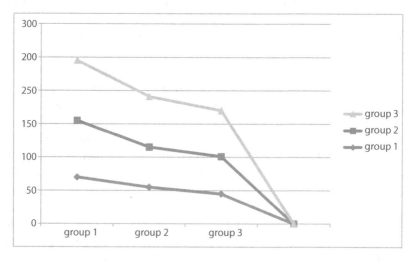

Figure 15.7 Machine learning (ML) relative performed on manual and machine model groups.

Evidence from patients' treatments is included in e-HCRs. Structured and unstructured data are both present in e-HCRs. In the proposed network, decisions are made in real time by both human experts and the fuzzy inference system (FIS). The FIS was k-fold cross-validated for use in generating predictions and taking actions. Figure 15.7 shows how the proposed framework fares in predicting 30-day readmissions for test patients.

15.4   FIS in Data Healthcare

A FIS approach for dynamic time slots is established. It was shown that a fuzzy allocation-based approach improved overall performance, communication reliability for mission-critical applications, and energy costs for packet routing in healthcare managing the data for WBAN sensors and wearable devices. Wireless body area network (WBAN) sensors and gadgets allow for the monitoring of vital biological signals; however, they have limitations owing to their small battery sizes and lack of network connection. The network has substantial challenges in the form of data delay, data scrambling, and an increase in jumping, since WBAN sensors are developed for life-or-death applications, such as those in the medical profession. Multiple access control (MAC) and IEEE protocols are only two of the many options for sharing data in a WBAN network. The WBAN incorporates a heuristic hybrid time slot fuzzy allocation approach to improve node-to-network coordinator communication. The proposed technique is now being used to keep tabs on 50 patients in real time using sensor data and wearable technology. Fifty patients are now being monitored in real time through the suggested algorithm, thanks to the use of sensors and wearable technology. Figure 15.8 displays the resulting boost in latency, energy efficiency, and packet delivery rate. The suggested model has better results than its competitors.

Recommendation systems in healthcare have been shown to accurately forecast risk and severity using an FL-based and CNN framework. The CNN analyzes data from the WBAN sensors and employs all mechanisms for categorizing diseases. After exchanging medical records and evidence-based suggestions, the incorporation of the FIS aids in calculating the patient's risk level and severity of illnesses. In response to the global spread of the COVID-19 epidemic, health recommender system (HRS) postings have gained widespread acceptance. The quality of HRS, however, may be improved by the combination of fuzzy and deep learning. A dataset of 102 patients is taken into account to evaluate the model's performance;

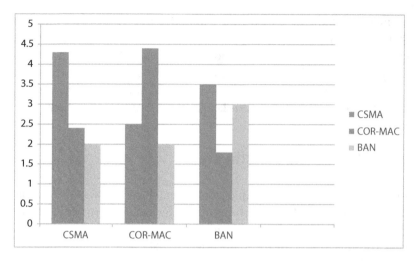

Figure 15.8 HHTSF model of energy consumption.

this dataset includes 42 characteristics and divides patients into three categories. Heart, liver, and renal illness patients' datasets were taken into account. The dataset is used for both instructional and evaluation functions. Sensitivity, accuracy, and specificity for different pairings of testing and training datasets are shown in Figure 15.9.

Low platelet counts and hemolytic anemia are common symptoms of preeclampsia, pregnancy-induced hypertension. Hemolysis, elevated liver

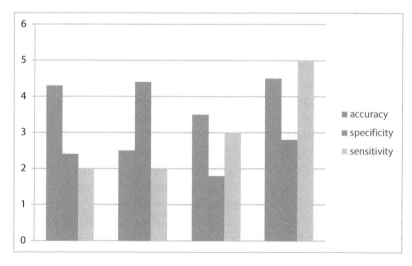

Figure 15.9 T2FLS system.

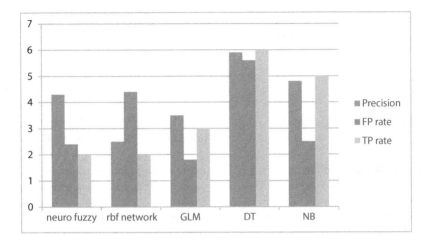

Figure 15.10 The neuro-fuzzy model similar to models for accuracy.

enzyme and low platelet count syndrome (HELLP) affects 8% of preeclampsia patients, according to the WHO. Its cause is unclear. Laboratory testing underpins medical diagnosis. Fuzzy logic algorithms and other ways may simplify syndrome diagnosis. Figure 15.10 compares strategies for diagnosing, treating, and improving pregnancy care. The radial basis function (RBF) network appears too good to be true. As seen in the graphic, RBF and neural fuzzy algorithms have a greater true positive rate than other methods, but their randomness makes them less reliable.

15.5   Conclusion

Health data ambiguity is the topic of this investigation. The ability to diagnose and treat patients relies on correct data. WBAN sensors, wearables, data gathering, and transmission are limited by low power. Reduced energy consumption makes detecting and sharing data easier. It is difficult for doctors to make diagnoses and provide prescriptions. Intuitive logical decision-making is difficult for machines. Healthcare data management makes use of AI and fuzzy logic when dealing with high levels of data heterogeneity, uncertainty, and noise, while fuzzy logic has been shown to be helpful in the organization of medical facts. Fuzzy logic models and algorithms for managing health data are currently being investigated by academics. To identify blind spots and unexplored territories in health data management studies, it must be openly dissected. In this study, the relative merits of several fuzzy logic-based model metrics are evaluated. In order to close gaps and fill in blanks in health data management studies, fuzzy logic models are introduced here.

Bibliography

Yang, Y., Que, Y., Huang, S., Lin, P., Multimodal sensor medical image fusion based on type-2 fuzzy logic in NSCT domain. *IEEE Sens. J.*, 16, 10, 3735–45, 2016 Feb 23.

Teng, J., Wang, S., Zhang, J., Wang, X., Neuro-fuzzy logic based fusion algorithm of medical images, in: *2010 3rd International Congress on Image and Signal Processing*, vol. 4, IEEE, pp. 1552–1556, 2010.

Barro, S. and Marín, R. (Eds.), *Fuzzy Logic in Medicine*, vol. 83, Springer Science & Business Media, 2001. file:///C:/Users/hp/Downloads/A-3.pdf

Khan, A., Li, J.-P., Shaikh, R.A., Medical image processing using fuzzy logic, in: *2015 12th International Computer Conference on Wavelet Active Media Technology and Information Processing (ICCWAMTIP)*, IEEE, pp. 163–167, 2015.

Teng, J. *et al.*, Fusion algorithm of medical images based on fuzzy logic, in: *2010 Seventh International Conference on Fuzzy Systems and Knowledge Discovery*, vol. 2, IEEE, 2010.

Tsai, D.-Y., Lee, Y., Sekiya, M., Ohkubo, M., Medical image classification using genetic-algorithm based fuzzy-logic approach. *J. Electron. Imaging*, 13, 4, 780–788, 2004.

Jayachandran, A. and Dhanasekaran, R., Multi class brain tumor classification of MRI images using hybrid structure descriptor and fuzzy logic based RBF kernel SVM. *Iran. J. Fuzzy Syst.*, 14, 3, 41–54, 2017 Jun 29.

Gurugubelli, S., Chekuri, R.B.R., Rajasanthosh Kumar, T., The method combining laser welding and induction heating at high temperatures was performed. *Des. Eng.*, 2021, 5, 592–602, 2021.

Chauhan, N. and Choi, B.J., Denoising approaches using fuzzy logic and convolutional autoencoders for human brain MRI image. *Int. J. Fuzzy Log. Intell. Syst.*, 19, 3, 135–139, 2019.

Yadav, S.P., Blockchain security, in: *Blockchain Security in Cloud Computing. EAI/ Springer Innovations in Communication and Computing*, K. Baalamurugan, S.R. Kumar, A. Kumar, V. Kumar, S. Padmanaban, (Eds.), Springer, Cham, 2022, https://doi.org/10.1007/978-3-030-70501-5_1.

Nguyen, T.M. and Wu, Q.J., A fuzzy logic model based Markov random field for medical image segmentation. *Evol. Syst.*, 4, 171–181, 2013.

Costin, H. and Rotariu, C., Medical image analysis and representation using a fuzzy and rule-based hybrid approach. *Int. J. Comput. Commun.*, 1, 156–162, 2006.

Yuvaraja, T. and Sabeenian, R.S., Performance analysis of medical image security using steganography based on fuzzy logic. *Cluster Comput.*, 22, 3285–3291, 2019.

Alawad, A.M., Rahman, F.D.A., Khalifa, O.O., Malek, N.A., Fuzzy logic based edge detection method for image processing. *Int. J. Electr. Comput. Eng.*, 8, 3, 1863, 2018.

Rani, P., Verma, S., Yadav, S.P., Rai, B.K., Naruka, M.S., Kumar, D., Simulation of the lightweight blockchain technique based on privacy and security for healthcare data for the cloud system. *Int. J. E-Health Med. Commun.*, 13, 4, 1–15, 2022, IGI Global. https://doi.org/10.4018/ijehmc.309436.

Ahmmed, R., Rahman, M.A., Hossain, M.F., Fuzzy logic based algorithm to classify tumor categories with position from brain MRI images, in: *2017 3rd International Conference on Electrical Information and Communication Technology (EICT)*, IEEE, pp. 1–6, 2017 Dec 7.

Javed, U., Riaz, M.M., Ghafoor, A., Cheema, T.A., Local features and Takagi-Sugeno fuzzy logic based medical image segmentation. *Radioengineering*, 22, 4, 1091–1097, 2013.

Jain, P. and Aggarwal, A., Text fusion in medical images using fuzzy logic based matrix scanning algorithm. *Int. J. Sci. Res. Publ.*, 2, 6, 1–6, 2012.

Torres, A. and Nieto, J.J., Fuzzy logic in medicine and bioinformatics. *J. Biomed. Biotechnol.*, 2006, 1–7, 2006.

Haq, I., Anwar, S., Shah, K., Khan, M.T., Shah, S.A., Fuzzy logic based edge detection in smooth and noisy clinical images. *PLoS One*, 10, 9, e0138712, 2015.

Ping, W. *et al.*, A multi-scale enhancement method to medical images based on fuzzy logic. *TENCON 2006-2006 IEEE Region 10 Conference*, IEEE, 2006.

Sinha, G.R., Fuzzy-based medical image processing, in: *Fuzzy Expert Systems for Disease Diagnosis*, pp. 45–61, IGI Global, 2015. https://core.ac.uk/download/pdf/34725337.pdf

Arnal, J. and Súcar, L., Fast method based on fuzzy logic for Gaussian-impulsive noise reduction in CT medical images. *Mathematics*, 10, 19, 3652, 2022.

Dey, N., Ashour, A.S., Shi, F., Balas, V.E.E., *Soft computing based medical image analysis*, Academic Press, 2018. https://www.researchgate.net/publication/313064270_Soft_Computing_Based_Medical_Image_Analysis/link/588f4da392851cef1363c8fd/download?_tp=eyJjb250ZXh0Ijp7ImZpcnN0UGFnZSI6InB1YmxpY2F0aW9uIiwicGFnZSI6InB1YmxpY2F0aW9uIn19

Hata, Y. *et al.*, A survey of fuzzy logic in medical and health technology. *World Automation Congress 2012*, IEEE, 2012.

16

Using IoT to Evaluate the Effectiveness of Online Interactive Tools in Healthcare

K. Suresh Kumar[1], Chinmaya Kumar Nayak[2], Chamandeep Kaur[3]
and Ahmed Hesham Sedky[4]*

*[1]MBA Department, Panimalar Engineering College, Varadarajapuram,
Poonamallee, Chennai, India*
*[2]Faculty of Emerging Technologies (Computer Science and Engineering),
Sri Sri University, Odisha, India*
[3]College of Computer Science and IT, Jazan University, Jazan, Saudi Arabia
[4]Arab Academy for Science, Technology and Maritime Transport, Egypt

Abstract

In cutting-edge contexts, including "smart cities," "smart homes," "healthcare," and "defense operations," the Internet of Things (IoT) is crucial. The healthcare industry may greatly benefit from IoT applications, since they allow for safe real-time remote monitoring of patients. In this survey, look at what is new. Implementation of IoT's function in healthcare monitoring systems. The ongoing progress of the Internet of Things will have a favourable influence that will enable customized treatments to improve patient results while also lowering healthcare management expenses. Through a comprehensive literature analysis, provide an update on the latest research on IoT-based healthcare monitoring strategies. In this literature study, examine and contrast the performance, efficiency, data security, privacy, and monitoring of several different systems. The article also categorizes healthcare monitoring sensors and investigates wireless and wearable sensors based on IoT monitoring systems. Investigate the difficulties and unanswered questions around quality of service (QoS), privacy, and security in healthcare. At last, the report lays out prospects connected to further technological developments and provides proposals and recommendations for IoT healthcare applications.

Keywords: Healthcare monitoring system, IoMT, analysis literature, QoS, technological development

Corresponding author: pecmba19@gmail.com

Satya Prakash Yadav, Sudesh Yadav, Pethuru Raj Chelliah and Victor Hugo C. de Albuquerque (eds.)
Advances in Fuzzy-Based Internet of Medical Things (IoMT), (239–254) © 2024 Scrivener Publishing LLC

16.1 Introduction

The Internet of Things results from years of study into the potential of interconnected digital devices. It has the potential to improve life for city dwellers. With the global population expanding at a rate never before seen and the prevalence of chronic illnesses rising, healthcare networks must be developed to efficiently manage and deliver a broad range of healthcare while cutting costs. IoT-enabled healthcare monitoring solutions are evolving. The Internet of Objects healthcare monitoring system tracks persons and links services and things worldwide through the Internet to collect, share, track, retail, and analyze data from these objects. Smart cities, smart homes, and innovative healthcare are just a few examples of intelligent applications that can use the IoT to remotely address and manage all linked physical devices they use. Using sensor networks on the human body will significantly aid disease diagnosis and patient monitoring. Moreover, the data may be accessed at any moment from anywhere in the globe. Patients with serious injuries or those living in remote places may have trouble getting to the hospital quickly. As a result, individuals may save both time and money by using video conferencing to talk to their physicians about improving their health. This system allows patients to keep track of their health data on their mobile devices. The positive effects are expected to the Internet of Things will be refined, leading to individualized therapy that improves patient outcomes and reduces healthcare administration costs. The IoT will enable robust data connectivity from several locations, unlocking the future of remote medical virtual consultations and care. Patients may also lessen their reliance on medical professionals and the probability of obtaining incorrect medical treatments in hospitals and clinics by enhancing the quality of care they receive at home. Because of this, it is possible that both the rate of medical treatment and patient safety will increase while the cost of care will fall. In healthcare, the Internet of Things has enormous promise. Shortly, people will be able to utilize a health-monitoring system from the convenience of their homes, which will significantly improve efficiency in healthcare facilities. To provide constant bodily and environmental monitoring, IoT sensors should be widely dispersed. Through this work, chronic illness management and rehabilitation may be monitored. The IoT will allow for reliable data connections from various locales, opening the door to the future of virtual consultations for remote medical treatment. Most current Internet of Things deployments and related research are still in their exploratory stages. They are primarily concerned with the deployment and configuration of technology in various settings and circumstances. However, few people employ these methods any more. Therefore, this study aims to assess existing literature about the development and deployment of an IoT-based healthcare monitoring system to enhance human well-being. These systems depend primarily on Internet of Things devices and sensors to match patients with the most appropriate healthcare professionals. This paper's primary contribution is a thorough examination of IoT-based healthcare monitoring systems, which will help future researchers, academics, and scientists better comprehend the state of the art in healthcare monitoring and more effectively address its shortcomings. In this article, present a holistic overview of the advantages, relevance, and a literature analysis of healthcare monitoring systems based on the Internet of Things.

Figure 16.1 Overview of the current research.

In addition, provide an IoT-centric discussion of the ideas behind wearables in medical infrastructure. The article also outlines obstacles and unresolved topics, as well as a taxonomy of healthcare monitoring sensors, and discusses security and standards for Internet of Things healthcare monitoring systems. provide future-proof recommendations for addressing these problems. Overview of the current research as shown in Figure 16.1.

16.2   Healthcare and Applications of the IoT

Applications of IoT-Based Healthcare Systems
Healthcare systems and apps built on the Internet of Things improve people's lives in many ways.

1. Healthcare on the go: In place of patients having to go to medical facilities, wireless Internet of Things-enabled technologies bring care to them.

   The IoT will enable robust data connectivity from several locations, unlocking the future of remote medical virtual consultations call care. Sensor data are gathered privately via the Internet of Things, processed by a lightweight algorithm, and shared with medical specialists for advice.

2. Real-time monitoring whereby extensive psychological data are gathered through noninvasive sensors powered by the Internet of Things. Data are stored and analyzed via gateways and the cloud.

3. IoT healthcare systems use sensor data, which aid in preventative care.

16.2.1   Healthcare Monitoring Systems

Researchers and medical industry experts are devoting a lot of time and energy into creating healthcare monitoring systems. There have been many fruitful studies in this field, and many more are in the works right now.

The rapidly expanding population of older persons and patients with chronic diseases is directly contributing to a dramatic increase in the number of care gaps experienced by patients. The main problem is that medical treatment is only available in hospitals, which is inconvenient and sometimes insufficient for those with special requirements or advanced age. Using sensor data and network connectivity, the Internet of Things offers a workable and efficient answer to the problem of continuous health monitoring for the elderly. The IoT and smart technologies have been demonstrated to provide better and more comprehensive services. Researchers have created a number of emergency systems with the use of sensors and wireless communication and intelligence technology. These methods have found many medical applications, most notably in the field of geriatric health monitoring. By recording crucial vital signs, information about health and potential dangers may be gathered.

16.2.2   Benefits of Using IoMT Healthcare

The IoT will have significant implications on the medical field. How software, hardware, and people work together to solve healthcare problems has undergone a sea change in recent years. The Internet of Things has given us new perspectives on the world, providing tools for a unified healthcare system that substantially improves the standard of treatment provided to patients. The Internet of Things has enabled the automation of previously labor-intensive and error-prone medical activities. The temperature and ventilation in many contemporary operating rooms, for instance, are controlled by networked equipment. There is an almost infinite number of ways in which the Internet of Things might enhance medical care, but here are a few of the most important:

1. Care costs have been reduced.
2. Errors made by humans are minimized.
3. Freedom from geographical constraints.
4. Less paperwork and fewer records to maintain.
5. Chronic illnesses are diagnosed at an earlier stage.
6. Medication management has been better.
7. The urgency of the need for medical attention.
8. Successful therapy more often.

16.3   Review of Related Studies

Various components comprise healthcare. Healthcare is provided through clinics, hospitals, pharmacies, home health agencies, nursing homes, pharmaceutical companies, and medical equipment manufacturers. The government, health insurance companies, and the sale of health-related products all have a role; services are aimed directly at the final customer. Research on healthcare monitoring using the Internet of Things is the focus of this section's review and analysis. Table 16.1 summarizes current IoT-based healthcare monitoring investigations. Pulse arrival time (PAT) may determine blood pressure (BP) from ECG and photoplethysmography (PPG). Because of their rigorous architecture, remote monitoring programs and people communicate easily. The gadgets can interact wirelessly and use little power to assess a particular physiological signal. Bilateral lower extremity (BLE) modules wirelessly communicate physiological measures to a gateway. For privacy and transmission security, sensor patches and gateways encrypt data. A smartphone and Raspberry Pi module gateway link the wearable sensor system to the cloud, allowing data retrieval and analysis. BLE technology is inappropriate for long-distance high-data rate wireless communication despite its low energy consumption.

Suggest a mobile phone-based IoT health monitoring system that remotely monitors patients' BT, ECG, and SpO_2. Arduino measured and processed this system. Wi-Fi sends data to Blynk, an IoT platform cloud service, where it may be seen and monitored live. Results are delivered to a doctor-monitored smartphone for confidentiality and privacy. Thus, Arduino and NodeMCU, which require improvement, are employed. Wi-Fi is unsuitable for long-distance transmission. Offer an

Table 16.1 Summary of healthcare monitoring according to the IoT.

Aim of the work	Used methodology	Developed model	Protocol
Developed a protocol of IoT	The system collects and sends to Raspberry 3	HR, BT, and GSR	IEEE80312
built a system using IoT to monitor patients in real time	Uses Wi-Fi and an ESP32 to measure vital data and send them to the cloud	Temperature, HR, BP	MOTT, BLE
developed an IoMT-enabled health signal-tracking platform	The body's sensor network includes numerous tiny electrical sensors	Uses 2 morcocontrollers	IEEES0211

Android-based IoT healthcare monitoring system for patients and older individuals. This prototype feeds Arduino Uno data from BT, HR, and galvanic skin response (GSR) sensors. Raspberry Pi uploads to the cloud storage. The Android app visualizes patient health parameters using Android Studio. The app lets doctors administer medications and monitor patient health. Gupta describes an IoT-based obesity monitoring system. A thoroughly functioning prototype monitors HR, SpO_2, BP, and BT. It is perfect for bodily condition monitoring. It stores medical data for numerous patients on an Arduino board and feeds them to healthcare professionals over Wi-Fi for remote monitoring. Clinicians may evaluate patients' health patterns to uncover changes suggesting an undiagnosed health issue. This makes long-distance communication difficult. An IoT-based monitoring system that can detect vital signs to assist doctors in diagnosing and monitoring patients. Sensors measure HR, BP, and BT. Raspberry Pi processes and uploads sensor data to the cloud. A smartphone app lets medical workers view the data remotely. The equipment was designed, tested, and assessed, as shown by vital sign data retrieval findings. Developed an IoT-based healthcare remote monitoring system utilizing NodeMCU and Arduino IDE. This article discusses IoT platform Ubidots. Open-source IoT software is needed. Its API lets users purchase and get data over HTTP and MQTT protocols while connected to the Internet or a local network. This IoT gadget measures pulse rate, temperature, and BP. This setup monitors vital indicators 24/7 and finds problems. ECG findings indicated 72 and 78 beats per minute for the individuals. SpO_2 was 94%, 97%, and 98%.

Finally, the experiment participants' temperatures were 94.78 degrees Fahrenheit. The design approach is cost-effective and easy to apply according to the authors.

16.4   IoWT

The objective of the Internet of Wearable Things (IoWT) is to enhance individuals' daily quality of life. The process entails the integration of sensors into wearable devices to track an individual's physical activity, health metrics, and other relevant parameters—applications to improve patient care and outcomes. The infrastructure facilitates clinicians' remote access to patient data during their routine activities. A new comprehensive framework for the Internet of Water Things (IoT) is presently under development based on the existing IoT architecture. The Internet of Wearable

Figure 16.2 Architectural elements of the IoT.

Things (IoT) is a groundbreaking technological innovation that holds significant promise in transforming the healthcare sector by establishing a self-sustaining environment for automated telehealth interventions. The diagram depicted in Figure 16.2 illustrates the structure of the IoWT and its interconnections, which comprise three fundamental components: the wireless body area network (WBAN), the gateway that is linked to the Internet, and the cloud. The wireless body area network serves as a primary interface of the IoWT. It is designed to encompass the human body to gather health-related information secretly. The wireless body area network acquires information from sensors that are either in direct contact with the human body or in the surrounding environment that can gather indirect data about an individual's conduct.

The wireless body area network has the capability to perform data analysis or transmit the collected data for analysis at a remote location. Furthermore, mobile computing devices, including smartphones, tablets, and laptops, require an Internet connection to transmit data to robust computing resources.

16.4.1   IoT Healthcare System

RFID tracks items, whereas BLE, LoRa, and Zigbee are wireless sensor network technologies. BLE transfers data between phones. Sigfox and Wi-Fi have extensive ranges. New IoT communication protocols like LoRaWAN, NB-IoT, and Sigfox are expected to boost the appeal of these applications, providing a widespread remote monitoring system. Wireless sensor networks (WSNs) power the IoT. The established IoT can link items to the Internet, enabling people to engage with computers and computer-to-computer communication. The IoT and WSN enable machine-to-machine communication. Figure 16.3 shows the WSN-IoT architecture. Sensor nodes communicate with a gateway in a distinct image. The

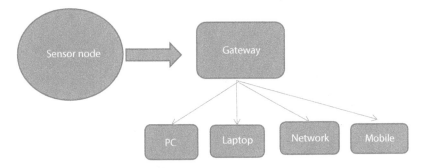

Figure 16.3 Relationship of WSN.

gateway connects several devices through Wi-Fi or the Internet, providing compatibility.

This research describes family mobile medical care system design and execution. The system includes data transfer, an Android client, and a server. Wireless data transmission is theoretical. Mobile healthcare's success is seen here. First, medical equipment sensors might record family members' signs. ECG, BP, SpO_2, respiration, and sleep are relevant. MySQL stores, computes, and analyzes data.

16.4.2   Classification of Health Sensors

They have classified medical sensors as contact (wearables) or noncontact (peripherals). Monitoring and therapeutic contact sensors exist. Again, noncontact sensors have three subcategories. All subcategories classify health-monitoring sensors with examples of their application.

On-body and peripheral health-monitoring sensors are the main types. Contact sensors detect physiological behaviors, chemical-level identification, and optical measurement. Medication, stimulation, and emergency monitoring employ contact sensors. Noncontact sensors track behavior, fitness, and rehabilitation. The different ways in which these sensors may be categorized are discussed below. Figure 16.4 shows a variety of wearable sensors used in different studies and used in IoT healthcare systems.

The usage of medical sensors and wearable devices may be useful in the following medical contexts:

1. Keeping an eye on patients' vitals at hospitals.
2. Large-scale medical and behavioral studies in the field. Support for mobile and independent aging.

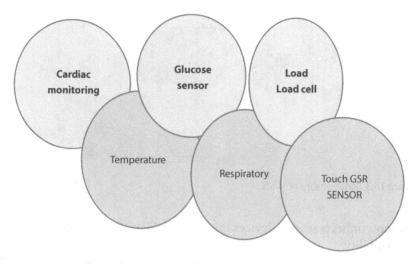

Figure 16.4 Use case and IoT sensors for healthcare.

3. Help for those with motor and sensory impairments.
4. Categorized health-monitoring sensors into subsets for comparative.
5. Performance of analyses based on their most common uses.

16.5   IoT Challenges of Healthcare

While the Internet of Things can potentially improve people's health, there are still many obstacles to overcome before it can be widely used in health-care monitoring systems. Consideration is given to various unanswered research questions, such as functionality, performance, data privacy, dependability, security, and stability.

Security, performance, computing intelligence, energy, and illness prediction are only a few of the bases on which the frequently asked questions and the rest of the questions are separated (Figure 16.5).

16.5.1   Security and Privacy

Privacy and security face moral difficulties. The cloud storage and digital format of medical records (held in electronic health records) make them vulnerable to hacking. If the cloud server is compromised, hackers will be able to access health records of a patient. There are issues with health

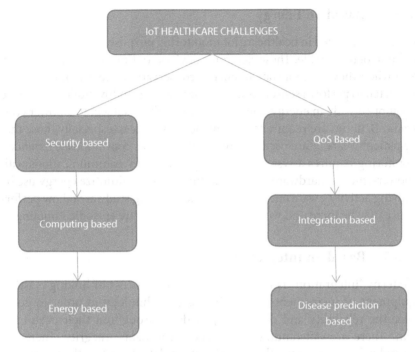

Figure 16.5 Healthcare challenges of IoT and open issues.

information usage, data ownership, data security regulations, and user authentication as a result of this. To boost trust in using the IoT in healthcare, designers and developers must take security and privacy into account from the start. Security procedures must be implemented at every level and in every part of the IoT to minimize vulnerabilities and ensure privacy. In order for customers to feel safe and confident in sensors, devices, gateways, and IoT services, developers must guarantee the security of these "things" and the systems they link to. Many consumer and enterprise solutions are developed without thinking about security or privacy. Integrating security procedures into the hardware and software of sensors and transceivers for wireless communications has a significant impact on the performance of various IoT-based remote monitoring applications in the field of healthcare. Data collected from these sensors and devices are normally stored and sent using robust authentication and encryption methods and other precautions built with user privacy in mind. Most of the time, healthcare applications like this connect to third-party data aggregators whose own security protocols are in place.

16.5.2   Based on Energy

IoT devices utilized in healthcare for monitoring purposes exhibit a restricted duration of battery life. These electronic devices continue to consume energy even when they are in a state of energy conservation and are not explicitly mandated to perform sensor readings. operational standby mode. The device is equipped with an energy-conserving mode, albeit subject to a power constraint. Batteries are required in many medical devices, especially those that the patient wears or are used to monitor their status continuously. Extended monitoring requires a system combining low-power communications with a power-efficient hardware design. Finding ways to minimize energy use by studying activity-aware energy models is an exciting study area. Low performance may be increased with the use of context-aware episodic sampling.

16.5.3   Based on Integration

The term "integration" is used to describe the process of linking existing equipment or instruments with third-party technology in order to guarantee the reliability and consistency of data throughout their useful life span. There are outstanding issues about the data's integrity. There are unresolved concerns over the integrity of the data. Based on the Internet of Things (IoT). Extending and fusing monitoring systems with other external devices that have different benefits would boost quality of life. Integrated information systems will greatly benefit from the creation of unified tools for communication, processing, and service delivery. This necessitates a wide range of cloud, software-defined network (SDN), and similar technologies are being used in the IoT health care monitoring system.

16.6   Results and Recommendations

Based on current research and their limitations, wearable healthcare devices should be enhanced and integrated with future technological trends to tackle communication issues and downsides. If companies desire delighted clients, they must make suggested technologies user-friendly, flexible, and secure. Wearable sensors in healthcare systems may improve disease management and treatment. The IoT can link health-monitoring gadgets and sensors to the cloud for 24/7 monitoring. Medical records are easily accessed and securely stored on a server. Combining technologies may boost IoT-based healthcare systems, and a plan to identify chronic illnesses and COVID-19 might aid physicians in making the best choice and optimizing patients' health. Using a fog/edge paradigm, processing tasks might be decoupled. Big data can potentially enable Internet of Things healthcare monitoring solutions to handle massive volumes of information effectively. In the future, healthcare delivery will be enhanced through IoT devices, SDNs, and augmented intelligence technology and infrastructure (TI).

16.7 Conclusion

The Internet of Things has limitless potential to advance healthcare. Among them include lower prices and more productivity, precision, and performance. The Internet of Things has allowed for the most effective automation of healthcare systems to date. Prior to the advent of Internet health care services, individual effort was reserved for more conventional fields. Medical care via the Internet is distinct from typical offline businesses. Based on the unique qualities of the online health market, this research broadened the application reach of efforts to include not only typical offline industry but also online health services and additional effort instruments (doctors' answers and mutual support groups). These work tools are exclusive to the eHealth industry and have not been the subject of research in the area of e-commerce. Moreover, the degree of sickness privacy is an original factor in other health coverage (OHCs) that has not been discussed in prior research on electronic services, such as electronic governance or electronic commerce. This paper is meant to serve as a primer for future professionals in the industry by offering a comprehensive resource on the Internet of Things and healthcare monitoring systems. This paper provides a comprehensive evaluation and analysis of current studies focusing on IoT-based health-monitoring systems. The study offers a comprehensive look at the advantages and relevance of these things, as well as a review of the relevant literature. It is possible to categorize health-monitoring sensors in IoT devices for healthcare systems based on their functionality and use cases. Future directions have been suggested. Additional research on the effectiveness of illness categorization systems and Internet of Things-based healthcare monitoring tools can be done. The next step will be to emphasize combining cutting-edge technologies like SDN and AI with Internet of Things-based healthcare monitoring systems.

Bibliography

Keikhosrokiani, P., Mustaffa, N., Zakaria, N., Abdullah, R., Assessment of a medical information system: The mediating role of use and user satisfaction on the success of human interaction with the mobile healthcare system (iHeart). *Cogn. Technol. Work*, 22, 281–305, 2020.

Subramaniyaswamy, V., Manogaran, G., Logesh, R., Vijayakumar, V., Chilamkurti, N., Malathi, D., Senthilselvan, N., An ontology-driven personalized food recommendation in IoT-based healthcare system. *J. Supercomput.*, 75, 3184–3216, 2019.

Vahdat, S., The role of IT-based technologies on the management of human resources in the COVID-19 era. *Kybernetes*, 51, 6, 2065–2088, 2022.

Sannino, G., De Pietro, G., Verde, L., Healthcare systems: An overview of the most important aspects of current and future m-health applications, in: *Connected Health in Smart Cities*, pp. 213–231, 2020.

van Gemert-Pijnen, J.E.W.C. *et al.*, A holistic framework to improve the uptake and impact of eHealth technologies. *J. Med. Internet Res.*, 13, 4, e1672, 2011.

Shneiderman, B. and Plaisant, C., *Designing the user interface: Strategies for effective human-computer interaction*, Pearson Education India, 2010.

Lee, G. and Kwak, Y.H., An open government maturity model for social media-based public engagement. *Gov. Inf. Q.*, 29, 4, 492–503, 2012.

Wathen, C.N. and Burkell, J., Believe it or not: Factors influencing credibility on the web. *J. Am. Soc. Inf. Sci. Technol.*, 53, 2, 134–144, 2002.

Farhan, M., Jabbar, S., Aslam, M., Hammoudeh, M., Ahmad, M., Khalid, S., Khan, M., Han, K., IoT-based students interaction framework using attention-scoring assessment in eLearning. *Future Gener. Comput. Syst.*, 79, 909–919, 2018.

Perry, S., Kowalski, T.L., Chang, C.H., Quality of life assessment in women with breast cancer: Benefits, acceptability and utilization. *Health Qual. Life Outcomes*, 5, 1–14, 2007.

Almeida, A. *et al.*, A critical analysis of an IoT—Aware AAL system for elderly monitoring. *Future Gener. Comput. Syst.*, 97, 598–619, 2019.

Ramón Gil-García, J. and Pardo, T.A., E-government success factors: Mapping practical tools to theoretical foundations. *Gov. Inf. Q.*, 22, 2, 187–216, 2005.

Preece, J., Nonnecke, B., Andrews, D., The top five reasons for lurking: Improving community experiences for everyone. *Comput. Hum. Behav.*, 20, 2, 201–223, 2004.

Pokhrel, S. and Chhetri, R., A literature review on impact of COVID-19 pandemic on teaching and learning. *High. Educ. Future*, 8, 1, 133–141, 2021.

Moorhead, S.A., Hazlett, D.E., Harrison, L., Carroll, J.K., Irwin, A., Hoving, C., A new dimension of health care: Systematic review of the uses, benefits, and limitations of social media for health communication. *J. Med. Internet Res.*, *15*, 4, e1933, 2013.

Asri, H., Mousannif, H., Al Moatassime, H., Noel, T., Big data in healthcare: Challenges and opportunities, in: *2015 International Conference on Cloud Technologies and Applications (CloudTech)*, IEEE, pp. 1–7, 2015 Jun 2.

Walvoord, B.E. and Anderson, V.J., *Effective grading: A tool for learning and assessment in college*, John Wiley & Sons, 2011. https://teaching.resources.osu.edu/teaching-topics/designing-assessments-student

Talal, M., Zaidan, A.A., Zaidan, B.B., Albahri, A.S., Alamoodi, A.H., Albahri, O.S., Alsalem, M.A. *et al.*, Smart home-based IoT for real-time and secure remote health monitoring of triage and priority system using body sensors: Multi-driven systematic review. *J. Med. Syst.*, 43, 1–34, 2019.

Awotunde, J.B., Folorunso, S.O., Ajagbe, S.A., Garg, J., Ajamu, G.J., AiIoMT: IoMT-based system-enabled artificial intelligence for enhanced smart health-care systems, in: *Machine Learning for Critical Internet of Medical Things: Applications and Use Cases*, pp. 229–254, 2022.

Rahmani, A.M., Naqvi, R.A., Malik, M.H., Malik, T.S., Sadrishojaei, M., Hosseinzadeh, M., Al-Musawi, A., E-learning development based on internet of things and blockchain technology during COVID-19 pandemic. *Mathematics*, 9, 24, 3151, 2021.

Saggi, M.K. and Jain, S., A survey towards an integration of big data analytics to big insights for value-creation. *Inf. Process. Manage.*, *54*, 5, 758–790, 2018.

De Savigny, D. and Adam, T. (Eds.), *Systems Thinking for Health Systems Strengthening*, World Health Organization, 2009. https://www.research-gate.net/publication/281649433_Systems_Thinking_for_Health_Systems_Strengthening

Victorelli, E.Z., Dos Reis, J.C., Hornung, H., Prado, A.B., Understanding human-data interaction: Literature review and recommendations for design. *Int. J. Hum.-Comput. Stud.*, *134*, 13–32, 2020.

Rowe, A.K., De Savigny, D., Lanata, C.F., Victora, C.G., How can we achieve and maintain high-quality performance of health workers in low-resource settings? *Lancet*, 366, 9490, 1026–1035, 2005.

Norman, C.D. and Skinner, H.A., eHealth literacy: Essential skills for consumer health in a networked world. *J. Med. Internet Res.*, 8, 2, e506, 2006.

17

Integration of Edge Computing and Fuzzy Logic to Monitor Novel Coronavirus

K. Rama Krishna[1]*, R. Sudha[2], G. N. R. Prasad[3]
and Jithender Reddy Machana[4]

[1]*Department of Information Technology, Vasavi College of Engineering, Hyderabad, Telangana, India*
[2]*Department of Computer Science and Engineering, Vasavi College of Engineering, Hyderabad, Telangana, India*
[3]*Department of MCA, CBIT, Gandipet, Hyderabad, Telangana, India*
[4]*Vasavi College of Engineering, Telangana, India*

Abstract

Opportunities in healthcare have expanded to recent advancements in the Internet of Things (IoT) technology, artificial intelligence, and machine learning. Furthermore, these technical developments equipped us to meet future healthcare concerns. Among these problems is the appearance of COVID-19, which has unfathomable consequences. In order to distinguish between patients with and without symptoms, the IoT architecture gathers symptom data in real time from users. In addition, the suggested system can track how well patients who are ill respond to therapy. FLCD is made up of three parts: a cloud-based infrastructure for storing data with a potential judgment (normal, moderate, severe, or critical), a rule-based FLC for combining the system, and symptom data collected through wearable sensors. Experiments with a fabricated COVID-19 sign dataset are done once the required characteristics have been extracted to enable efficient and perfect identification of corona cases. This allowed FLCD to achieve a 95% success rate, 99.35% recall, 95.3% precision, and an error rate of no more than 3.53%.

Keywords: COVID-19, IoT technology, FLCD, wearable sensors, ML

Corresponding author: k.ramakrishna@staff.vce.ac.in

Satya Prakash Yadav, Sudesh Yadav, Pethuru Raj Chelliah and Victor Hugo C. de Albuquerque (eds.) *Advances in Fuzzy-Based Internet of Medical Things (IoMT)*, (255–270) © 2024 Scrivener Publishing LLC

17.1   Introduction

Initially dubbed SARS-CoV-2 (severe acute respiratory syndrome coronavirus 2), the new coronavirus COVID-19 was released into the wild in December 2019. This recently discovered coronavirus-caused illness transmits easily from person to person. Pandemic status for the viral epidemic was announced by the World Health Organization (WHO). Due to its rapid growth and infectious nature, it is predicted to peak on March 11, 2020. Table 17.1 contains the abbreviations used in this document. There were 211,746,699 cases of infection in the globe as of August 2021, with 3,431,960 fatalities recorded and 179,493,324 patients cured. Researchers in the medical field throughout the globe worked tirelessly to develop many vaccinations that have been given the green light for urgent use by national regulatory bodies and the World Health Organization. The WHO has designated seven vaccinations for use in extreme situations, allowing for their worldwide distribution and use to lessen the likelihood of contracting the COVID-19 virus. Since December 2020, just 22.3% of the global population has been completely immunized against COVID-19, whereas 42.3% have gotten at least one dose. In low-income nations, just 2.4% of the population has gotten at least one dose of vaccination. There have been reports of vaccine-related adverse effects, although they normally only last a few days at most. Therefore, social isolation and separation are the only proven methods of prevention. To stem the spread of the virus, governments throughout the globe have implemented work from home and lockdown restrictions. Standard operating procedures (SOPs) as suggested by the World Health Organization are shown in Figure 17.1. Despite conventional barriers to interaction rules, a second wave of COVID-19 spread internationally within 6 months, and other outbreaks occurred once limits were relaxed. The extremely contagious Delta strain has been on the rise around the globe in the fourth pandemic wave, making it the most dangerous of the four.

The fact that no notable effects were seen after the third and fourth rounds adds an extra layer of difficulty. Initial signs were a high temperature, difficulty breathing, sore throat, and a diminished sense of taste and smell. Diarrhea and exhaustion may be followed by subsequent waves like discomfort and a sore throat. However, most patients exhibit no outward signs of illness, making them a severe global hazard due to their invisibility and infectiousness. Transmission control is most effective when it relies on early case detection, fast testing, and self-quarantine. To prevent the spread of illness, it is crucial that both healthcare providers and the general public

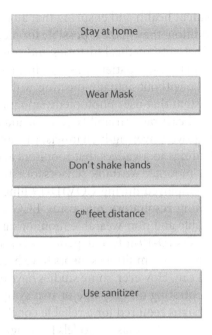

Figure 17.1 WHO-recommended SOPs for COVID-19.

practice rapid identification and careful surveillance. Recent publications recommend Internet of Things (IoT)-enabled frameworks for COVID-19 case detection and monitoring using wearable sensors. These structures help locate and maintain tabs on possible COVID-19 patients. While potentially effective, such technologies for identifying criminals in large groups seem unfeasible due to their high cost and resource requirements. As a result, there is a pressing need to create a framework that requires fewer people to intervene and fewer sensors to identify the sign of the illness. This study aims to create a low-cost, robust, and efficient Internet of Things-based platform that anybody may utilize.

17.2 Literature Review

When it comes to handling the COVID-19 pandemic and lockdown circumstances, the IoT technology has been shown to be effective. In order to solve this difficult issue, researchers have created smart wearable gadgets and mobile apps that make use of the Internet of Things. Rapid illness detection, real-time patient monitoring, and containment are all made possible by technological advancements. Furthermore, these technologies aid in monitoring patient health and ensuring that all infectious individuals are isolated. In addition, they make it possible for medical professionals to maintain track of patients' medical histories and conduct remote monitoring. Using these methods, a patient may get in touch with his doctor or specialist for advice without actually meeting with them. Suggested a wrist-worn sensor system that uses photoplethysmography (PPG) data to track heart rate (HR), heart rate variability (HRV), and blood oxygen saturation (SpO_2). Using two wavelength channels, the authors of this study demonstrated the findings in a gadget that monitors activity in real time. Suggested using chest-mounted wearable sensors for estimating respiratory rate. It is commonly employed during COVID-19 illness and proposed a technique for estimating respiratory rate using ECG and pulse position (PPG) sensors. Wearable and non-wearable monitoring device is used for quickly diagnosing COVID-19-infected people with sensor data. With wearable sensor technologies, multiple sensors have been suggested to log your symptoms if you can. However, some studies have only employed one or two sensors, concentrating on only one or two symptoms while disregarding other crucial signs required for a reliable conclusion. Due to their restricted capabilities, these IoT-based models have significant drawbacks. Nearly 15 symptoms of COVID-19 must be taken into account for a correct diagnosis. If a different sensor is used for each sign, it amounts to 15 sensors—an expensive and unworkable number. However, relying on only one or two sensors for COVID-19 detection while disregarding other vital indicators leads to inaccurate findings. If an accurate and trustworthy diagnosis is needed, consider additional symptoms. During the ongoing COVID-19 fourth wave, a substantial proportion of individuals infected with the virus remain asymptomatic, rendering their detection challenging, given that most individuals do not exhibit any symptoms until the condition deteriorates. In the majority of contemporary research endeavors, pulse oximetry is commonly employed for the measurement of arterial oxygen saturation (SpO_2). It is uncommon for the primary sensor for asymptomatic detection to be a mix of HR monitoring and a polyelectrolyte humidity sensor for RR monitoring. Obtained from these sensors and subsequently merging them, it is possible to enhance detection and prevention. Hence, it is imperative to establish an Internet of Things framework that can promptly and autonomously identify individuals afflicted with COVID-19, whether they exhibit symptoms or not. The current demand is for an efficient Internet of Things framework that utilizes cost-effective sensors to detect a wide range of vital signs, thereby offering an affordable solution that can be widely adopted.

17.3 COVID Detection

The schematic representation of the FLCD's overall design is depicted in Figure 17.2. The detection of asymptomatic patients has gained significance due to the rising number of such cases. The primary objective of the proposed model is to identify individuals who are asymptomatic. The objective is to identify asymptomatic individuals by monitoring their vital signs through the utilization of wearing sensors. Likewise, it can have a significant impact on SpO_2 levels. The measurement of arterial oxygen saturation (SpO_2) plays a crucial role in the management and assessment of disease progression and severity in individuals affected by COVID-19.

17.3.1 Function and Workflow of FLCD

The infection causes severe damage to the lungs. Chronic coughing, wheezing, and damage to lung tissue are all symptoms of COVID-19, an infection that causes swelling of the lower breathing tract. So, for early diagnosis, tracking infected people's progress and treatment is critical. Detecting the sickness in the initial stage by any abnormalities in the respiratory system. In addition to temperature and respiration rate (HR), oxygen saturation (SpO_2) is another fundamental and crucial marker for identifying asymptomatic suspects. Symptoms may often be predicted by keeping an eye on a patient's heart rate. SpO_2 is another parameter that may be significantly impacted. The SpO_2 is very important for individuals infected with COVID-19.

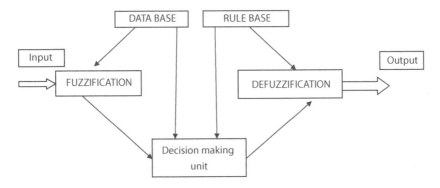

Figure 17.2 RBFL classifier for COVID-19 detection.

17.3.2   Data Collection Layer

Fusion-based data normalization in in-memory or edge processing. After data processing, a judgment is given that specifies whether a person has a light, moderate, or severe case of COVID-19 infection or if he or she is not infected by any virus. A motion sensor to track interpersonal distance and a cloud database including gathered data with created judgments are available to users, local medical units (hospitals/doctors), and city cations. A motion sensor can tell whether someone is touching or being touched by another person. Image processing from closed-circuit television and drone-based crowd surveillance is at the forefront of current research into measuring social distance. To the best of our knowledge, no currently suggested social distance monitoring methodology makes use of motion-based sensors able to identify people. Within a specific range, the motion detector may pick up on the presence of a human being. It sends out ultrasonic sound waves, which bounce off of people and other surfaces and return to the source. An alert will inform whether someone has crossed the restricted area. The Bluetooth Low Energy (BLE) module and integrated Wi-Fi enable it to interact with other smart devices. Figure 17.3 shows examples of sensors that may be worn. Wearable sensors include thermometers, pulse oximeters, motion detectors, and humidity

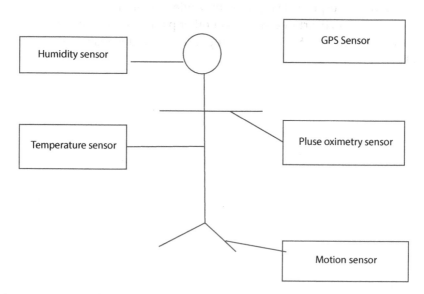

Figure 17.3 Sensor location on the human body.

Table 17.1 To collect information for a specific user.

User ID				
Time	Loc	SpO_2	Hormone replacement therapy (Hrt)	Inhalation therapy (It)

monitors, while a global positioning system (GPS) reader may be found in every modern smartphone. However, using the phone's built-in sensor is the most cost-effective option. The practicality of wearable sensors is questionable, although all of the necessary components are present in today's smartphones. Sensors on smartphones allow users to check their body temperature, heart rate, oxygen saturation, and breathing rate, as well as track their social distance, and locate themselves using the phone's GPS.

17.3.3   Cloud Layer

A cloud database is utilized to establish Table 17.1, which serves as a repository for the data about a single user. "User ID" refers to the unique identifier assigned to an individual user. The variable "time" denotes the moment the reading is captured. "Loc" represents the current geographical position. The variable "temp" signifies the numerical rate of the body temperature. Lastly, "SpO_2" denotes a numerical rate of the oxygen saturation level. The abbreviation SpO_2 refers to the measurement of peripheral oxygen saturation.

17.4   Setup of FLCD

The FLCD system under consideration is found upon a mechanism for collecting and processing symptom data in real time. This entails the collection of COVID-19 symptom data in real time from various sources. Wearable sensors collect information and provide a transmission mechanism to computers. This model analyses data and finds relevant patterns. However, in order to conduct experiments and tests, a dataset is utilized as an input consisting of symptom data from individuals who have tested positive and negative for COVID-19.

17.4.1   Data Refinement Phase

The characteristics that have been chosen for the preprocessing stage are then modified. The degree to which information is refined depends on two things:

1. the overall piece mass and
2. quantity and information conveyed by the feature.

The chosen characteristics and their relative importance are evenly spread throughout the various classes. In Table 17.2, the feature weight is broken down into four groups: typical, moderate, severe, and catastrophic.

FCG graphs have the same representation as any other graph, FCG = (V, E), where V denotes the vertex and E denotes the edge. The edges are represented by the letter E. The FCG is shown in Figure 17.4 when the sets of feature weights W = (w1, w2, w3, w4, w5) and feature weights X = (x1, x2, x3, x4, x5) are taken into account. Inter Feature Weight (IFW) is a weight matrix that represents the connections between nodes.

Table 17.2 The refined weights.

Symptoms	Choice	Weight	Choice	Total
TEMP-f	93.9	0	98.0-1001.1	6
SOP2%	90-100	0	92-93	8
SOCD-ft	10 -12	0	15-19	10

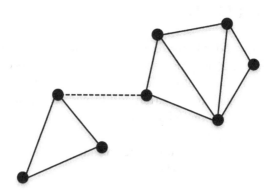

Figure 17.4 Feature connectivity graph.

17.4.2 Fuzzification

Fuzzification refers to the procedure of partitioning a collection of input values into multiple fuzzy sets. The process involves utilizing the association method to determine the extent to which input data are associated with the respective fuzzy set. During the process of fuzzification, the FIS logic system utilizes a specific method to convert crisp input values into fuzzy sets. The input values designated for testing are converted into association results referred to as "normal," "mild," "serious," and "critical." Each fuzzy set utilizes a membership function to generate a numerical value ranging from 0.0 to 1.2. Figure 17.5 illustrates association functions associated with the chosen FIS sets and one verdict set.

17.4.3 Defuzzification

An output obtained from the rule introduction phase is subjected to a defuzzification process. The values of crisps, which are the results generated by the inference engine, are primarily essential for practical applications in real-world scenarios. Hence, it is imperative to perform defuzzification on the output of the fuzzy rules. The process involves converting a fuzzy set into a well-defined value. The procedure involves transforming a FIS into a crisp set, resulting in a measurable outcome. This is achieved by utilizing fuzzy sets and their respective membership degrees. The comprehensive procedure of the FIS is depicted in Figure 17.6. Cognitive (COG) and

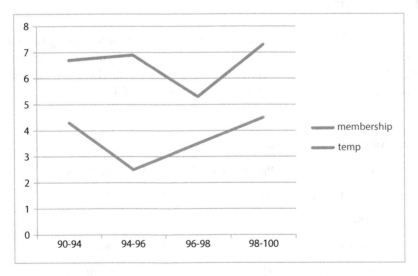

Figure 17.5 The membership function of temp, SpO_2, heart rate, social distance.

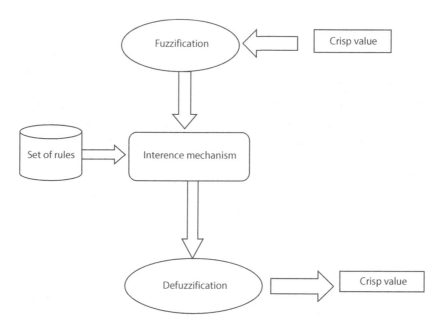

Figure 17.6 The structure of the FIS.

Motivation, observation, method (MOM) are widely recognized as the two most commonly employed techniques for defuzzification.

17.5   Result

The results of FLCD systems are discussed in this chapter. Using support vector machine (SVM), decision tree, naive Bayes, K-nearest neighbour (KNN), and logistic regression, the FLCD is analyzed. These are categorization methods in this research. Data are shown in Table 17.3.

Table 17.3 A comparative analysis.

ACT	Planned model	SVM	Naive Bayes
ACCURACY	98	90	90.92
EEROR	90	92	30.94
F-SCORE	78	94	50.56
ROC	92	98	91.20

17.5.1   Confusion Matrix

A confusion matrix, shown in Figure 17.7, is used in the performance matrix calculations. Typically, the performance of a binary classifier is evaluated using the matrix compares the actual target values with those predicted. class; nonetheless, a multiclass matrix may be generated and will help to evaluate the effectiveness of a multiclass overall learning issue. Since there are four possible categories, a 4-by-4 matrix is constructed, with false positive, true positive, true negative, and false negative values occupying each of the 16 cells. The examples belonging to the calculated and predicted classes are shown in the matrix's columns, while the instances belonging to the real classes are displayed in the matrix's rows. Clarity, perfection, misclassification rate, and occurrence are among the variables generated.

The FLCD system might easily replicate the harmful impacts of earlier iterations. COVID-19 virus, and lowering mortality rates by early detection will reduce the death rate. Patients may be monitored and potentially unreported incidences found to this technique, which might lead to better

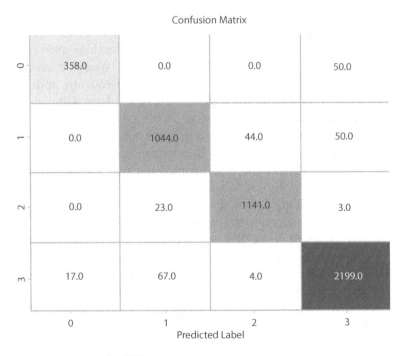

Figure 17.7 Matrix for the FLCD system.

treatment and results. Take a preventative rather than a defensive stance, allowing me to foresee the conclusion of any scenario with amazing precision. While waiting for government involvement, it also provides a tailored solution based on the needs of the individual. Systems to help people survive in space, radar detection, and the use of sophisticated digital infrastructure to hide social dominance hierarchies at a huge scale. FLCD also allows for the observation of a patient throughout the isolation of 14 days and after back to normal.

17.6 Conclusion

The fast global expansion and ongoing mortality risk from the COVID-19 virus. As a result, stopping the disease's transmission and curing the infected person depend on prompt and early identification of a person suspected of having COVID-19. A person with the Internet of Things capabilities is the focus of this study. In order to expedite the process of diagnosis and mitigate the transmission of the highly contagious COVID-19 virus, this study introduces a framework for rule-based fuzzy logic detection and patient monitoring. The proposed system for COVID-19 detection, known as the FLC for COVID-19 Detection (FLCD), includes three main components: data gathering, data fusion, and a cloud layer. Wearable sensors are utilized to collect data pertaining to symptoms, subsequently undergoing preprocessing and filtration through the data fusion layer. Ultimately, the data and the derived assessment are stored within the cloud infrastructure, ensuring accessibility for all users. The findings regarding precision, recall, accuracy, error rate, specificity, and F-score provide convincing evidence that the proposed FLCD system performs better than current techniques in diagnosing people who are suspected of having COVID-19 as well as in accurately identifying potential cases of COVID-19. The FLCD system has demonstrated a success rate of 95%, a mistake rate of 2.52%, precision of 94.73%, recall of 93.35%, and specificity of 98.06%, thus indicating the system's successful attainment of its objectives. The predictions of the FLCD model are compared to those of various other machine learning algorithms, such as the decision tree, K-nearest neighbor, support vector machine, naive Bayes, and logistic regression. The results indicate that the FLCD algorithm demonstrated superior performance compared to the other machine learning algorithms that were evaluated.

References

1. Energy Information Administration, *Household energy consumption and expenditures, consumption by end use,* Energy Information Administration (EIA), Washington, DC, USA, 2010.
2. Conti, J., Holtberg, P., Beamon, J., Schaal, A., Sweetnam, G., Kydes, A., Annual energy outlook with projections to 2035, Report of U.S. Energy Information Administration (EIA); EIA, Washington, DC, USA, 2010.
3. Ahmad, M.W., Mourshed, M., Yuce, B., Rezgui, Y., Computational intelligence techniques for HVAC systems: A review. *Build. Simul.,* 9, 359–398, 2016.
4. Borenstein, S., Jaske, M., Rosenfeld, A., *Dynamic pricing, advanced metering, and demand response in electricity markets,* Center for the Study of Energy Markets, University of California, Berkeley, CA, USA, 2002.
5. Keshtkar, A., Arzanpour, S., Keshtkar, F., Ahmadi, P., Smart residential load reduction via fuzzy logic, wireless sensors, and smart grid incentives. *Energy Build.,* 104, 165–180, 2015, [CrossRef].
6. Javaid, S., Javaid, N., Iqbal, S., Aslam, S., Rahim, M.H., Optimizing energy consumption of air-conditioning systems with the fuzzy logic controllers in residential buildings, in: *Proceedings of the 2018 International Conference on Computing, Mathematics and Engineering Technologies,* Sukkur, Pakistan, 3–4 March 2018.
7. Grygierek, K. and Ferdyn-Grygierek, J., Multi-objectives optimization of ventilation controllers for passive cooling in residential buildings. *Sensors,* 18, 1144, 2018, [CrossRef] [PubMed]
8. Iqbal, S., Boumella, N., Garcia, J., *Fuzzy controllers-recent advances in theory and applications,* InTech, London, UK, 2012.
9. Woolley, J., Pritoni, M., Modera, M., Center, W.C.E., Why occupancy-responsive adaptive thermostats do not always save-and the limits for when they should, in: *Proceedings of the 2014 ACEEE Summer Study on Energy Efficiency in Buildings,* Asilomar, CA, USA, 17–22 August 2014.
10. Lu, J., Sookoor, T., Srinivasan, V., Gao, G., Holben, B., Stankovic, J., Field, E., Whitehouse, K., The smart thermostat: Using occupancy sensors to save energy in homes, in: *Proceedings of the 8th ACM Conference on Embedded Networked Sensor Systems,* Zürich, Switzerland, pp. 211–224, 3–5 November 2010.
11. Khan, T.A., Abbas, S., Ditta, A., Khan, M.A., Alquhayz, H., Fatima, A., Khan, M.F., IoMT-based smart monitoring hierarchical fuzzy inference system for diagnosis of COVID-19. *Comput. Mater. Contin.,* 65, 3, 2591–2605, 2020.
12. Kumar, S., Kalra, G., Bhardwaj, H.K., Rajoria, Y.K., Kumar, D., Boadh, R., Internet of Medical Thing and FIS evaluation for selecting and delivering the best health insurance coverage. *J. Pharm. Negat. Results,* 13, Special Issue 8, 3438–3446, 2022.

13. Silva-Ramírez, E.-L. and Cabrera-Sánchez, J.-F., Co-active neuro-fuzzy inference system model as single imputation approach for non-monotone pattern of missing data. *Neural Comput. Appl.*, 33, 8981–9004, 2021.

14. Khanmohammadi, S., Chou, C.-A., Esfahlani, F.Z., Hourani, A., A fuzzy inference system for predicting human error and its application in process management, in: *IIE Annual Conference. Proceedings*, Institute of Industrial and Systems Engineers (IISE), p. 2032, 2014.

15. Zanbouri, K. *et al.*, A new fog-based transmission scheduler on the Internet of multimedia things using a fuzzy-based quantum genetic algorithm. *IEEE Multimedia*, Volume 30, 1–14, 2023.

16. González, J.C., Dalforno, C., Suppi, R., Luque, E., A fuzzy logic fish school model, in: *Computational Science–ICCS 2009: 9th International Conference Baton Rouge, LA, USA, May 25-27, 2009 Proceedings, Part I 9*, Springer Berlin Heidelberg, pp. 13–22, 2009.

17. Patro, P., Azhagumurugan, R., Sathya, R., Kumar, K., Kumar, T.R., Babu, M.V.S., A hybrid approach estimates the real-time health state of a bearing by accelerated degradation tests, machine learning. *2021 Second International Conference on Smart Technologies in Computing, Electrical and Electronics (ICSTCEE)*, pp. 1–9, Bengaluru, India, 2021, doi: 10.1109/ICSTCEE54422.2021.9708591.

18. Parthiban, K. and Venkatachalapathy, K., Internet of things and cloud enabled hybrid feature extraction with adaptive neuro fuzzy inference system for diabetic retinopathy diagnosis. *J. Comput. Theor. Nanosci.*, 17, 12, 5261–9, 2020 Dec 1.

19. Ramadan, A., Kamel, S., Hamdan, I., Agwa, A.M., A novel intelligent ANFIS for the dynamic model of photovoltaic systems. *Mathematics*, 10, 8, 1286, 2022.

20. Yadav, S.P. and Yadav, S., Fusion of medical images in wavelet domain: A discrete mathematical model. *Ing. Solidaria*, 14, 25, 1–11, 2018, Universidad Cooperativa de Colombia- UCC. https://doi.org/10.16925/.v14i0.2236.

21. Mokni, M., Yassa, S., Hajlaoui, J.E., Omri, M.N., Chelouah, R., Multi-objective fuzzy approach to scheduling and offloading workflow tasks in Fog–Cloud computing. *Simul. Modell. Pract. Theory*, 123, 102687, 2023.

22. Abo-Sennah, M.A., El-Dabah, M.A., Mansour, A.E.B., Maximum power point tracking techniques for photovoltaic systems: A comparative study. *Int. J. Electr. Comput. Eng.*, 11, 1, 2088–8708, 1–22, 2021.

23. Roy, S. *et al.*, A multi-criteria prioritization-based data transmission scheme for inter-WBAN communications. *J. Inst. Eng.s (India): Ser. B*, 104, 1, 1–7, 2023.

24. Kaur, J., Saxena, J., Shah, J., Fahad, Yadav, S.P., Facial emotion recognition, in: *2022 International Conference on Computational Intelligence and Sustainable Engineering Solutions (CISES)*, IEEE, 2022, https://doi.org/10.1109/cises54857.2022.9844366.

25. Quan, Y., Chaoyang, D., Qing, W., A fuzzy adaptive fusion algorithm for radar/infrared based on wavelet analysis, in: *2007 IEEE International Conference on Control and Automation,* pp. 1344–1348, IEEE, 2007, May.
26. Vyas, S., Gupta, S., Bhargava, D., Boddu, R., Fuzzy logic system implementation on the performance parameters of health data management frameworks. *J. Healthcare Eng.,* 2022, 1–12, 2022.

18

Implementation of IoT in Healthcare Barriers and Future Challenges

Aravindan Srinivasan[1]*, Veeresh Rampur[2], Munagala Madhu Sudhan Rao[3] and Ravinjit Singh[4]

[1]Department of CSE, Koneru Lakshmaiah Education Foundation, Vaddeswaram, AP, India
[2]Department of Electronics, Government First Grade College, Bidar, Karnataka, India
[3]English Department, Koneru Lakshmaiah Education Foundation, Vaddeswaram, AP, India
[4]Faculty of Business & Management (FABM), Akademi Laut Malaysia (ALAM), Bidar, Malaysia

Abstract

The Internet of Things (IoT) is used in many areas, including healthcare. This technology improves medical service efficiency and patient care. Thus, its full integration into the healthcare industry is a shared goal. Many IoT-based healthcare system applications enhance diagnosis and treatment. Globally, healthcare is unique. Aging, chronic and lifestyle diseases, and growth goals affect the global population. Healthcare expenditures rise. Technology could fix this. Mobile health checks, where doctors visit people instead of hospitals, may be a solution. This paper examines the IoT in healthcare. This article visualizes the cognitive functions, enabling elements, and operational workflow of the IoT as part of healthcare. This report examines notable healthcare IoT installations. The essay discusses the healthcare sector IoT performance challenges. The IoT technology in healthcare has benefited several aspects of the patient–system interaction. Healthcare practitioners may acquire vital health data from clever medical equipment connected to a smartphone app. A doctor may assess a patient's health to enhance therapy. This healthcare technology might improve the patient healthcare management system.

Keywords: IoT healthcare system, real-time monitoring, patient healthcare

*Corresponding author: Kkl.aravind@gmail.com

Satya Prakash Yadav, Sudesh Yadav, Pethuru Raj Chelliah and Victor Hugo C. de Albuquerque (eds.)
Advances in Fuzzy-Based Internet of Medical Things (IoMT), (271–286) © 2024 Scrivener Publishing LLC

18.1 Introduction

The Internet of Things (IoT) is crucial to solving healthcare's many problems. The IoT in healthcare may provide personalized solutions based on the patient's medical history and lifestyle [1]. Patients, doctors, hospitals, carers, and insurers benefit from healthcare IoT solutions. Fitness trackers and wireless gadgets may help people measure their activities and make healthy choices [2]. Medical specialist to stay often updated about the advancement of new treatments and to smear their knowledge for future challenges. IoT system enhances data and high-tech equipment utilization, enabling a timely response [3]. Disease management systems may be improved using widely available sensors and gateways. The IoT can monitor hospital staff and equipment. The IoT companies monitor and manage hospital systems, nurses, patients, and equipment. Location sensors connect hospital patients, physicians, and medical equipment through the IoT [4, 5].

Connected to the Internet, healthcare data and administration systems manage the numerous directions in which medical procedures might travel. The IoT has immense untapped possibilities to transform healthcare delivery systems. The IoT is becoming common in healthcare institutions around the globe [6]. By facilitating the mobilization of consumer demand patterns and improving data-tracking methods, the IoT has an opportunity to transform the healthcare industry. Data gathered from patients are analyzed by IoT-enabled healthcare equipment [7–9]. IoT monitoring in healthcare aims to provide access to timely diagnosis and care. Medical alerts and records may be monitored in real time, thanks to IoT apps. This paves the way for doctors to give patients the care they need and improves the quality of that care.

The spread of COVID-19 has helped medical technology develop. IoT service workers may prioritize and advance the upcoming of the IoT in healthcare. Healthcare modernization, new preventative platform development, and efficient data management might all benefit from this technology [10]. Wheelchairs, nebulizers, pumps, scales, defibrillators, and testing devices may all benefit from having IoT sensors attached to them for easy identification. Rapid changes in the healthcare business make it difficult to foresee the next game-changing innovation [11, 12]. Processing and understanding the long-term influence of the Internet of Things on health care needs to be consider. There have been significant developments in the use of the IoT in healthcare, especially in exercise science, medical study, and treatment.

Low- and middle-income nations may benefit significantly from the IoT's linked devices for healthcare because of how cheap they are. In addition, it offers a mechanized approach to monitoring various conditions and improving the security of patients [13]. This technology is often used for monitoring purposes to ensure the safety of a healthcare facility's assets. This technology is well-known for its efficiency in monitoring things or people with little investment of time or money. Monitoring medicine delivery, ensuring the correct dose, and keeping tabs on possible adverse effects are now accomplished by utilizing IoT devices [14, 15].

Also, it could help patients remember to take their meds on time and in the right amount [16]. Using IoT devices in healthcare is cool! These things are super helpful for IoT applications. They can help cut down on wait times in emergency rooms, make things better for patients and staff, ensure people take their meds, keep track of inventory, and ensure that all of the necessary hardware is available [17].

There were several obstacles to building a sensitive and competent framework for implementing the IoT in the global healthcare industry. Improvements in patient care's efficiency and administration rely heavily on the IoT's reliable operation. The IoT has become more valuable to patients in the healthcare industry [18]. Warbles, a new kind of attractive and cutting-edge IoT gadget, has helped patients gain a deeper understanding of their health status. Since this innovation allows for constant patient health tracking, it has found more widespread use in the healthcare industry [19, 20]. Connected to mobile devices, these tools expedite the dissemination of real-time data, allowing medical professionals to quickly obtain them and use them to make critical decisions in patient care. A few years back, there has been encouraging progress in the healthcare industry's use of IoT technologies. The delivery of medical care is being transformed by the IoT [21, 22].

IoT devices can streamline communication processes, leading to precise data transmission between medical professionals, personnel, and individuals seeking medical attention, ultimately enhancing the quality of healthcare services [23]. The integration of the IoT technology within the healthcare sector represents a notable advancement, as it enables the ongoing monitoring of patients and the acquisition of real-time data, thereby facilitating the identification of illnesses. Retrieving essential data is typically feasible during a crucial need period. IoT devices can reduce data categorization into suitable classifications, enabling the relevant medical practitioner to process them. Pharmacy and medical device management are crucial components of the healthcare industry [24]. Using IoT devices with sensors enables the facile tracking of medical equipment. The integration of the IoT in the healthcare sector has emerged as a significant development in recent times [25].

Medical practitioners spend a lot of time and effort caring for their patients [26–28]. The application of the IoT in healthcare is a fascinating area of study. Through voice commands, physicians can access critical health information about a patient's diagnosis, medical history, prescriptions, progress reports, care plans, allergies, examinations, findings, and immunization plans [29–31]. The healthcare sector has recently adopted the IoT technology to enable remote monitoring, which ensures patient safety and security [32–34]. This technology allows medical practitioners to deliver quality care even when not physically present [35].

The paper's research objectives are segmented as follows:

- The present research intends to inquire about the IoT's intelligent features in the medical field.
- The study aims to investigate the many enabling parts of the IoT in healthcare systems.
- The purpose of the study is to examine the healthcare IoT's operational workflow and to identify and investigate the critical uses of healthcare IoT.
- The study intends to look into possible challenges and opportunities associated with integrating the IoT technology into healthcare delivery.

18.2   The IoT in Healthcare

The healthcare industry has diverse applications for the IoT. IoT systems can gather and communicate human health data in real time [36, 37]. Medical reports are commonly kept in cloud-based systems and can be accessed by authorized individuals from any location, at any time, and using any computer [38–40]. Integrating the IoT technology in the healthcare industry involves linking the healthcare management framework with IoT devices, cloud-based data management, and fog computing [41–43]. The IoT implementation in the healthcare segment is illustrated in Figure 18.1.

The IoT may also aid in making the medical staff more productive [44–46]. Hospitals and other healthcare institutions can have a complex organizational structure with many different departments, making it essential to identify and direct staff correctly [47]. The IoT aids in coordinating efforts and streamlining care administration. Many healthcare facilities, doctors, and patients embrace the IoT despite its challenges [48–50].

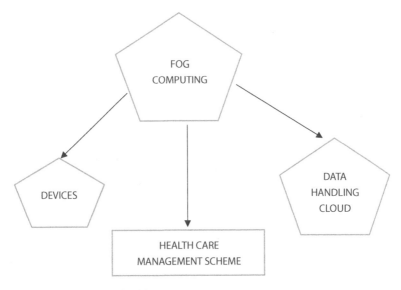

Figure 18.1 The IoT in the healthcare system.

18.3   IoT Smart Features

Figure 18.2 depicts the diverse intelligent functionalities and capabilities of IoT services within the healthcare sector. The text delves into the fundamental underpinnings of connected health theory, the utilization of intelligent care units and online information trailing, and their amalgamation for the betterment of society.

This nascent technological advancement has made it possible to meet all healthcare needs effortlessly. The rise of chronic illnesses and the global aging phenomenon pose significant healthcare challenges that constrain healthcare providers' capacity to deliver superior care and enhance patient outcomes. Developing novel benchmarks for healthcare providers to furnish exceptional healthcare services is imperative. The IoT satisfies contemporary standards by enabling instantaneous monitoring, providing dependable approaches for collecting patient data, and monitoring both the patients and personnel activities. Medical practitioners can utilize the information collected from wearable technology and other medical apparatus to monitor the health status of their patients, establish suitable treatment protocols, comply with treatment regimens, and attain the intended outcomes.

Surveillance data may be used to detect healthcare insurance fraud and keep patients and their providers informed. Information from the IoT may

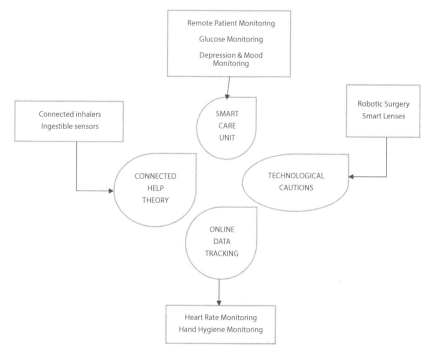

Figure 18.2 Functionalities of the IoT.

be used across operational processes and patients to confirm underlying issues and advise the best option. Other sectors have widely adopted the IoT and linked devices. In the future, healthcare workers can make their jobs more accessible, productive, and automated. The IoT facilitates the gathering of huge quantities of data, which will be effectively analyzed by segmenting them into smaller units. This approach avoids the pitfalls of excessive precision and yields superior outcomes. Planning the integrating process thoroughly may help healthcare companies and institutions avoid safety risks and interoperability difficulties. After integrating IoT systems, it is essential to choose trustworthy devices, ensure they are compatible with current infrastructure, keep things running smoothly, and do regular security checks. The IoT includes intelligent gadgets that can monitor a person's health records and help reduce the likelihood of future ailments.

Figure 18.3 discusses some crucial enablers and elements that comprise IoT services in the healthcare industry. Supporting healthcare delivery and associated services in their entirety using the IoT starts with cases of real-time alerts, remote medical assistance, gathering and analyzing information on the cloud, and so on.

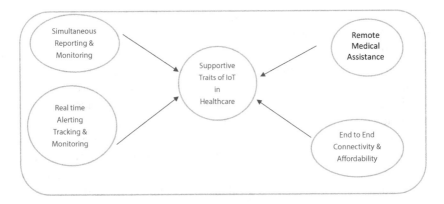

Figure 18.3 IoT enablers.

With its potential to improve healthcare technology and usher in a new era of digital healthcare delivery, the IoT is well-positioned to bring about a dramatic shift in the sector. To offer high-quality medical treatment, healthcare professionals must meet additional requirements. One of the many benefits of the IoT is that it allows for constant monitoring. As a result, the IoT is forecasted to mature into a potent remedy for gathering patient information and documenting all activities of patients as well as healthcare providers, allowing them to conform to the latest regulations.

Due to IoT healthcare devices, patients can get in touch with clinicians rapidly and have their questions answered. Early detection of health issues via IoT devices may save both time and money for healthcare professionals. Dispensing medications to patients by their doctors' orders might be made more efficient with IoT devices in healthcare. The patient's body may be connected to the computer in this way. One of the many applications of the IoT is inpatient monitoring.

The prompt diagnosis and treatment help to save lives. However, appreciate that a medical institution and an IoT app development company worked together to effectively fix this problem as a result of their excellent cooperation. IoT devices' data will help physicians decide what treatment and monitoring are best for each patient. The IT business does not only provide IoT products for healthcare, it serves a wide range of industries. The IoT is a vast system of interconnected electronic gadgets constantly collecting and exchanging data online.

Healthcare will get even more incredible with the IoT. It will be a game changer for individual healthcare, pharmaceuticals, insurance, and construction facilities. Using medicine and cool healthcare gadgets like activity trackers can help with medical issues. Activity monitors monitor cancer patients to see how much they are moving around and how tired and active they are. Doctors better grasp things if they have data from before and after treatment.

Through increased connection and cutting-edge tools, IoT implementation in healthcare will boost teamwork and ease the flow of information. Disease monitoring and diagnosis may be made more accessible and time-efficient with Bluetooth, Wi-Fi, and other technical elements. The time and money spent on patient visits are cut down with this method. The introduction of this new technology may help reduce healthcare expenditures. Any IoT endeavor in healthcare requires massive data collection on individual patients and their medical histories. The IoT infrastructure must also be able to transmit information to other devices reliably. Data from IoT devices may be collected, analyzed, monitored, shared, and received with ease to a cloud-based architecture. Due to its enormous dimensions, establishing a cloud foundation is required.

18.4   The IoT Process in the Health Process

The initial step involves the gathering of data from various pertinent sources. Subsequently, the data proceed to the analysis phase, wherein cloud services are utilized. The aforementioned facilitates the provision of reasonable and practical decisions and assistance in patient care. These decisions provide patients with guidelines to enhance their overall satisfaction within the healthcare system. The utilization of IoT devices equipped with sensors has the potential to facilitate real-time monitoring of equipment location for environmental surveillance and pharmacy inventory management. Implementing the IoT technology in the healthcare industry supports hospitals' patient care efforts. The escalation of population growth has led to an increase in the overall number of individuals afflicted with illnesses, advanced age, and other health-related concerns. However, implementing the IoT in the healthcare sector has proven to be a viable solution to these challenges. The IoT technology has enabled medical professionals to monitor the real-time symptoms of patients, thereby mitigating the risk of critical events such as heart failure, asthma, cardia arrest, and diabetes.

This would have far-reaching effects on medicine and pave the way for developing cutting-edge new treatments. The IoT has several applications in healthcare, including improving efficiency and providing a more unified user experience. Incorporating different mobile app development solutions into healthcare allows doctors to assess patients and categorize disorders simultaneously. Most hospitals' priority is patient safety.

On occasion, it is necessary to employ multiple devices to monitor an individual patient. The integration and utilization of various devices pose a challenge due to the variations in their standards and protocols. Furthermore, the integration of the IoT technology by prominent healthcare institutions globally has propelled the healthcare sector to unprecedented levels. The ubiquitous nature of the IoT is expected to significantly impact the global healthcare industry, particularly in terms of enhancing operational efficiency. Individualized healthcare services are provided to patients. IoT-enabled methods are engineered to gather, transmit, and examine information from individuals within a dynamic and evolving context.

18.5   Applications

The IoT has facilitated the convergence of various technological aspects within the healthcare industry. The technology in question has established an extensive network using expanding Internet connectivity to tangible devices and commonplace entities. These methods and objects can link via the Internet and be conveniently supervised and controlled. In addition to the benefits above, implementing the IoT technology in the healthcare sector yields various avenues for enhancing operational efficacy. Hospitals are susceptible to vulnerability, and the transmission of infections is a notable concern. Integrating the IoT technology into hygiene monitoring systems can significantly improve the efficiency and effectiveness of intelligent hygiene monitoring. The system can monitor patients' adherence to their rehabilitation protocols and identify the necessity for urgent medical attention.

The implementation of the IoT has resulted in enhancements in patient protection, hospital resource managing, and environmental observation, including dampness and disease control, within the healthcare industry. A significant trend will likely involve the continual expansion of healthcare policies in conjunction with integrating the IoT connectivity. The process of medical research typically spans multiple years, and the integration of the IoT technology has the potential to expedite this process. This phenomenon can be attributed to the dependable and expeditious gathering and evaluation of data. Consequently, utilizing IoT applications preserves time and resources, facilitating more comprehensive and superior medical research and treatments. As noted in previous studies, healthcare professionals may use the IoT to enhance their vigilance and compassion when interacting with patients.

Medical professionals and private nurses may monitor patients using wearables and other home monitoring gadgets. Medical professionals can keep tabs on patients, better prepare for their care and rehabilitation, and be alert for those needing immediate treatment to the IoT sensors included in these gadgets. With the IoT, patients' medical records and future care may be kept in one place. It uses information from various high-quality sensors to monitor the patient's health and detect the slightest changes. Healthcare providers need to put their patients' needs before their own. Management solutions provided by the IoT can save people from becoming sick.

18.6   IoT Barriers and Future Challenges

Various barriers impede the application of the IoT in healthcare amenities. Safeguarding the confidentiality of personal health information is paramount, as it is a perpetual possibility of its vulnerability to unauthorized access. Despite significant efforts, achieving comprehensive privacy remains a formidable task. Another crucial factor is the inadequate training provided to healthcare professionals. Despite the digitalization of the healthcare sector, the authorities have allocated minimal attention to this aspect.

More infrastructure poses a significant obstacle to implementing the IoT in healthcare systems. The previous paper highlights the multifaceted nature of the IoT for heart health care, which involves numerous stages. The task of ensuring the availability of said devices presents a significant challenge.

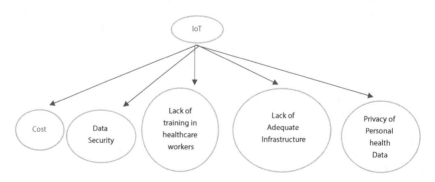

Figure 18.4 Barriers of the IoT.

Moreover, it is imperative to regularly update the infrastructure, as outdated infrastructure poses a significant obstacle. Figure 18.4 illustrates a range of obstacles that interfere with implementing the IoT technology in the healthcare sector.

18.7   Discussion

The IoT has been integrated into various sectors, including manufacturing, logistics, retail, and healthcare. The implementation of IoT devices has enabled hospitals, physicians, and patients to engage in patient monitoring, hospital procedure management, and health tracking. The technology has had a significant impact on individuals, particularly the elderly population, as it allows for promptly monitoring their health status. A device designed to provide a warning signal to family members and healthcare professionals in the event of any disruption or modification in an individual's daily routine. The utilization of IoT devices, if employed appropriately, has the potential to inundate medical professionals with copious amounts of data, yet it may also facilitate the process of diagnosis. IoT systems have the potential to monitor patients' movements and responses to medication, thereby enabling the development of more individualized treatment plans and reducing the incidence of medical errors.

Integrating IoT medical systems involves utilizing intelligent connected devices capable of monitoring a patient's health status and detecting potential health issues before they manifest into a full-blown disease. The data collected through IoT devices will aid medical professionals in identifying the underlying factors contributing to a patient's ailment. Wearable devices can monitor the health of individuals with chronic conditions by collecting data, identifying patterns, and issuing notifications. The insights derived from this data can facilitate accurate diagnosis, effective treatment, and improved customer service. Medical devices monitor equipment utilization for each patient and analyze the data to gain insights and assess their condition. When integrated with a system for tracking positions in real time, these wearables and stickers will aid healthcare practitioners in expediting their tasks.

Utilization of this technology is associated with various potential hazards. The fundamental concern pertains to the safeguarding of privacy and security of data. The abundance of information presented poses challenges to decisions regarding care. The demand for skilled personnel in human resources and healthcare is evident. In the forthcoming health-care industry, implementing an electronic health record system is poised to yield advantages for patients and physicians. Medical practitioners will assess the latest laboratory test outcomes and the patient's medical records. Conversely, individuals afflicted with ailments stemming from their lifestyle can schedule appointments with medical practitioners at their convenience. Wearables are diminutive intelligent devices with mobile applications that track and assess physical well-being. The IoT is poised to revolutionize a burgeoning industry, rapidly expanding its reach to remote regions worldwide. Numerous digital enterprises are investing substantially in developing novel IoT-enabled commodities incorporating computer vision technology. Contact lenses allowed with the IoT tech-nology can detect an individual's glucose level and assess the likelihood of developing diabetes. This IoT application has been widely recognized as highly beneficial for hospitals globally. Numerous healthcare facilities are anticipated to utilize this application in the forthcoming years due to its ability to promote hospital hygiene and facilitate staff focusing on high-priority responsibilities.

18.8   Conclusion

The IoT significantly impacts medical science, enabling the implementa-tion of comprehensive and efficacious medical treatments. It finds appli-cation in various medical devices that enhance the caliber of healthcare facilities rendered to patients. The IoT is improving existing devices by inte-grating intelligent microchips. The IoT presents significant data protection and privacy risks. The proliferation of the IoT generates enthusiasm across many industries due to its versatility in serving various applications. The company also introduced a series of wearables and accessories that have facilitated patients' lives. These devices are interconnected and capture an increasing amount of data, thereby exacerbating the issue. The IoT tech-nology in the medical field facilitates the monitoring of blood coagulation systems daily for individuals with diabetes. This enables them to maintain their blood coagulation levels within the therapeutic range, mitigating the likelihood of experiencing bleeding or stroke. Healthcare professionals will encourage patients to intimate their blood clot tests. The utilization of IoT applications can be expanded to encompass a diverse range of ill-nesses within multiple healthcare industry settings. Healthcare profession-als can leverage the information obtained from wearable technology and other medical devices to monitor the well-being of their patients, ascertain the most suitable treatment regimen, comply with prescribed therapeutic interventions, and attain the desired medicinal outcome.

References

1. Abdulmalek, S., Nasir, A., Jabbar, W.A., Almuhaya, M.A.M., Bairagi, A.K., Khan, M.A., Kee, S.H., IoT-based healthcare-monitoring system towards improving quality of life: A review. *Healthcare (Basel)*, 10, 10, 1993, 2022 Oct 11, doi: 10.3390/healthcare10101993. PMID: 36292441; PMCID: PMC9601552.

2. Nguyen, H.H. *et al.*, A review on IoT healthcare monitoring applications and a vision for transforming sensor data into real-time clinical feedback, in: *2017 IEEE 21st International Conference on Computer Supported Cooperative Work in Design (CSCWD)*, IEEE, 2017.

3. Selvaraj, S. and Sundaravaradhan, S., Challenges and opportunities in IoT healthcare systems: A systematic review. *SN Appl. Sci.*, 2, 1, 139, 2020.

4. Ugrenovic, D. and Gardasevic, G., CoAP protocol for web-based monitoring in IoT healthcare applications, in: *2015 23rd Telecommunications Forum Telfor (TELFOR)*, IEEE, 2015.

5. Wu, T., Redouté, J.-M., Yuce, M., A wearable, low-power, real-time ECG monitor for smart t-shirt and IoT healthcare applications, in: *Advances in Body Area Networks I: Post-Conference Proceedings of BodyNets 2017*, Springer International Publishing, 2019.

6. De Michele, R. and Furini, M., IoT healthcare: Benefits, issues and challenges, in: *Proceedings of the 5th EAI International Conference on Smart Objects and Technologies for Social Good*, pp. 160–164, 2019, September.

7. Zgheib, R., Conchon, E., Bastide, R., Engineering IoT healthcare applications: Towards a semantic data driven sustainable architecture, in: *eHealth 360°: International Summit on eHealth, Budapest, Hungary, June 14-16, 2016, Revised Selected Papers*, Springer International Publishing, pp. 407–418, 2017.

8. Kumar, S. *et al.*, A wristwatch-based wireless sensor platform for IoT health monitoring applications. *Sensors*, 20, 6, 1675, 2020.

9. Rathi, V.K. *et al.*, An edge AI-enabled IoT healthcare monitoring system for smart cities. *Comput. Electr. Eng.*, 96, 107524, 2021.

10. Kashani, M.H. *et al.*, A systematic review of IoT in healthcare: Applications, techniques, and trends. *J. Network Comput. Appl.*, 192, 103164, 2021.

11. Mishra, S.S. and Rasool, A., IoT health care monitoring and tracking: A survey, in: *2019 3rd International Conference on Trends in Electronics and Informatics (ICOEI)*, IEEE, 2019.

12. Nandyala, C.S. and Kim, H.-K., Green IoT agriculture and healthcare application (GAHA). *Int. J. Smart Home*, 10, 4, 289–300, 2016.

13. Bibani, O. *et al.*, A demo of IoT healthcare application provisioning in hybrid cloud/fog environment, in: *2016 IEEE International Conference on Cloud Computing Technology and Science (CloudCom)*, IEEE, 2016.

14. Bhoomika, B.K. and Muralidhara, K.N., Secured smart healthcare monitoring system based on IoT. *Int. J. Recent Innov. Trends Comput. Commun.*, 3, 7, 4958–4961, 2015.

15. Yadav, S.P. and Yadav, S., Fusion of medical images using a wavelet methodology: A survey. *IEIE Trans. Smart Process. Comput.*, 8, 4, 265–271, 2019, The Institute of Electronics Engineers of Korea. https://doi.org/10.5573/ieiespc.2019.8.4.265.

16. AL-Mawee, W., Privacy and security issues in IoT healthcare applications for the disabled users a survey, 2012.

17. Yadav, H., Singh, S., Mishra, K.K., Srivastava, S., Naruka, M.S., Yadav, S.P., Brain tumor detection with MRI images, in: *2022 International Conference on Computational Intelligence and Sustainable Engineering Solutions (CISES). 2022 International Conference on Computational Intelligence and Sustainable Engineering Solutions (CISES)*, IEEE, 2022, https://doi.org/10.1109/cises54857.2022.9844387.

18. Alansari, Z. *et al.*, The Internet of Things adoption in healthcare applications, in: *2017 IEEE 3rd International Conference on Engineering Technologies and Social Sciences (ICETSS)*, IEEE, 2017.

19. Selem, E. *et al.*, THE (temperature heterogeneity energy) aware routing protocol for IoT health application. *IEEE Access*, 7, 108957–108968, 2019.

20. Alekya, R. *et al.*, IoT based smart healthcare monitoring systems: A literature review. *Eur. J. Mol. Clin. Med.*, 7, 11, 2020, 2021.

21. Godi, B. *et al.*, E-healthcare monitoring system using IoT with machine learning approaches. *2020 International Conference on Computer Science, Engineering and Applications (ICCSEA)*, IEEE, 2020.

22. Mustafa, T. and Varol, A., Review of the internet of things for healthcare monitoring, in: *2020 8th International Symposium on Digital Forensics and Security (ISDFS)*, IEEE, 2020.

23. Patro, P., Azhagumurugan, R., Sathya, R., Kumar, K., Kumar, T.R., Babu, M.V.S., A hybrid approach estimates the real-time health state of a bearing by accelerated degradation tests, machine learning, in: *2021 Second International Conference on Smart Technologies in Computing, Electrical and Electronics (ICSTCEE)*, pp. 1–9, Bengaluru, India, 2021, doi: 10.1109/ICSTCEE54422.2021.9708591.

24. Abdulmalek, S. *et al.*, IoT-based healthcare-monitoring system towards improving quality of life: A review. *Healthcare*, 10, 10, 1–32, 2022, MDPI.

25. Singh, K. *et al.*, Role and impact of wearables in IoT healthcare, in: *Proceedings of the Third International Conference on Computational Intelligence and Informatics: ICCII 2018*, Springer Singapore, 2020.

26. Dziak, D., Jachimczyk, B., Kulesza, W.J., IoT-based information system for healthcare application: Design methodology approach. *Appl. Sci.*, 7, 6, 596, 2017.

27. Wu, F., Wu, T., Yuce, M.R., Design and implementation of a wearable sensor network system for IoT-connected safety and health applications, in: *2019 IEEE 5th World Forum on Internet of Things (WF-IoT)*, pp. 87–90, Limerick, Ireland, 2019, doi: 10.1109/WF-IoT.2019.8767280.

28. Ud Din, I., Almogren, A., Guizani, M., Zuair, M., A decade of Internet of Things: Analysis in the light of healthcare applications. *IEEE Access*, 7, 89967–89979, 2019, doi: 10.1109/ACCESS.2019.2927082.

29. Rajput, Singh, D., Gour, R., An IoT framework for healthcare monitoring systems. *Int. J. Comput. Sci. Inf. Secur.*, 14, 5, 1–7, 2016.

30. Maksimović, M., Vujović, V., Perišić, B., A custom Internet of Things healthcare system, in: *2015 10th Iberian Conference on Information Systems and Technologies (CISTI)*, IEEE, 2015.

31. Hussain, A. *et al.*, Security framework for IoT based real-time health applications. *Electronics*, 10, 6, 719, 2021.

32. Durga, S., Nag, R., Daniel, E., Survey on machine learning and deep learning algorithms used in internet of things (IoT) healthcare, in: *2019 3rd International Conference on Computing Methodologies and Communication (ICCMC)*, IEEE, 2019.

33. Robel, Md.R.A. *et al.*, IoT driven healthcare monitoring system, in: *Fog, Edge, and Pervasive Computing in Intelligent IoT Driven Applications*, pp. 161–176, 2020.

34. Zamfir, M. *et al.*, Towards a platform for prototyping IoT health monitoring services, in: *Exploring Services Science: 7th International Conference, IESS 2016, Bucharest, Romania, May 25-27, 2016, Proceedings 7*, Springer International Publishing, 2016.

35. Khan, M.A., Challenges facing the application of IoT in medicine and healthcare. *Int. J. Comput. Inf. Manuf. (IJCIM)*, 1, 1, 1–15, 2021.

36. Ghosh, A., Raha, A., Mukherjee, A., Energy-efficient IoT-health monitoring system using approximate computing. *Internet Things*, 9, 100166, 2020.

37. Alshamrani, M., IoT and artificial intelligence implementations for remote healthcare monitoring systems: A survey. *J. King Saud Univ.-Comput. Inf. Sci.*, 34, 8, 4687–4701, 2022.

38. Badotra, S. *et al.*, IoT-enabled healthcare network with SDN, in: *2020 8th International Conference on Reliability, Infocom Technologies and Optimization (Trends and Future Directions) (ICRITO)*, IEEE, 2020.

39. Dhanvijay, M.M. and Patil, S.C., Internet of Things: A survey of enabling technologies in healthcare and its applications. *Comput. Networks*, 153, 113–131, 2019.

40. Kaur, H., Atif, M., Chauhan, R., An internet of healthcare things (IoHT)-based healthcare monitoring system, in: *Advances in Intelligent Computing and Communication: Proceedings of ICAC 2019*, Springer Singapore, 2020.

41. Milovanovic, D. and Bojkovic, Z., Cloud-based IoT healthcare applications: Requirements and recommendations. *Int. J. Internet Things Web Serv.*, 2, 60–65, 2017.
42. Pradhan, B., Bhattacharyya, S., Pal, K., IoT-based applications in healthcare devices. *J. Healthcare Eng.*, 2021, 1–18, 2021.
43. Kaur, P., Kumar, R., Kumar, M., A healthcare monitoring system using random forest and internet of things (IoT). *Multimedia Tools Appl.*, 78, 19905–19916, 2019.
44. Hossein, K.M. *et al.*, BCHealth: A novel blockchain-based privacy-preserving architecture for IoT healthcare applications. *Comput. Commun.*, 180, 31–47, 2021.
45. Amaraweera, S.P. and Halgamuge, M.N., Internet of things in the healthcare sector: Overview of security and privacy issues, in: *Security, Privacy and Trust in the IoT Environment*, pp. 153–179, 2019.
46. Zagan, I. *et al.*, Design, fabrication, and testing of an IoT healthcare cardiac monitoring device. *Computers*, 9, 1, 15, 2020.
47. Saleem, K. *et al.*, IoT healthcare: Design of smart and cost-effective sleep quality monitoring system. *J. Sens.*, 2020, 1–17, 2020.
48. Jeong, J.-S., Han, O., You, Y.-Y., A design characteristics of smart healthcare system as the IoT application. *Indian J. Sci. Technol.*, 9, 37, 52, 2016.
49. Kim, S. and Kim, S., User preference for an IoT healthcare application for lifestyle disease management. *Telecommun. Policy*, 42, 4, 304–314, 2018.
50. Dhruba, A.R. *et al.*, Development of an IoT-based sleep apnea monitoring system for healthcare applications. *Comput. Math. Methods Med.*, 2021, 1–16, 2021.

Index